MELTDOWN ICELAND

HOW THE GLOBAL FINANCIAL CRISIS
BANKRUPTED AN ENTIRE COUNTRY

ROGER BOYES

B L O O M S B U R Y
LONDON · BERLIN · NEW YORK

First published in Great Britain 2009

Copyright © 2009 by Roger Boyes

The moral right of the author has been asserted

Bloomsbury Publishing Plc
36 Soho Square
London W1D 3QY

www.bloomsbury.com

Bloomsbury Publishing, London, New York and Berlin
A CIP catalogue record for this book is available from the British Library

ISBN 978 1 4088 0233 5

10 9 8 7 6 5 4 3 2 1

Typeset by Hewer Text UK Ltd, Edinburgh
Printed in Great Britain by Clays Ltd, St Ives plc

Mixed Sources
Product group from well-managed
forests and other controlled sources
www.fsc.org Cert no. SGS-COC-2061
FSC © 1996 Forest Stewardship Council

MELTDOWN ICELAND

Contents

Author's Note

The Icelandic telephone book is ordered according to first, rather than family, names. You look for Jon or indeed Björk rather than Eriksson or Gudmundsdottir. Iceland has a patronymic name system. Children take the name of their father. Jon Stefansson is the son of Stefan. If Jon has a son, he will be given a first name, but his surname will be Jonsson. If Jon has a daughter, she will be Jonsdottir, the daughter of Jon.

Icelanders therefore use first names when talking of each other. The prime minister is commonly referred to as Johanna. *Meltdown Iceland* sometimes sticks to this convention, calling the former prime minister David Oddsson by his first name, or using Jon Asgeir to denote the businessman Jon Asgeir Johannesson. No disrespect is thus intended. For the most part the book uses surnames in the manner familiar to non-Icelandic readers.

The book also uses the Latin alphabet. Icelandic uses accents on its vowels, but for the convenience of the reader these have generally been deleted. The umlaut qualifying the letter *o* has been deleted, except in a few cases of internationally known figures, such as the singer Björk. And one runic letter has been rendered as *th*.

Preface

Hvelreki = "good luck" in Icelandic
It translates as "May a whole whale wash up on your beach."

The geological fault line between America and Europe, the Mid-Atlantic Ridge, runs through Iceland. Every year the gap between the tectonic plates is tugged apart by another inch; it is a place of collision and division, a junction between two zones.

In October 2008, many Icelanders felt they had been tugged into that cleft, disappearing into a netherworld. The events that were to unfold in the following months—the first major financial crisis of the global era—traumatized the island. Iceland had thought itself strong and independent, but was instead bankrupt and beholden to creditors. Its fall from grace was caused in part by the blighted lending practices of U.S. mortgage banks, by the crumbling of confidence, the sudden death of credit. How was a small, indebted island in the North Atlantic supposed to survive? But Iceland had also brought the problems down on itself; it had allowed itself to be misgoverned; it had let its market revolution—an earnest and enthusiastic copy of the changes introduced by Reagan in the United States and by Thatcher in Britain—get out of hand. There was greed, incompetence, feuding, revenge, and deceit: the themes of the ancient Viking sagas transplanted onto a modern age.

The calamity that hit Iceland was, in short, a microcosm of what was happening elsewhere in supposedly more complex societies. When the United States catches cold, the world sneezes. When the United States catches pneumonia, though, smaller states take to their sickbeds and are lucky to survive. How lucky is Iceland? This book charts Iceland's progress from the years of poverty, through to the good years, the manic years, and on to the Kreppa, the Icelandic word for "crisis." *Kreppa* actually connotes something more: the roar of a volcano perhaps; the approach of catastrophe. In telling this story I want to do more than sympathize with the Icelanders. I want to show the human narrative to this international meltdown, and demonstrate that we—Icelanders and non-Icelanders alike—are not just powerless victims caught in the spokes of the vast machinery of capitalism.

Meltdown Iceland tries to bring the crisis down to scale. The meltdown can be understood, I believe, only when broken into the smallest of units. The United States, ten months after the sinking of Lehman Brothers, had spent $4 trillion to mitigate the pain of the crisis and offered about $12.7 trillion in guarantees to the U.S. financial sector. That is written $12,700,000,000,000. Such figures numb the brain, obscure rather than enlighten. Iceland, by contrast, has the population of a small Midwestern town. Walk across this craggy island and you can go for days without meeting a human. The entire financial and political decision-making class could fit into a bus, with a couple of seats free for paying passengers. The difference between a prosperous Icelandic future and a three-generational epoch of belt-tightening is about $20 billion, a mere drop in the U.S. water barrel. Yet somehow America's problems have become those of Iceland. And the questions raised by Icelanders about how to live in the globalized era, how to be the master of capital, not its servant, about finding one's own rhythm, are questions bothering us all.

1 : Fall

Sunset, December 31, 2008: 3:28 P.M.
Sunrise, January 1, 2009: 11:14 A.M.

Here we go! Here we go! Here we goooo! Encouraged by the crowd, a ginger-bearded student, made clumsy through drink, clambered close to the head of Leif Eriksson, the Viking explorer who discovered North America. The area around the Eriksson statue, in front of the imposing Hallgrim's Church, is the best spot for viewing the New Year's fireworks over Reykjavik. It is the moment when Icelanders try to turn night into day, an act of defiance on this subpolar island where the midwinter sun is at best a fleeting, always anemic visitor. The 2009 celebrations followed the modern traditions: first, a meal at home with the extended family, then a pagan moment around a glowing, tall bonfire—a luxury on an island devoid of timber—followed by an extravaganza of Catherine wheels and Bengal tigers, exploding over the harbor. The night is dedicated to beery revel, at home, at neighbors', on the street. Outside the capital, beyond the lava fields, the New Year's Eve barn dance is the place to flirt and size up future partners. The fishing fleets are at anchor, the backbreaking routines of the farmstead briefly set aside.

The Reykjavik student, egged on by his drunken friends, took a rocket out of his pocket. He used his thighs to keep a grip on the great Viking and fumbled for his lighter.

"Happy New Year!" he shouted, peering down at a cluster of teenagers near the podium. It was the last we heard from him as he lost his perch and tumbled twenty feet to the ground. He landed on his back; blood trickled from his mouth. Within minutes four ambulances were on the scene.

"Stupid boy," said Olafur, a university instructor and our New Year's host, "you can't drink and climb."

"Stupid Iceland," chipped in his wife, Aldis. "Stupid, stupid Iceland for trying to climb and not knowing how to fall."

In October 2008, Iceland—perched at the top of the international happiness and satisfaction scales, a tiny, poor country that had become rich—came crashing down to earth. The prime minister, the dour Geir Haarde, battered by the winds of a gathering global storm, became the first Western leader to admit that his country had gone bust. "There is a very real danger, fellow citizens, that the Icelandic economy in the worst case could be sucked into the whirlpool, and the result could be national bankruptcy." More followed throughout the autumn and the winter; as the temperatures dropped and the days shortened, Haarde started to reread his favorite author, Winston Churchill, and prepare his three hundred thousand citizens for the worst. Until then Iceland had gloried in its newfound reputation as the essence of Cool, a successful nation where people couldn't stop partying. Its swashbuckling entrepreneurs had embraced the new global economy, taken the modern equivalent of the Viking longship—the executive jet—and flown around the world, buying up companies. In Britain, Iceland had in a few short years bought a stake in most of the fashion outlets on the high street: Moss Bros., Karen Millen, Whistles, House of Fraser. The old Vikings had specialized in rape and pillage; the New Vikings put clothes on the backs of British womanhood. The Icelanders pushed into the United States, setting up a network of hundreds of Bonus supermarkets, and throughout Scandinavia. Partly it was trophy shopping—London's flagship toy shop, Hamleys, the soccer team West Ham United—and it later emerged that many of the stakes had been funded with unsecured loans provided by complaisant banks.

From the turn of the new millennium, Icelanders had been feeling good about themselves. For the first time in its history, their island was no longer governed solely by the soil and the sea: it was part of the global economy. And it busily mimicked the lifestyles of the rest of the capitalist world, which had also bought into the frenzy. Elton John was flown in to perform at a birthday party—routine to Russian oligarchs, perhaps, but until then, not for Icelanders. Russian ostentation has deep historical roots, justified to some extent by the innate wealth of a country that controls so much oil and gas. Even in bad times, Russian wealth is not fool's gold.

But the Icelanders are not of that ilk. The island is rich only with sheep, fish, and thermal energy, the hot water forcing itself up through the thin crust of the earth. It does not even have trees. Although about a third of the island was forested when the first Vikings arrived in the late ninth century, today Iceland is bare, the trees long since chopped down for timber. Iceland is a rocky outcrop in the North Atlantic, not an emirate on the Gulf. Its new role as a global player, its sudden wealth—those fat Jeeps in the center of Reykjavik, the Max Mara outlet—was created by sleight of hand, by the financial alchemists who tried to change the rules of economics. Iceland's wealth was illusory; its bankruptcy real. Iceland's banks did not meddle in the U.S. subprime mortgage market, one of the few things that can be said in their defense. But when the lies at the heart of the U.S. real estate boom came to light, all the many deceits, big and small, underpinning the world economy inevitably tumbled out helter-skelter, eroding trust, destroying credit. Welcome then to the Flat World, where a defaulting homeowner in Florida can help bankrupt a distant island; and where that same crash can wipe out the savings of hundreds of thousands of British, German, and Dutch depositors who had rashly accepted the myth of a Cool, stable Iceland, a place where one could make money and live a long, comfortable life.

Understandably then, New Year's celebrations in 2009 in Reykjavik had a slightly hysterical undertone. Icelanders set off more fireworks per person than the people of any other country in the world. This time, with no cash for explosions, a loan had to be negotiated with the Chinese fireworks manufacturers. The Chinese freighter moved alongside a boat sent by Nissan to collect three hundred unsold cars. The rockets, the blaze of artificial light, the drunkenness, the search for oblivion: there was little doubting that Iceland saw itself as the prime victim of the global crisis.

The last time that Iceland was at the hub of the world's attention was when the Laki volcano blew its top. That was back in 1783, but the modern New Year's fireworks orgy is supposed to simulate that literally explosive event. The lava shot up to heights of 1.4 kilometers (.9 miles). More than 120 million tons of sulfur dioxide were released into the atmosphere—equivalent to three times the annual European output in 2006. It was a tragedy for Iceland—a quarter of the population died in the resulting famine—but it also transformed the world. In Britain, the summer of 1783 was known as the "sand-summer" because of the ash fallout. A toxic cloud spread to Norway, then south to Berlin and Prague. The English Channel was blocked because the volcanic ash formed such a dense fog. The climate of the whole planet was affected: by the winter of 1784 (the volcano continued to erupt until February of that year), New Jersey was recording its largest ever snowfalls, the southern Mississippi River froze over, and the Gulf of Mexico iced up. In Egypt, there was a drought; in Japan, a famine. Most dramatic of all, the change in the atmosphere played havoc with the harvests in France, stoking the anger of rural workers and preparing the ground for the French revolution in 1789.

Pastor Jon Steingrimsson saw the lava rolling toward his parish and gathered the congregation into his church on the banks of the Skafta River for a chance to pray before it was engulfed. "The church was shaking and quaking from the cataclysm that threatened it from upstream. We called fervently and earnestly upon God, who so ordained that the lava did not advance a single foot." The lava stopped in front of the church and piled up, layer on layer, and as the water from the local lakes surged, it cooled the molten fire.

The parish survived. Will Iceland survive the latest disaster that, like Laki, has turned local into global misery?

The Laki eruption was a violent act of nature that had devastating effects on the planet. The current meltdown is man-made, but it has struck Iceland with the force of a natural catastrophe. Certainly it took Iceland by surprise. There were early warning signs—just as there are before a volcano erupts—but they were brushed aside. Regulators and monitors failed Iceland in a spectacular way; there was an institutional breakdown, an utter dereliction of duty on the part of a political class that had become intimately intertwined with big business and bankers.

Interrelated, educated at the same schools, motivated by ancient rivalries and encyclopedic grudges, Iceland's rulers were unable to handle or anticipate the brewing financial volcano.

But the fault did not lie solely with the elite. Icelanders, since the beginning of the twenty-first century, had begun to feel rich. They bought Range Rovers—now colloquially known as Game-Overs—on complex loan packages involving Japanese yen, Swiss francs, and euros. Inflation soared and interest rates rose to keep it under control. The bankers explained to fishermen and farmers that they needed to wait no longer for coveted cars or new homes or winter holidays in Thailand. Credit, denominated in exotic currencies, was always available. So Icelanders went global and got greedy; they did not want to hear that things were going wrong. Of course, the Icelanders were not alone. The *Financial Times*, on October 10, 2008, issued the "Bonus" edition of its glossy *How to Spend It* supplement. One suggestion: the Dunhill Mechanical Belt, which automatically expands or contracts by up to 35 millimeters after a business lunch. No embarrassing fumbling! Cost: £5,895. Ten days later the business newspaper had realized it was lagging behind the times. Its advice columnist was being asked by an (anonymous) banker whether he should hide his profession at dinner parties to avoid public opprobrium. He was advised to pretend that he was writing his first novel, apparently an all-purpose device for those hiding a shameful secret.

The questions that are now being raised by the Icelanders can be heard in corporate boardrooms and around dinner tables in New York, Frankfurt, and Paris. How did we lose control over our lives? Icelanders, like Americans and Britons, took on record amounts of debt compared to income. They were told—and did not question—that this was acceptable because the debt was supported by high stock prices and, when that bubble burst, staggeringly high house prices. Since the 1990s Iceland's unemployment rate had been barely 1 percent; thousands of Poles came to the island to do the dirtiest of the fishing jobs, to work on building sites, to push old people in their wheelchairs. All that contributed to a sense of well-being. As in America, low unemployment was taken as proof that the economic model was working. Yes, wages were stagnating, but that was not deemed to be a sign of failure—rather of international competiveness.

In the United States, four out of five dollars of lending to business and consumers was conducted by financial companies that were not regulated or overseen by the Federal Reserve. As the central bank of the United States, the Fed is primarily responsible for ensuring the stability of the financial system, dealing with banking panics, and supervising and regulating banking institutions. By 2008 it was clear that the Fed had been sleeping on the job. In Iceland the shortcomings were even more spectacular. David Oddsson—the self-proclaimed Margaret Thatcher of the northern economies—had presided over a privatization wave as prime minister in the 1990s. This led inevitably to the privatization of the state-owned banks. But almost no accompanying regulatory apparatus was put in place; there were no insider-trading rules. In 2003, Oddsson became central-bank governor, the one man on the island who could have blown the whistle on the rampant overseas expansion of the banks. But of course to do so would have been to recognize his own previous fallibility as prime minister. He didn't. Icelandic banks—Landsbanki, Kaupthing, and Glitnir, housed in three unobtrusive buildings near the Reykjavik dockside—had accumulated assets that dwarfed the country's gross domestic product. When the assets turned into liabilities, Iceland became a failed state.

The scale is different; the problem universal. In the lead-up to the global crisis, the earnings of American financial institutions rose to more than one third of all the country's profits. Economists failed to spot this as a cause for concern; it was merely taken as proof that manufacturing was a twentieth-century anachronism.

Iceland's collapse even today should be sending out warning signals to countries with overextended banking sectors such as Switzerland, Denmark, Sweden—and Britain. In a polemical study of the roots of the Icelandic meltdown, Willem Buiter of London University pointed out that Britain's banking system accounted for 450 percent of GDP—and asked, could London become "Reykjavik-on-Thames"? For, like Iceland, Britain does not have a global reserve currency in the form of the euro or the dollar to draw on if things go horribly wrong.

The crisis in Iceland then presents a micro-version of the crisis facing the rest of the capitalist world as it stumbles through the worst financial meltdown since the Great Depression. Though Reykjavik with its 120,000 inhabitants is almost Toy Town small—the prime minister's office is barely more than a cottage, which feels crowded if more than eight people are there at work—its size actually makes it easier to understand some of the forces that are upsetting the planet.

Here on the island, some light can be shed on the murkier corners of capitalism. How, for example, are regulatory boundaries, the essence of democratic control, eroded by personal friendship, family ties, and back-scratching deals? The economist Vilhjalmur Bjarnason calculates that Iceland's meltdown was caused by a mere thirty people: the core of the country's decision-making elite. Naturally, the networks in the United States and Britain were larger, more diffuse. But Iceland can serve as a scale model, an anthropological field study, at a time when politicians are losing themselves in numbers, throwing hundreds of billions of dollars at failing banks and industrial sectors. The island is an antidote to vertigo, to the dizzy abstraction of unfathomable numbers.

The ability of the new financial instruments—the credit-default swaps and the complex mortgage-based obligations—to draw a veil over investment and trading has helped to dupe supposedly sophisticated investors. And the Icelanders are indeed financially sophisticated. I recall one trip from Keflavik Airport where the taxi driver—a former trawlerman—spent forty-five minutes discussing the strengths and weaknesses of the Japanese economy. Part of his home loan was factored in yen, and so, naturally, he was hungry for information. He needed to assess his exposure. How did Icelanders become a society of risk-takers? How did they come to abandon centuries-old caution about taking on debt? Do they share the responsibility for the meltdown? How does the island society now change? Can it reject being part of a global society and go back to the old ways?

For the time being, the Icelanders are looking—like the Americans and the British—for someone to blame. The radicalizing effect of national bankruptcy became clear on New Year's Eve. It was early afternoon. A cold drizzle fell and the light was beginning to fade. Students, mothers with children, pensioners, and teachers came together to form a critical mass of perhaps two hundred angry protesters outside the Hotel Borg in downtown Reykjavik. Every year at this time the country's politicians meet for a live, usually jocular, sometimes tipsy TV discussion on the coming year; it is supposed to have a calming effect on the population before the fireworks. This time it was different. The protesters manhandled the prime minister, stopping him from entering the hotel lobby. They cut the TV cables and in a great surge tried to push into the hotel, a venerable place that used to be the watering hole for British officers during the Second World War.

The police moved in and sprayed Mace into their eyes. Two men in suits lunged into the midst of the demonstrators, fists flaying, shouting, "Bloody communists!" One, it emerged later, was a central-bank economist; the other was his brother. For Icelanders, this was a deeply shocking moment. Protest culture was something new, but since the October meltdown people had taken to the streets. Icelanders were furious that no one had resigned or claimed any responsibility for bankrupting their country. Their hope was that the spirit of protest would eventually gather sufficient strength to crack open the political class and create a new kind of governance. It was an honest but naïve goal in a society where almost everyone had a relative working in the discredited banks or the disabled commercial empires or the distracted public administration.

So, until New Year's Eve, the cusp of 2009, the Icelandic revolution was a quixotic affair, little more than a way of broadening out the grumbling in the coffee bars of Laugavegur Street. Lit by tea candles, painted in warm and reassuring shades of ocher or salmon pink, these cafés are cozy centers of sedition. At Hljomalind, the cellar has been converted into a communal space for late-night bands—there is no other way of paying the bills—and the list of featured musicians includes groups such as Face the Anger, Gone Postal, and Stick in the Knife. All innocent enough—until the Hotel Borg riot. Then it became clear that the Icelanders were not simply frustrated and shell-shocked—an emotion shared in 2009 by many, many communities on at least three continents—but polarized. In power, and reluctant to abandon it, was an elite that still believed in the innate superiority of market power and a form of globalization fueled by the free movement of capital and labor. Out of power, and irate, were people who felt cheated by their leaders and who were demanding a change in tone—an end to the patronizing manner of the born-to-rule politicians—and a change in substance. The island, a year after the crisis broke on its shores, was demanding a reevaluation of Iceland's future.

Iceland has always had boom-and-bust cycles—bad harvests, bad fishing years. There is no fear of going without. But the level of personal debt—the sense that not one, but two generations may be forced into emigration to pay for the incompetence or cupidity of the rulers and their market dogmatism—has stirred the islanders.

In the Antarctic Kerguelen Islands lives a species of butterfly that has lost the ability to fly. The high storm winds destroyed too many of the species, so by some regressionary reflex, the insect's wings have withered and it has become a land creature. The Icelanders may adopt a similar strategy, staying on the ground and retreating from the high-flying world of global finance, its decadence and iniquities, its curling deceits. If so, we should all be watching. For it takes the desperation of a bankrupt state to ask these questions, and ask them on our behalf. More: to prod us into the debate we should all be having, about values and priorities, about vulnerability and solidarity.

I have spent some months in Iceland following its rhythms. It took a while for an essentially urban reporter to penetrate the tribal complexity of the society, scratch away at its secrets and self-doubts. Iceland puts on an inscrutable face to foreigners and does not much welcome inquiry. But one thing became clear: the hunch that the island would adopt a "back to basics" approach to the financial crisis is proving wrong. The assumption was that the island, so heavily dependent on imports, would automatically return to a traditional way of life. Visiting journalists reported that the old delicacies, such as ram's testicles, flattened sheep heads, and grilled whale were returning to the dining table in the absence of white truffles flown in from Copenhagen. It was back to the unforgiving land, so difficult to farm, and to codfishing. Yet global capitalism cannot simply be stigmatized or dismissed. The abiding concern of the Icelanders has been the search for economic security and for a form of modernization that can be squared with the Icelandic temperament—the Viking temperament.

The tycoons who through complex patterns of cross-ownership tapped into a seemingly endless flow of credit were accepted for so long by the Icelanders because they were indeed Viking heroes. Long-haired, womanizing, impulsive hunters, they appeared to come straight out of the ancient sagas. The old Vikings were not just marauding pirates— they were modernizers. It was the Vikings who—at a time when there were no roads, little trade, and almost no communication between closed communities—gave Europeans a sense of the size of their continent and its relationship to the outside world. They were free men in pursuit of profit. In doing so they revolutionized global trade in metals, timber, and humans. Because they controlled the sea-lanes with their high-speed, technologically advanced vessels, they also became the best-informed people in the world: they knew exactly how badly guarded were the walls of Paris and the current prices for slaves on the Baghdad market. The New Vikings, Iceland's advance-guard entrepreneurs, were also concerned with global influence, intelligence, and profit. They wrought untold damage on the economy—most Icelanders are agreed on this—but also contributed to a new national self-regard. Iceland thus has a tangled idea of the modern: its creative power, its potential for destruction. But Iceland has understood that it is on the fault line of something important. That the world is in the grips of not just a financial crisis, but a deeper reappraisal of the rights and wrongs of capitalism.

And so it was that I decided to rent a place in Reykjavik from Hildur Helga. Through my windows, smeared by sea salt, I can monitor the meltdown. I see the fashionable forty-year-old taking a bag of dresses to the Red Cross secondhand shop, now the busiest place on the main street. The newly unemployed banker setting out for a café with free Wi-Fi. The teenagers contemplating emigration. "We were happy," says the woman at the Salvation Army hostel. "But we wanted to be happy and rich. That was a mistake."

Yes, I nod, anxious to move on before the sun disappears. Perhaps it was a mistake.

2 : Pride

Iceland is not a myth; it is a solid portion of the earth's surface.
Pliny Miles, 1854

From Hildur Helga's house it is a short walk to parliament, the Althing. "Downtown," as the Reykjavikers say, though the bustling hub of the capital is made up of barely six streets. On the way to the parliament building on Austurvoellur square, one passes some improvised architectural gems, built with Siberian driftwood or covered with the brightly painted corrugated iron that protects the houses from the corrosive sea air. The effect in the capital's better corners is of being in a particularly progressive kindergarten where children are allowed to smear everything in reds and blues and pin paper suns to the windows. Some of the money that has flowed into Iceland has clearly gone into restoration, but the capital, little more than a few farmsteads until the late eighteenth century, has no great architectural tradition. Houses are nests, offices are fortresses—the money has been spent mainly on prettification. So one wends one's way past these oversize dollhouses toward the harbor, past the brutalist architecture of the three banks—Landsbanki, Glitnir, and Kaupthing—where Icelanders now settle their electricity bills rather than check their offshore portfolios, and past the whitewashed cottage where the prime minister works. Outside Iceland's White House are two statues, one of Hannes Hafstein, leader of the first home-rule government, and the other of King Christian IX of Denmark, with the Icelandic constitution firmly in his hand. Only the statues indicate that the building is anything more than a modest family home. Out along the harbor one sees the new concert hall, doomed never to be finished because it was sponsored by one of Iceland's crippled banks; a thriving hot dog stand where Bill Clinton once dined; a covered flea market selling stockfish and Herman's Hermits LPs.

Austurvoellur Square comes as a relief from the jumble. It is a green, cheerful space, quietly distinguished, with another statue, of Jon Sigurdsson, Iceland's nineteenth-century hero, the man who tried to liberate the island from Denmark, facing the house of parliament. When the chamber is in session, on the first floor, the speaker has his back to Jon Sigurdsson, but all the other deputies can see the statue through the high window. They see not just the revolutionary Sigurdsson—they can, with growing frequency, take in the anger of the Icelandic nation. Every Saturday since the autumn of 2008, a swelling mob of islanders has gathered in the square to yell at politicians. At first they threw eggs. Then eggs, with Iceland's galloping inflation, became too expensive, and they threw stones, bricks, and briefly, inspired by the attack on George W. Bush, a few shoes. One protester clambered up the building and draped a FOR SALE banner. Speeches were made, by poets, by dissident economists, by an eight-year-old girl. As the autumn turned to winter, then to the spring of 2009, it became clear to everyone present that something important was happening. The numbers were not huge—perhaps two thousand at a time—but as a proportion of the population, difficult to shrug off. "Two thousand out of a Reykjavik population of one hundred thousand, two thousand, come rain or snow, with many more sympathizers," says blogger Alda Sigmundsdottir. "To get the equivalent in the U.S., you would need two million on the streets. This is real people power."

For young Icelanders, the spring of 2009 was the time when the crisis began to bite. "We can't transfer cash to our two daughters studying in Boston," a retired teacher told me. "So, they said, 'We're coming back home, we've got to change the place!' But I told them 'Stay where you are, get jobs, save—the krona is going to be worthless!' And my heart hurt when I said that." Unemployment was something new for young Reykjavikers, frightening even. By March 2009, most young employees in the international departments of banks were out of a job, had quit their big apartments, and had moved in with their parents or into shared living quarters. There was still plenty of food in the shops—though growing more expensive by the week—and the financial crisis had not become a survival issue, except for heavily indebted single mothers or the elderly dependent on imported medication. The welfare state continues to function, after a fashion, even in conditions of bankruptcy; the state budget is ransacked to pay the doctors; the private budget to pay for the essentials. Financial crisis translates rather into psychological distress; the world becomes uncertain. The rent and mortgage are unpayable, so they are not paid, and power slips away into the hands of erratically managed, barely functioning banks that have the authority to evict you at any moment. Loans on cars become too expensive to pay; the debt grows, the cars stay parked on the street. The great anchors of life—the assets, the mortgaged houses that were in effect a way of saving for the future—become unsellable, and so people who felt wealthy and free feel poor and trapped.

Across the globe, governments were throwing billions at a crisis, to head off a slump, to avert deflation, and in so doing were saddling future generations with higher taxes and higher debts, snuffing out prospects. What was worse: The expensive life vests thrown by governments to inefficient, arguably corrupt banks? Or that politicians had let the situation arise in the first place with deregulation and sloppy monitoring of the financial establishments? Rioters from Bulgaria to Latvia could not make up their minds. All they knew was that no one in government was taking the blame. The same went for the Icelanders. "We have no concept of ministerial responsibility, of politicians stepping down for something they have not personally done," said Urdur Gunnarsdottir, a shrewd thirty-eight-year-old diplomat. The result was a sense of arterial blockage in the political corpus. Without change at the top—with plainly compromised politicians declaring themselves to be indispensable in their country's darkest hour—there seemed no serious chance of restoring trust in the mechanical workings of capitalism. The New Zealand economist Robert Wade—who had been one of the most trenchant analysts of the Asian economic crisis of 1997—drew a packed audience in Reykjavik's university cinema when he transferred his knowledge to the case of Iceland. He sensed the collective intake of breath when he told the Icelanders that a second wave of trouble would follow the breakdown in banking. The sudden surge of unemployment, the quick flip-flop from prosperity to sacrifice, the sheer inability of institutions to deal with the looming challenges—all that was going to spawn serious unrest. "The tipping point will be caused by the rise of general awareness throughout Europe, America, and Asia that hundreds of millions of people in rich and poor countries are experiencing rapidly falling consumption standards; that the crisis is getting worse, not better; and that it has escaped the control of public authorities, national and international."

Iceland, first to be hit, first to respond, was embracing the new protest culture. There was a passion to it that could only be experienced on a closely knit island. As I sidled through the crowd after a February protest, I found that some of the demonstrators outside parliament were related to deputies inside. And some of the riot cops were cousins of the protesters. This was a hot-blooded family affair, played out against a global backdrop.

"There's been nothing like this since the great protests against joining NATO," said a seventy-year-old who had been using her walking stick to bang a pot. We regrouped a safe distance from the strangely un-Icelandic, black-suited riot police. One of the first responses to the crisis and its social aftermath had been to boost funds for the riot units while cutting them for the antifraud squad. Not a move that inspired confidence in the government. The NATO comparison was important. It highlighted what was at stake: the existential struggle on the island between the need to modernize, to achieve a kind of economic security that went beyond the fishing waters, and the desire to preserve independence, the limited ability of a small country to define its future. Size has become central to the unfolding of the global crisis. The equations Small Country = Small Problem and Big Country = Big Problem do not hold water. Iceland was the first country to be totally overwhelmed by the crisis because it could not cope with massive cash outflows and the sudden end to credit. It had made itself totally dependent, through its swollen financial sector, on the whims of global markets. The use of finance to secure the independence of small countries with little manufacturing or economic muscle was an illusion entertained not only by Iceland, but by the Baltic republics of Estonia, Latvia, and Lithuania and by the many tiny states that had made themselves rich by becoming tax havens. Both the United States and the European Union, spending hundreds of billions of dollars to stave off a depression in 2009, turned on these tax-haven states, furiously insisting on tighter banking controls. Iceland began 2009 as a pariah state because of its inability to pay back its debts. But in the course of the year, tax havens such as Switzerland and Liechtenstein were also being put in the stockades. This was indeed an asymmetrical crisis, one that punished smaller societies for their ambition.

Iceland's reluctance to join NATO in the 1950s presaged some of these issues. Was it desirable to have big partners such as the United States and Britain? How much sovereignty should one surrender? How intrusive could the culture of these outside societies become? The Icelanders wanted NATO membership because it promised to bring prosperity, and prosperity would bring security. But how many foreigners can one accept without diluting and ultimately losing one's identity? And crucially, who can be trusted to make those judgments?

The Icelanders are proud of their independence, but most will accept that it is relative. The island was originally settled—between A.D. 870 and 930—by Norwegians. Some came to Iceland indirectly from Britain, Ireland, Orkney, and the Hebrides, bringing Celtic wives and slaves. The Vikings were having a hard time—defeated by Alfred the Great in Wessex and Mercia; thrown out of Dublin in 901. Iceland, with its pastureland and hot springs, seemed a good place to go. Other settlers came from western Norway, fleeing the rule of Harald Fairhair, who was trying to unify Norway by bending petty chieftains to his rule. They were, in essence, freethinking tax dodgers. That is the founding myth of Iceland: a place of refuge for proud, independent-minded frontiersmen.

Iceland remained under some kind of Norwegian control until 1380, but the Icelanders, even with their technologically sophisticated, high-speed longships, were four difficult days away from the motherland. In 930 they established the Althing, the world's first parliament, a law-making assembly, and it quickly became clear that Norway had to negotiate rather than merely assert its control over the Icelanders.

It was the parliament that in effect laid the foundations of an organized resistance to the Norwegian king. In 1024, a messenger was sent from Norway by King Olaf Haraldsson (later Saint Olaf) to address the Icelandic clans at the Althing. The king, he said, wanted the Icelanders to pay tribute: "He will be your king if you will be his subjects, and both be friends and help one another in all things of good report." The king's first demand was that he be given the island of Grimsey, at the mouth of a strategic fjord in northern Iceland. The Icelandic chieftains were divided in what became the quintessential Icelandic argument about independence. Some chiefs wanted the "friendship" of King Olaf. Others resisted "bondage" to a colonial power. Led by Einar Eyolfsson, the dissidents carried the day. It was all right, said Einar, to send King Olaf presents— hawks, horses, that kind of thing—but not to pay fixed taxes. As for Grimsey, it should stay under Icelandic control. "If some army from abroad made it their base and sailed from there with warships, I think many a cottar would find himself in a predicament."

When the kingdoms of Norway and Denmark were united in 1380, Iceland essentially became a Danish colony and lost the autonomy it had enjoyed under the Norwegians. The Danes held the monopoly in the Icelandic fish and wool trade, controlled the prices, and restricted entry to ports. Throughout much of the nineteenth century, Icelanders pushed for—or at least talked about—home rule. It took time, under the Danish yoke, for a proper Icelandic mercantile class to establish itself. One small milestone on the road to a modern society was the first submarine telegraph cable, in 1902. That marked, in the words of one Icelandic scholar, the end of the Middle Ages. But the devastating European war to end all wars gave Iceland the prospect of becoming a prosperous, self-governing society. World fish prices boomed during the First World War, and the country had a large, modern trawler fleet. Iceland realized that it could grow rich by analyzing and exploiting gaps in global markets. A distant war had made Iceland less of an island.

An Act of Union between Denmark and Iceland in 1918, followed by a new constitution in 1920, awarded the Icelanders a degree of home rule. It also, however, built in the possibility of Iceland's repudiating the Act and declaring full independence. The German invasion of Denmark in April 1940 gave the Icelanders the opportunity they were waiting for. The Althing announced that since Denmark was under foreign occupation, Iceland was going to sever ties with the Danish crown.

But Iceland was soon to be reminded that its independence was conditional, limited by the strategic interests of greater powers. On May

10, 1940, barely a month after the Germans marched into Copenhagen, the British army took over Iceland. The British logic was clear: German submarine technology was advanced and threatened to cut off the life-line between America and the United Kingdom. The fjords of Iceland would have made perfect submarine pens for the Germans. If Hitler controlled the North Atlantic, U.S. food and energy supplies to the United Kingdom would dry up. So too would the supply of fish and fish oils. There had been hints of German interest. Heinrich Himmler, head of the Nazi security machine, had set up a mission to visit Reykjavik in March 1939 with a view to making a genealogic chart of the island. For Nazi ideologues, Iceland was almost racially "pure" and one of the mystic roots of Nordic-Viking culture. Prominent Nazis, Himmler believed, could be shown to have Viking ancestors if one simply searched hard enough on the island. The Nazi mission was called off at the last moment because of the German invasion of Bohemia-Moravia; Himmler and his Gestapo suddenly had a pressing appointment in Prague.

But Nazi interest in Iceland remained strong. Hermann Göring had sent experts to make precise maps of the island, supposedly to work out the flight paths of falcons. Since Göring became Luftwaffe minister, it was reasonable for the British to entertain suspicions In fact, as early as 1936, the poets W. H. Auden and Louis MacNeice noted the presence of Göring's brother in the breakfast room of their Reykjavik boardinghouse. "The Nazis have a theory that Iceland is the cradle of the Germanic culture," wrote Auden in a letter home. "Well, if they want a community like that of the sagas they are welcome to it. I love the sagas, but what a rotten society they describe, a society with only the gangster virtues . . . I saw Goering for a moment at breakfast next morning and we exchanged politeness. He doesn't look in the least like his brother." Lurking offshore, there was the German cruiser *Emden*; the Nazis claimed it was simply acting as the mother ship for a fleet of German fishing steamers netting cod in Icelandic waters. Lufthansa had asked for landing rights, and German "glider clubs" had become frequent visitors.

Then there was the Icelandic Nazi Party, founded in 1934 by a handful of pro-German ultranationalists. They were marginal—in 1939 three pro-Nazi Icelanders absurdly asked a German prince, the Nazi Friedrich

Christian zu Schaumburg-Lippe, to become king of Iceland as soon as the German army moved in. Yet they were frequently in tune with the xenophobic ranting in the mainstream parties. A Danish diplomat, C. A. C. Brun—who had made it his duty to defend the few Jews on the island—approached the Icelandic prime minister, the muscle-bound former wrestling champion Hermann Jonasson, on behalf of a Jewish merchant. The man, Hans Rottberger, a Jew expelled from Berlin by the Nazis, had set up as a leather trader in Iceland and had been denounced by his competitors.

C. A. C. Brun records in his diary, apparently without irony, how he buttonholed the prime minister after a dinner at the Danish legation.

"He showed extraordinary understanding for my arguments and authorized me to announce to the little Jew that he definitely has to leave—it is a principle in Iceland; Iceland has always been a pure Nordic country, free of Jews, and those who have entered in the last years must leave."

The prime minister agreed to delay the expulsion order for a couple of months. When the trader was eventually thrown out in May 1938, moving to Denmark, the largest Icelandic newspaper praised the expulsion of the Jews. "It must be welcomed that the authorities have shown firmness in dealing with these vagabonds . . . Hopefully the authorities will ensure that foreigners who are still here without a residence permit will be sent out of the country immediately."

So British and U.S. suspicions that Iceland could drop into the lap of Nazi Germany were justified. The effect of having a society based so transparently on intermarriage among a few families, with bloodlines that can be traced back centuries, is a paralyzing fear of the Other, the outsiders. Foreigners are treated generously, as guests, but they are also a source of nagging anxiety. And of course the isolation of Iceland had always been its true line of defense. The plague had come twice to the island in the fifteenth century, each time brought in by a foreigner in a ship. The feeling prevailed that all that is bad comes from across the water, from outside the island family. That was enough, in the 1930s, to create an anti-Semitic climate in a place that had given shelter to at most a few dozen Jews. Soon the worry about the Other, about the moral corruption of the supposedly purebred island race, would be transferred to the British and then to the Americans, as military occupiers and later as globalizers.

The British moved into Iceland in May 1940. Since the country had declared itself neutral, the arrival of the British—tired, seasick, more afraid of the cold than of the Germans—was depicted as an invasion. Many Icelanders saw it that way. Ron Rawle, arriving from Britain in May as part of a Field Ambulance team, remembers driving trucks of tents through Reykjavik. They passed a woman in national costume, wearing an apron and tall black headdress. "She was cleaning the front of her house with mop, bucket, and broom. We waved to her as we had been instructed. She shook her mop at us and, with a stream of Icelandic invective, disappeared inside her house and slammed the front door behind her." The Icelanders were divided not so much between those who hated the British and those who loved them, as between those who told the soldiers, "Leave us alone, this is not our war," those who were nervous ("You're making us a target"), and those who preferred the Germans because of the implicit promise of a privileged status under the Nazis. Brigadier Procter of the 146th Infantry Brigade scribbled in his diary, April 4, 1942, "A young Icelander at North Quay Reykjavik drew a swastika on the wall, was arrested and handed over to the civil police." The local police chief released the Icelander immediately. The British were allowed some cautious fraternization, but for the most part they stayed in their Nissen huts and kept their distance. Their rations were too scant to feed a black market. The British established an arctic warfare training center in Iceland and thus unwittingly paved the way for the island to become part of a strategic postwar constellation. It was no good Iceland pretending that it could behave like those ministates of Europe—neutral San Marino or Andorra—that survived on selling colorful postage stamps to philatelists. If it was to be fully independent of Denmark, then it had to establish that it was of global military importance. By the time that U.S. Marines replaced the British soldiers, the Icelanders were beginning to understand the link between occupation by a (well-wishing) foreign army with a future and independence. Small countries need protectors. If one shed the quasi-colonial rule of the Danes, a vacancy was created (reminiscent of the French-British financier Jimmy Goldsmith's aphorism "When you marry your mistress, you create a vacancy"). The British occupiers had not radiated a sense of prosperity and confidence; for the most part they seemed like shabbier versions of the Icelanders themselves, careful with their money, complaining about the weather, unwilling to stray too far from camp. There were few Anglo-Icelandic courtships. The Americans by contrast swept the Icelanders off their feet with their brashness, wealth, generosity, naïvité, loudness, friendliness—the GI syndrome.

"Well dressed, well fed, and virile, the GIs moved in, swelling Reykjavik's population by two thirds," wrote Amalia Lindal, an American woman who had married an Icelandic engineer. "The Britishers who were to leave soon looked resentfully at their natty successors, and the housewives in Reykjavik were often in a dilemma. A nice British boy came to visit one Sunday bringing, as he always did, his weekly ration of one orange and one apple, there being no fruit at all among the Icelanders . . . Some minutes after a GI entered bearing not a piece of fruit, but a basket of assorted fruits, and a box of chocolates to boot."

Iceland had opened a diplomatic mission in New York City following the invasion of Denmark. It made inquiries as to whether it could secure U.S. protection under the Monroe Doctrine; Iceland seriously thought it could—by dint of its closeness to U.S. waters—offer itself as a part of Washington's sphere of interest. The United States declined, but Winston Churchill was intrigued. Iceland could become a way of nudging neutral America into the war against Hitler. The United States was neutral, so was Iceland, but by May 1941, Franklin Roosevelt—concerned by the deepening American involvement in the German U-boat campaign in Atlantic waters—had offered to take over the protection of Iceland. It was legally and politically complicated, in an isolationist America, to occupy a foreign neutral. An invitation was required from Reykjavik, and it duly arrived with fifteen provisions—including full recognition of Iceland's independence and a promise to withdraw "immediately on conclusion of the present war."

The Americans broke their promise, however, and as the wartime garrison mutated into a Cold War strategic base, Icelanders groaned publicly about being betrayed. But the U.S. presence marked the beginning of a sense of wealth. At the onset of war in 1939, Iceland was deeply in debt, with a severe shortage of foreign-exchange reserves. By the end of the war, thanks to the investment of U.S. forces, Iceland was a creditor nation, with strong currency reserves, and a good balance of trade—the fishing fleet had been able to trawl without competition for five years and had no shortage of international customers. In 1941, the Americans had started to build a major air base at Keflavik, a forty-minute drive out of the capital. During wartime, the airfield had been used as a refueling stopover for aircraft flying between the United States and United Kingdom. The harbor had been expanded and deepened. Farmers had grown rich supplying sheep, milk, and chickens to the U.S. bases. Across the island, construction equipment used by the Americans and the British was, as the war ended, handed over to the Icelanders. Roads were built; there was no shortage of work for out-of-season fishermen.

The attraction of America as a modernizing force, a global pacesetter, was already apparent to Icelanders before the war. Halldór Laxness—who was to win the Nobel Prize for Literature in 1955—set out for the United States in 1927 to make his name in Hollywood. It didn't quite work out, but while he was there writing scripts, he became friendly with one Icelandic emigrant after another, from Bill Cody, a star in cowboy movies (from Skagafjoerdur), to the comedian Barney Bronson (real name Bjaerni Bjoernsson). These émigrés—Western Icelanders, as they are still called in Reykjavik—embody the island's search for the modern. All, including Laxness, were deeply skeptical of capitalism, a society that tolerated so much urban poverty, yet they were hungry for information about how the world of money functioned, how the pace of life could be accelerated. The claustrophobia of the island was set against the wide-openness of the United States. There was, too, the sheer materialistic pull of America. Laxness, a skeptical Catholic-turned-Communist, was quick to buy a luxurious American limousine after winning the Nobel Prize. At a news conference in Iceland, a journalist asked him if it was not ridiculously expensive to drive a long, sleek car designed for cruising around Beverly Hills on the bumpy gravel farm tracks that made up the island's road network. The audience fell silent; then, as now, it was not usual in Iceland to pose provocative questions in public. After a moment, Laxness sighed and replied, "It is generally very expensive to be an Icelander."

The view of America, of its power and its temptations, was thus a confusing amalgam of fears and ambition. Yes, the United States was helping to make Iceland richer than it had ever been before. Most Nordic societies could boast a golden age, but not Iceland, unless one counted the long-ago bounty and loot of the Vikings. No, this was it: the modernization not only of its hospitals, the building of hotels, but also the modernization of Icelandic society, its transformation from an atomized, individualistic, and clan-bonded culture to a proper nation-state with a global role.

Yet the Icelanders also saw the global intrusion as something impure, fickle. When Iceland became a founding member of NATO in 1949—prompting fierce, angry protests—the Americans started to expand the air base at Keflavik, and the island began to fear contamination. Icelandic girls fell for the apparent charms of the American soldiers, became pregnant, aborted. Icelandic society has always been relaxed about single motherhood, but only because parentage was so easy to establish since everyone takes his or her father's name. The daughter of Olafur may be called Kerstin, but her surname will be Olafsdottir—daughter of Olafur. Olafur's son takes the name Olafsson. Family pressure meanwhile ensured an active, responsible paternal role. But bearing the child of a foreigner due to leave the island and never return? That was shaming. Tension crackled between the Icelandic menfolk and the seemingly more sexually successful Americans. Until the 1960s, Icelandic governments—in various political constellations—asked the U.S. military authorities not to send black soldiers to the NATO bases on the island. The U.S. government complied, withdrawing its (racially) "mixed" units. And the tension spilled over into other areas. U.S. television shows beamed out to the soldiers on the base were deemed corrupting and were banned from Icelandic sets. This marked the birth of an independent Icelandic television service, family friendly and purged of American influence.

This prejudice against the new, the foreign, the strange, was very provincial. The Icelandic political class was indeed rurally based, sometimes only a generation away from relatives living in turf cottages. But there was another anxiety about America and the way it was changing Iceland that revolved around Keflavik. Yes, the establishment of the base had unlocked international funding. Thanks to U.S. interest, Marshall Plan money was drummed up to build the Icelandic cement works and its fertilizer plant, to drain the marshland and begin a proper program for hydroelectric power. The Icelandic government of Olafur Thors was justifiably worried that the economic boom of the war years would quickly be followed by a slump, a depression, if the Americans withdrew. The Icelanders were accustomed, with bad harvests and erratic fishing years, to boom-bust cycles, but the war had done more than enrich the country. It had raised expectations to extraordinarily high levels and had started a new wave in the island's long, chronic struggle with inflation. If Keflavik remained a base, if the Icelanders in effect abandoned the neutrality that was anchored in their 1920 constitution, then the country could continue the path toward prosperity and modernity. That was the dilemma confronting the postwar government, and these underlying issues—the restricted options of a small country seeking to maintain independence in the face of big global interests—remain to this day.

"Couldn't we have done it without the Americans?" asks writer Andri Snaer Magnason. "Did we, through depending on others, fail to cultivate our own independence and creativity and choose instead to reward other things? Was it good that shipping companies were given monopolies for the transportation of certain goods, or that the contractors with contacts in the right places cleaned up on building projects on the Keflavik base, all with pretty certain guarantees of easy profits?" This kind of dependency on the outside world as a wealth-creation machine, argues Magnason, ultimately impoverishes a society. "In the long run, sudden wealth and rapid growth can undermine the foundations of a society and lock people into a system where some have it so easy that they no longer dare take risks."

Keflavik grew to be a mammoth base, complete with a hospital, schools, beauty shops, its own bank, bowling facilities, and a Wendy's hamburger restaurant. The aircraft—AWACS reconnaissance planes, F-15 Eagles— roared over Iceland for more than four decades. At least until the collapse of the Soviet Union and the Warsaw Pact, the Pentagon saw Keflavik as a vital part of its forward defense. More than one thousand Soviet planes were intercepted and turned back over Icelandic airspace; Moscow's submarines were monitored as they moved into the Atlantic. U.S. strategic bombers were refueled. The initial U.S. idea was to make the island into *Battleship Iceland*, heavily armed and ready—if the Soviet Union wiped out NATO bases in West Germany—to become a launchpad against Moscow. Iceland's geography, which had always been a mixed blessing—rich in fish but too remote to make any political impact on the world—could, in the Cold War, be translated into cash advantages.

By 1955, four years after the NATO base became fully operational, it was generating 18 percent of all Iceland's foreign earnings. There was a hidden price, though: a lurking sense of insecurity, of having become a target. That gave a boost to the local Communist Party. Significantly, the Soviet embassy in Reykjavik became one of the largest in northern Europe. During the Cold War, Iceland was a potentially interesting prize for the Russians, and remains so today. Thriller writer Arnaldur Indridason set one of his well-researched books (*The Draining Lake*) during the Cold War, at a time when Icelandic Communists were being sent to study at East German universities—and returning as spies. The KGB's interest in American intentions for Iceland was almost bottomless. The author depicts a Russian diplomat saying, "Obviously we would have wanted to observe the base, the transportation of military hardware, movements of warships, aircraft, submarines . . . not just in Keflavik. There were activities all over Iceland."

The statement, though fictional, rings true. Iceland was, in the 1970s and 1980s, a magnet for spies. Mainly Western diplomats spying on Eastern diplomats and vice versa. But Icelanders were recruited too, and though everyone is silent about those days—the country is so small that an indiscretion quickly becomes known—the mere presence of the Keflavik base plainly polarized families, forcing people to choose sides in public. "How could one be against the presence of an army that made us richer and protected us from harm? An army that introduced us to Elvis and rock 'n' roll?" Björn is in his sixties and has been sent to the Kringlan shopping mall by his wife to make the week's purchases. The shelves still reflect American appetites—Betty Crocker, Ben & Jerry's ice cream—rather than dried fish or squashed lamb heads. "But you can also say, how could one sustain an army on a base that irritated superpower relations, that took us a step further from world peace, that eroded trust and solidarity within society?" Iceland no longer lies on a strategic fault line—not at the moment anyway—but it is playing a significant role in a global collapse. "We're just the bloody canary in the coal mine," says Björn, adjusting his baggy Pepe jeans. "We die first—just as we were supposed to do in the Cold War." He took a box of Cheerios and placed it carefully in the shopping cart.

But in the 1950s, the Keflavik base—now something of a ghost town, housing a few student hostels—drew real passion in Iceland. Thousands marched the thirty miles from the capital to the base, down the windy Reykjanes Peninsula, across the rusty-brown lava fields, to demonstrate their hatred of the place. It was not just about war, about the loss of neutrality, the branding of a proud community as a mere garrison. Rather, it was the touchstone of modernity. How much were they willing to change; how much of their identity could they surrender? No one wanted to live in the Middle Ages, go back to turf cottages—but was the price of progress Americanization?

By the 1990s, with the Cold War no more than a week's worth of teaching on the high school curriculum, many Icelanders started to be less dogmatic. Since there was no Soviet Union, there was no danger to Iceland. The base had become irrelevant and harmless—so why not keep it? Closure would have put as many as a thousand Icelanders out of work, a large number for a tiny country and a strain on the welfare budget. The Independence Party—Iceland's conservatives—argued that if the country was going to plead for the continuation of the base, reversing decades of hostility, the government would have to be more understanding of U.S. policies. Everything—economic growth, security, independence—had its price.

The logic of the Keflavik U-turn later became part of the existential debate about whether—or how far—Iceland should open itself to the global economy. Many (by no means all) Icelanders came to see that the opposition to the U.S. Air Force base had been little more than an attempt to stop the clock, to control events that were ultimately out of the island's control. When, in 1991, the Independence Party came up with a forceful prime minister, David Oddsson, ready to privatize industry, to borrow ideas from Ronald Reagan and Margaret Thatcher, to take Iceland to the next level, his natural critics bit their tongues. Perhaps they had been wrong about Keflavik. Was American television so bad? Was American-style dating really so immoral? Weren't we all a bit more American now, and none the worse for it? More: Hadn't capitalism just won the war against socialism? Shouldn't Iceland be on the winning side?

How humiliating, though, to make concessions to the outside world. Those who read the transcript of David Oddsson's 2004 visit to the White House understood the gritty reality: a small power is doomed to surrender. "That's the way it is," says Björn, "you swallow your pride three times a day with your meals, like headache pills. And maybe for a while, the migraine recedes."

David Oddsson's mission to Washington was clear: to persuade George Bush to keep the Keflavik base.

George Bush's agenda was even simpler. To celebrate his fifty-eighth birthday.

> President Bush: It's my honor to welcome the prime minister of Iceland to the Oval Office . . . Mr. Prime Minister, thank you for coming.
>
> Prime Minister Oddsson: Thank you very much, Mr. President. I'm very happy to be here, not least on the president's birthday. It's a privilege.
>
> Pres. Bush: Thank you for remembering . . .
>
> Press question: Mr. Prime Minister, did you reach an agreement on the defense treaty with Iceland?
>
> PM Oddsson: That was never—the meeting—was to have an agreement. Now, today I had the opportunity to explain my

view of the issue to the president, and he is looking into my position on the Iceland position, but he had an open mind.

Pres. Bush: Yes. Let me comment on this, about—this is an issue related to the F-15s. For the American press, we've got four F-15 fighters stationed there. The prime minister pressed very hard for us to keep the fighters there. He was very eloquent, very determined that the United States keep the troops there . . . I told the prime minister I'm—I appreciate our alliance, I appreciate his friendship. I fully understand the arguments he's made, and we will work together to solve the issue. Holland, where are you?

Press question: Here, sir. Thank you. There's a story today that the CIA held back information from you that Iraq had abandoned its WMD [weapons of mass destruction] programs. Is that true? . . .

Pres. Bush: This is information from the report of the United States Senate . . . I will look at the whole report. I will tell you, however, that I know that Saddam Hussein was a threat. He was a threat to the neighborhood; he was a threat to the people of Iraq. He harbored terrorists.
. . .

PM Oddsson: Well, I just—on this, I must say I agree with the president about Iraq . . .

Pres. Bush: Thank you, Mr. Prime Minister.

The reporters in the Oval Office start to sing "Happy birthday, Mr. President." David Oddsson joins in.

Pres. Bush: Thanks. You actually call that singing? [Laughter] It was beautiful.

3 : Carve-up

*The Icelander's temperament is nervoso-lymphatic
and at best nervoso-sanguineous.*
Richard Burton, 1875

It is dark when I leave Hildur Helga's house, but not pitch-black. As I walk to the university to talk to yet more economists, the texture, the feel of the day before dawn—it is ten A.M.—is of damp brown gabardine. Or more charitably, of a painterly chiaroscuro; faces appear green and scooped-out under the streetlight, then disappear. The harbor is far away, maybe a mile, but the dockside sounds—the clatter of chains, the busy hooting—seem to carry up through the town, so complete is the sensory deprivation of an early-morning winter meeting in Reykjavik. I am looking for some clarity, some precision in the gloom. Perhaps no single profession has so consistently disappointed in this crisis as that of the economist. Yet all I want is a simple answer to the question, when did the global meltdown begin? Establish that and you are halfway to understanding.

The straightforward response that I expect from the dissident economist Gylfi Magnusson is September 15, 2008, when the United States pulled the plug on Lehman Brothers. It was a deeply shocking event. The magnate Jon Asgeir Johannesson, whose own bank, Glitnir, was nationalized, appeared on an Icelandic talk show shortly afterward and briefly abandoned his swagger to blurt out, like a baffled child, "Why would they do that? Why did they let Lehman go?" But identifying the trigger for a panic attack—however sustained, however frightening—is not the same as establishing the causes of the underlying neurotic condition.

Some have argued that we were gripped by a collective madness at the turn of the millennium. We expected the Y2K, a global computer bug, and instead caught the get-rich-quick bug. Tina Brown, whose former job as editor of *Vanity Fair* was to monitor how people get rich, took the pulse as Bernard Madoff's hapless investors found they had been robbed. "*Something* went wrong on or about the dawn of the millennium, that's for sure—and it keeps on going wrong. Did the 2000 election and 9/11 and Iraq and now maybe Great Depression II—in short, the Bush years—unhinge us into some strange collective suicide spree of self-indulgence, self-delusion, and blind pursuit of money money money till we drowned in it?" Tina Brown may have been a little breathless in her questioning, but the framework was right: an element of hysteria, of irrationality, crept into the business world and into everyday commercial dealings. When I reach Gylfi's office, as neat as a ship's cabin, I find him reading a paperback edition of John Kenneth Galbraith's *A Short History of Financial Euphoria*, and I know that I am not going to get a short answer. The fifteen-year-old work identifies Tina Brown–style adrenaline rush as the hallmark of a bubble: "The euphoric episode is protected and sustained by the will of those who are involved, in order to justify the circumstances that are making them rich."

But the roots of Iceland's crisis, and those experienced elsewhere, run deeper, in the imperfect privatization waves, the era of Reagonomics and of Thatcherite dismantling of the nanny state. The transfer of state assets into private hands was seen as a liberating moment for arthritic, stagnant societies weighed down with egalitarian ideas. Margaret Thatcher swept into power in 1979 as the result of popular disillusion with the inept financial management of the previous Labour government. This was symbolized by the return of a suntanned Prime Minister Jim Callaghan from an international summit in Guadeloupe to a strikebound London, its streets clogged with rubbish left uncollected by striking garbagemen. "Crisis? What crisis?" he declared. Ronald Reagan, elected president in 1981, similarly took over a messy, stagnant situation left by the outgoing administration of Jimmy Carter, including 11.8 per cent inflation—the highest since 1947—high unemployment, and high interest rates. Stagflation, in other words, though I share Galbraith's aesthetic doubts about the term ("There are some additions to the English language that are too wretched").

In 1984, three years into Reaganomics and four years into Thatcherism,

their economic guru, Milton Friedman, traveled to Reykjavik to debate his policies on television with leftist skeptics and to deliver a public speech. In the audience he had a group of fans, including the then young mayor of Reykjavik, later to be prime minister, David Oddsson. Mayor Oddsson, surrounded by some of his young, conservative acolytes, enthusiastically applauded Friedman. The American economist was asked by an outraged Icelander why the audience had to pay an entry fee for the lecture: free education had always been an essential part of Icelandic culture at the core of its civil society. "There's no such thing as a free education," snapped Friedman. Oddsson laughed out loud and slapped his chair. That is what Iceland needed—a shake-up of the old egalitarian values that were stifling competition and growth.

That lecture was a milestone of an intellectual and ideological odyssey that led ultimately to the near-bankruptcy of Iceland. Like Thatcher, Oddsson was a polarizing figure, capable of strong friendship. His main criteria for political selection—as he rose to be prime minister and then central-bank governor—were unquestioning loyalty, commitment to a free market ideology, and a readiness to laugh at his sardonic and inter-mittently funny quips. Administrative competence came a distant fourth. He grew up with his mother and grandmother—whom he would quote at length on important occasions—in Selfoss, a small town on the south coast of Iceland, famous only for its oversize grocery store. His father, a doctor, was a distant figure, not married to his mother, and both parents had other children with other partners. Young David was indulged by his various female relatives, who encouraged him to perform on the stage and try on fancy dress. Apparently, he spent a lot of time in front of the mirror.

Reykjavik has two grammar schools, and they have been the breeding ground for the political and business classes. In this hothouse—"a mosquito swamp," in the words of one Icelandic writer—future rulers bonded, initiated lifelong feuds, argued about girlfriends, and sorted out their political views. Oddsson's school, the Menntaskolinn—or more pompously, the Sigullum Schola Reykjavicencis—can trace its origins back to 1056, one of the oldest Icelandic institutions, and has been on its current site, long and brown and squat, since the mid-nineteenth century. Almost all of Iceland's prime ministers were educated there. Oddsson is remembered for his extravagant hairstyle, vaguely influenced by Elvis Presley, but which now, essentially unchanged with age, seems to owe more to the flamboyant Serb war criminal Radovan Karadzic; a combative poet's graying quiff. At school, he played the lead role in Alfred Jarry's *Ubu Roi*, the absurd, arrogant leader. Since then he has been nicknamed King Bubbi, *Bubbi* being the Icelandic version of Ubu. His best school friends included Geir Haarde (who was to succeed him as inspector scholae, chief school prefect, and later as prime minister—in January 2009 Haarde let his government coalition collapse rather than fire his schoolboy mentor Oddsson as central-bank governor). Then there was Kjartan Gunnarsson (who would later be made vice chairman of the board of Landsbanki), Hrafn Gunnlaugsson (who became head of production of state TV under the Oddsson prime ministership), Kari Stefansson (CEO at Decode, the genetic-research group enthusiastically promoted by Oddsson), and Jon Steinar Gunnlaugsson (appointed a Supreme Court judge despite criticism from other lawyers, claiming he was underqualified). These became the hub of the Oddsson system as he moved from the mayor's office to the prime ministership. It was a team, but more than that, a kind of freemasonry. Two men who collaborated with Oddsson on devising a successful radio-show format never wanted for work; others who helped him with his literary endeavors (he wrote volumes of short stories) had their careers nudged along or were bailed out of trouble.

The Icelandic nation is ancient; the state relatively new. So there was little to hold up a strong character such as Oddsson from using state institutions—solely in the service of the nation, of course—as a means of supplying favors to those loyal to the leader. If all that smacks of a cult of personality, well, that's what it was. Oddsson branded himself— big hair, big talents—and created a court that maintained a checklist of who could be considered a Friend of David, and who not. It was a Manichaean world, thronged with enemies who wanted, but could not be allowed, to hinder Oddsson's holy mission of modernizing Iceland. Margaret Thatcher famously dismissed an internal critic as "not one of us." The common link between Oddsson and his heroine Margaret Thatcher was ideological conviction, a certainty that the relationship between the state and the individual had to be changed, that the nation could only gain mettle if more competitors and more choice were introduced—and this shift, this revolution, could only be ushered in by a tight-knit avant-garde. Many of the neocons who rose to power under George W. Bush had a similar flair for conspiratorial organization. Oddsson shared their fascination with conspiracy.

So much for Oddsson's political romanticism, his absolute belief that only he could save the Icelandic nation. There were, however, two problems. First, Iceland, though it had a large Communist Party, strong unions, and a broadly egalitarian ethic, was not on the verge of collapse in the 1980s. It was muddling through. The economy needed an overhaul, but it was not exactly crying out for a Thatcherite revolution led by the disciples of Milton Friedman. Inflation was high, but the Icelanders had lived with that for decades. Nor was there any major social opposition—as there was in other Nordic countries—to privatization, providing it was done for pragmatic, commercial reasons. Before Oddsson got to work on his privatization program, one bank had already been taken out of state control. As mayor of the capital he had carried out modest, practical disposals of state assets. By most accounts, Oddsson was a successful mayor. Forceful—he pushed through the development of the "Pearl," an attempt to introduce architectural novelty to a complex of giant hot-water tanks—but also briskly efficient. To become a Thatcherite leader, however, demanded different skills. In essence he had to reinvent Iceland, convince the people that they were living in a run-down state that would never be able to cope with modern society. It was indeed a nanny state: beer was banned until 1989; television shut down on Thursdays to give families time to talk, sing, and read books. It was a tribute to Oddsson's powers as a persuader, in the Reagan mode, that he convinced Iceland it was an unhappy society, waiting for him to lead it to prosperity and contentment. Oddsson had a stage actor's feel for his audience: once they were made aware of a problem, they were ready to participate in the solution. "It's like that passage in Orwell's *Road to Wigan Pier*," a translator tells me. "He goes to a bunch of coal miners and asks, 'How long have you suffered from the housing shortage?' And they answer, 'Since we were told about it.' That's what David has always done well—he has raised consciousness. People listen to him, even if they can't stand him."

Iceland had grown up with a tradition of chieftains, of *gothar*, the men who offered up the sacrifices to the gods. Now, after decades of indifferent rule, it had one again. He had levered his way into the vice chairmanship of the Independence Party, the conservatives, in 1989, and took control two years later, ousting his school chum Thorstein Palsson. Around him was his revolutionary cell who had worked together on a magazine, *Locomotive*, propagating the ideas of Friedman and Friedrich von Hayek: Kjartan Gunnarsson, Jon Steinar Gunnlaugsson, the ever-faithful lapdog Geir Haarde. One of the contributors was Palsson; now he had been pushed out by his former friends. It was a characteristic Oddsson putsch. David duly became prime minister in 1991 with the Social Democrats as a coalition partner. Inflation was high; state coffers almost empty. "Let's get to work!" Oddsson told his cabinet.

First, though, Oddsson had to reassure the old, established wealthy families of Iceland that rapid, systematic privatization was not going to impoverish them or dilute their power. These families—known as the Octopus in Iceland because their tentacles gripped the island—had grown rich primarily by gaining control over transport routes. This is the key to power on a remote island. At its heart was the Eimskip steam-ship firm, formed in 1914: the publicly owned company had caught the popular imagination. Some thirteen thousand—out of a popula-tion of one hundred thousand—bought into the firm. Fathers would proudly take their sons to the dockside to inspect the large-funneled steamers. Eimskip's harborside headquarters—now a Radisson hotel—was burnished with polished teak and was as solid (as they used to say) as a bank. The swastika, a Nordic rune that used to be Eimskip's symbol, has since been removed. The directors grew nervous about the possible competition from air travel, and by the 1920s the shipping magnates were forming the first Icelandic airline: a single Avro 504 bought from Britain. After a year the plane had to be sold, and not until the 1940s did a proper airline began to take shape—Flugfelag Islands, later named Icelandair—using the airfields laid by the British and the Americans.

Almost immediately, Flugfelag Islands faced competition. Three young Icelandic pilots studying in Canada bought their own plane and brought it to Iceland after independence was declared in 1944. When Flugfelag Islands refused them jobs, they formed their own airline, Loftleidir. The two young airlines competed furiously, a testimony to Icelandic entrepreneurship and initiative. In the 1950s one of Loftleidir's ramshackle DC-3s carrying an interesting cargo of industrial diamonds, performing dogs, and the body of an American colonel crashed into Vatnajökull, Iceland's highest glacier. The U.S. Air Force sent a ski-fitted C-47 to retrieve the coffin of the colonel. But this too crashed. The Icelanders ended up rescuing both crews, but Loftleidir typically struck a deal with the Americans: $700 for the wreckage of the C-47. The salvage team, in extraordinarily hazardous conditions, carried the aircraft sixty miles across sheer ice down to a lower valley. There, the Icelanders repaired the engines. The next stage was to give the plane a lick of paint—and sell it for $80,000 to a Spanish airline. That profit helped Loftleidir finance the first of a modern fleet.

Flugfelag Islands found it difficult to compete against this kind of energy and decided to raise capital so that it could move into major international routes. Eimskip bought a quarter of the airline's shares—and insisted that an Eimskip man became chairman. They then set about crushing the competition. The government paid its dues to the Octopus and locked Loftleidir out of domestic routes. The Loftleidir managers responded by becoming the world's first low-cost airline on transatlantic routes—with the beguiling slogan "We fly slower, but we're lower"—and succeeded in annoying established airlines across mainland Europe. When the International Air Transport Association (IATA) loosened its pricing regulations in 1970, Loftleidir's risk-takers were doomed. They merged with Flugfelag and became the modern Icelandair—enjoying a monopoly on all flights in and out of Iceland and giving Eimskip unprecedented power on the island.

This was a triumph for the mercantile barons of the Octopus. Only in 1990 did it become clear that Eimskip—once the Icelanders' introduction to popular capitalism—was part of a tightly knit clique of businessmen and politicians. The company's books, reluctantly opened, revealed that 40 percent of the stock was owned by fourteen people, who controlled the board. The board had been buying up stock sold by shareholders without putting it on the market. Steered by the magic fourteen, Eimskip had snatched one third of the shares in Icelandair and swallowed up its biggest competitor, the shipping company Hafskip. Fourteen families, the families of the Octopus, controlled all movement in and out of the island. The timber trade, for example, was in the tentacles of the Octopus. Since there were no trees on Iceland, timber had to be imported, on ships run by Eimskip. Access to timber was the key to controlling the construction industry. Since the timber and paper trade worked hand in hand, it was inevitable that newspapers too landed in the grasp of these business elites. The families did not just make money, they made policies that suited them. Of the fourteen, two clans are important: the Engey family and the H. Ben family. Both were influential within the Independence Party, and each had supplied its own prime minister.

The Engey family takes its name from the tiny island of Engey just offshore from Reykjavik. Bjarni Benediktsson—prime minister between 1963 and 1970—was the godfather of the Engey clan. His grandson, who bears the same name, became the leader of the Independence Party in 2009 in succession to Geir Haarde. The Engey family controlled over the years not only Eimskip and Icelandair, but also the NI oil company and Islandsbanki, and the powerful Sjova insurance company was founded by Bjarni Sr.'s brother, Svein Benediktsson. Since the 1970s, an iron rule has been that no one rises within the Independence Party without paying his dues to the family; Oddsson in particular regarded Bjarni Benediktsson Sr. as a model for the prime ministership.

The other important Octopus clan were the so-called H. Bens, named after Hallgrimur Benediktsson. They too produced an Icelandic leader—Geir Hallgrimsson, who was prime minister between 1974 and 1978, for the Independence Party of course. Their economic interests included Shell Iceland, car dealerships, and a sweets factory.

The Octopus was not a formal group; it was essentially an owner-ship pattern. The families did not own everything, it just felt that way. A smaller grouping, nicknamed the Squid, was rooted in the Icelandic cooperative movement and offered its adherents—the island's fish smok-eries for example—a degree of protection. By the late 1980s, however, companies were dropping out of the Squid's clammy embrace. In some ways the Octopus resembles the old Mafia structures of Sicily—but without the crime. "You know, I've been talking about the Octopus. for years," says a veteran journalist, "but I still don't know what it really means." Many Italians say something similar about the Mafia; it is a way of doing business. Unlike the Sicilians or the Calabrians, however, the Octopus families do not settle differences with bloodshed. They have become venerable establishment figures, firmly holding a slice in every lucrative activity on the island. But this, at least, they demanded from a young, aspiring conservative politician: respect. The Octopus could make things happen, or it could block them. A good prime ministership therefore depended on the goodwill of the families.

What were they to make of Oddsson? He was, perhaps, a touch too flamboyant, but he had been a good mayor of Reykjavik, passing one of the traditional tests for aspiring prime ministers. His privatization of the HB Grandi fishing concern had been carried out without seriously infringing Octopus interests. The Octopus families had by 1990–91 watched for more than a decade Thatcherite privatization across the water in Britain and had seen that it could make society wealthier. More to the point, Thatcherism had made it respectable to display wealth; for some younger members of Octopus dynasties that could be a relief; for the older generation, the model of Thatcher and Reagan remained ineffably vulgar. But of course as long as Oddsson would allow Octopus companies to enrich themselves through the sale of state assets, there could be no serious objection.

And so it was. Before ordinary Icelanders got greedy, their business elite sensed that Oddsson was about to open a treasure chest. With the faithful Geir Haarde as his finance minister, he began his mission of bringing wealth to a poor island: abolition of government funds propping up unprofitable entrepreneurs; liberalization of the currency; lowering the corporate income tax from 45 to 18 percent. It was the Milton Friedman hymn sheet, already used by Thatcher and Reagan. But there was also a rougher, more knockabout model for transition: Icelandic privatization and its opening up to the world happened in parallel to the unlocking of the Russian economy. The Russian push toward the market was, like the Icelandic, driven by the popular wish to live according to what was perceived as the Western norm, to somehow align their lives with the lives depicted in the U.S. television series watched across the country, across the generations. On paper the Oddsson program was clearly Reaganesque and Thatcherite: to transform society, to empower the individual, to offer choices. As expressed by Geir Haarde (in a 2001 speech to the Icelan British chamber of commerce), they were on a holy mission:

> Since 1991 we have been pursuing four main objectives:
> 1. to increase private saving—by selling shares in public offerings,
> 2. to increase efficiency,
> 3. to broaden share ownership and develop the Icelandic stock market,
> 4. and to raise capital to reduce Treasury debt.

The same cannot be said of the Russian privatizations; there was no empowerment of the many involved, only enrichment of the few. "Russia's new capitalist elite grew dizzyingly rich in a remarkably short time," says Chrystia Freeland, author of *Sale of the Century*, "but its fortunes were not based on new technologies, more efficient services or more productive factories." Rather, they were built by capturing pieces of the collapsing Soviet state. The Oddsson team was later accused by one of Iceland's dissident economists, Thorvaldur Gylfasson, of reproducing Russian behavior in their privatization of the banks. "One beneficiary of the banks' privatization—a politician whose private-sector experience consisted of running two small knitwear factories in the 1970s, a few months each—became an instant billionaire. Iceland became Russia." But at the outset, there was a kind of ideological clarity. The government tried to disentangle itself within the first eighteen months from its state-owned travel company, fertilizer plant, fish-processing factories, printing works, and alcohol production. As the Oddsson team cut through this collection of companies, it became clear to ordinary Icelanders how deeply the state was involved in their lives, and where a large chunk of their taxes was going.

"For decades, beginning in 1927 when a farmers' party gained a parliamentary majority," says Thorvaldur Gylfasson of the University of Iceland, "the Icelandic economy was more heavily regulated than most in Western Europe. Interference and planning were the norm." Oddsson followed the neoliberal textbook. Tax rebates were offered for those who bought shares; entrepreneurship was encouraged. A deal with the trade unions to curb wage agreements helped bring down inflation; so too did a recession in the early 1990s that brought down consumer demand. Although Oddsson was resolutely against the European Union and the euro, he accepted the need to belong to the European Economic Area. From 1994, this helped his modernization project, forcing competition onto the island.

The Icelandic equivalent to oil and raw materials in the Russian privatization was fish. Oddsson's ambition was for Iceland to move from fish to finance, to realize the dream of Iceland's only Nobel Prize–winning author, Halldór Laxness: "We have to prove to the rest of the world that the fish can sing just like a bird." Fish could make life beautiful and should be treasured like songbirds. Oddsson knew the figures: fishing contributed 12 percent to the GDP, but stocks were dwindling. His deep opposition to joining the European Union was not just a nod to the politics of Thatcher but also a straightforward expression of the national interest—joining the EU meant its fisheries policy would open up Icelandic waters to foreign fleets and the slow death of the island's trawlers. Oddsson's Independents were in coalition with the Social Democrats, who insisted that fishing companies should pay a so-called resources fee. The money would go toward replenishing the fish stocks. Oddsson said that would be too much of a strain on business. Instead, he promoted a system of individual transferable quotas whereby each fishing boat was given a quota for each species caught, on the basis of the average catch of the previous three years. This was monitored with high-tech electronics as soon as the fish were landed in any of the country's fifty-three ports. The Fisheries Directorate knew precisely how much fish was being caught, as did the trawlermen, who could be guided by the market on whether to stay in port or net some more. The quota is the property of the fishing-boat owner—he can, if he so chooses, sell a chunk of it to someone else. The system has been praised: the fishing fleets are no longer overcapacity, the catch per boat is increasing, and prices are stable.

"There is nothing really wrong with the economics or biological consequences of a quota fishing system," Gylfi Magnusson tells me. "Before that we had restrictions on what days you could fish, what kind of fishing tackle, and it didn't work well."

The problem, though, was that the government was handing over something for nothing. "Anyone who wants to start fishing now has to purchase the rights from those who got it free," admits Magnusson. Although the system was merely streamlined by Oddsson, it came to symbolize his approach to the economy. Margaret Thatcher popularized capitalism by giving people in subsidized council housing the right to buy the homes they lived in. That allowed the state to save money, created a new home-owning working class, and shifted attitudes to saving; it was intelligent populism. When the political elite in Iceland gave away a public good free of charge, it enriched only a few fishing-vessel owners and their political sponsors. It was the greatest wealth transfer in Icelandic history.

The Irish have their "mackerel millionaires"; the Icelanders suddenly found themselves with quota kings.

"Until then," says Gylfi Magnusson, "the well-off Icelanders conformed to a certain norm. He had his own three-bedroomed house, a summer house in the countryside, two cars, and he took holidays abroad. Then came the quota millionaires with a surge of wealth, and the upper-middle class stood aghast!" By buying and selling quotas, by concentrating them, owners of even relatively small fleets became dollar millionaries within weeks. They were rough, uncultured, and suddenly—like lottery winners—they were next door. "What are you going to do with nineteen rooms—your children have left, and your wife has run away," the seventy-eight-year-old Yrsa Gunnarsdottir asked her neighbor who had hired hard-drinking Polish construction teams to bang and hammer away at a flashy mansion overlooking the sea in what used to be a staid middle-class district of Reykjavik. The millionaire just grinned—old women enjoy privileged status—but she had hit a sore point. In the wake of the enriched fishermen came a new phenomenon: the fish-quota wife, slightly brassy, with a taste for leopard-skin sofas and gold faucets, who moved with unusual swiftness toward the divorce courts. For them, the fish did indeed sing like birds.

The quota fortunes were to become part of the overall crisis in Iceland. Since quotas were now regarded as property, loans could be taken out using them as security. The money, plowed into foreign adventures, secured by fish that had not yet been taken out of the ocean, was lost when the banks crashed. Now most fishery companies are saddled with heavy foreign-currency debts. Deutsche Bank, in effect, owns the haddock still swimming freely in the Atlantic.

But that could not be predicted at the beginning of the Oddsson years. As far as Icelanders were concerned, a few fishermen had got lucky, but the main thing was that privatization had served the national interest. The first investment that really stirred the imagination of the Icelanders was not in fish but in genes. In 1996, five years after assuming the prime ministership, Oddsson had helped his school chum Kari Stefansson to return to Iceland from the United States. Kari was a poster boy for Oddsson's Iceland: handsome with icy blue eyes, he had trained as a doctor, done well as a medical researcher in the United States, and was now returning with his wife and children to an island that had a bright new future. More, he had a compelling idea that linked up the essential nature of the nation with the new capitalism. Just as the singer Björk had used Icelandic tradition to market herself for global success, so Kari Stefansson was ready to transform the Icelanders' fascination with their ancestors into a profitable, market-leading concern. All he needed was a state guarantee to underwrite the expansion of his genetic database so that it included the whole of the island. The Icelanders have become a little more multicultural over the past twenty years, but they remain a basically homogeneous nation, with a precise knowledge of their genealogical heritages. "I can trace my family back to the Settlement, to the ninth century," says Hildur Helga, without registering any particular pride. "So can most of us." The information gleaned can be used to track and explain the evolution of hereditary diseases—and could in theory be a gold mine for pharmaceutical companies. The Icelanders were enthusiastic and bought up clusters of shares in the company Decode, marking a big step into popular capitalism, comparable in emotional terms to the German enthusiasm for Telekom shares. The state support made it seem like a sure thing.

Then things started to go wrong. The surgeon general warned in the Icelandic equivalent of the *Lancet* or the *Journal of the American Medical Association* that the personal data could be abused in the future—by private insurance companies, for example, assessing health risks and raising premiums. The Union of Icelandic Physicians registered their opposition.

Icelanders were then given an opt-out clause: they could withhold their data. By 2001 the share price of Decode wobbled, then collapsed. Many Icelanders had taken out loans to buy the shares, especially after hearing the repeated blandishments of Stefansson's deputy Hannes Smarason. Both Smarason and Stefansson went on to make fortunes, and Decode survives. But thousands of Icelanders took a dive. For them, it was the first signal that privatization could be flawed, that the grand drama of modernization through popular capitalism might be acted out at a cost to ordinary investors. Iceland was supposed to be on the winning side of globalization—that was the Oddsson pledge. In reality, the winners were often his old schoolmates. The spirit of the Menntaskolinn had survived into middle age.

Does Thatcherism—or Reaganomics—encourage cronyism? From the moment that a government announces itself to be pro-business, the conduits are opened. Businessmen were admired at the courts of Thatcher (she was, after all, married to a doting former executive of Castrol) and Reagan, given easy access, consulted on key legislation. Under Thatcher, British politicians took to accepting free holidays at lakeside resorts and trips in private planes. Cabinet ministers often found themselves with director-ships or consultancies after leaving office. The relationships stemmed from a structural interdependency: the state was divesting some of its economic power, through deregulation and privatization, yet it wanted to retain influence. How did it do so? Through networks that ensured the place-ment of like-minded people in the economic engine room. The golf course became an important part of the political process: a place to consolidate and test alliances with promising businessmen (Denis Thatcher took on these arduous putting-green duties for his wife). Does the risk of lucrative state assets handed on a plate to friends and allies compromise privatiza-tion? Did it feed into the global meltdown of trust? It did in the Oddsson years in Iceland, not just because of his own tribal system of loyalty—of dues to be paid, favors to be dispensed—but because the Icelandic political class demanded it. Regularly Iceland appeared high up in Transparency International's annual list of least corrupt nations. Yet the ruling class, so small, so tightly bound by obligations, by blood and money, had become desperate for reward. That was the trend before Oddsson arrived in the prime minister's office, but his rule accelerated it.

Above all, the Octopus demanded its slice of privatization profits. But it had reckoned without a new, upstart business class that was getting ready to seize its share of the cake. In the late 1990s a group of businessmen had formed the Orca SA group, named after a killer whale that feeds on octopus meat. Oddsson's Social Democratic partners had held up his cherished plan—the very heart of his ambition to make Iceland a global player—of privatizing the banks. But after changing coalition partners in 1995, swapping the Social Democrats for the Progressive Party, a start could be made. The easiest bank to put on the market was the investment bank FBA, Fjarfestingarbanki Atvinnulifsinns. To the sounds of trumpets, FBA was put on the block in 1999. But within months, Orca rather than ordinary punters had bought a 26 percent interest in the bank. Who were the men behind Orca? There was Thorsteinn Mar Baldvinsson, who ran Samherji Fisheries in competition with Eimskip. The boss of Eimskip, still part of the Octopus, was Hoerdur Sigurgestsson—a friend of David Oddsson's. Thorsteinn Mar's involvement was thus a direct challenge to the Octopus, a way of saying that it would have little say in the future constellation of the banking sector.

The other Orca players included Jon Olafsson, no friend of Oddsson's, with big media interests. In addition there was Eyolfur Sveinsson, a former media mogul and formerly an assistant to Oddsson in the prime minister's office. Now he was working against the interests of Oddsson—and the Octopus.

And there was Jon Asgeir Johannesson, owner of a growing retail empire—and soon to be Oddsson's nemesis.

David Oddsson began to understand the challenge mounted by these businessmen. If Iceland was going to privatize its banking system—and the FBA sale was merely a toe tentatively dipped in the water—then that would unravel the fabric of the Icelandic establishment. Jon Asgeir Johannesson and Jon Olafsson were seen by Oddsson as hustlers; Eyolfur Sveinsson as an ungrateful turncoat. Yet they had made a successful grab for FBA and clearly wanted more. True, a 26 percent stake was hardly revolutionary. Eventually, over 50 percent of the shares found their way to Octopus families; so, for the time being, all was well with the world.

But David Oddsson now grasped that deregulating and modernizing

Iceland entailed the rise of a new class, a class that did not respect convention or the traditional patterns of power. The most unruly of all was Jon Asgeir. A personal rivalry was already taking shape between Jon Asgeir and David. The duel between the two men was to take on some of the epic dimensions of the sagas. No blood was shed or decapitations made, but the long contest was filled with a passionate hatred that dragged Iceland to the brink of bankruptcy.

FBA was after a few years sucked into Johannesson's empire, becoming part of the Glitnir bank, a useful cash machine for Jon Asgeir. At the time Oddsson barely noticed. He was focused entirely on the privatization of the two big state banks, Landsbanki and Bunadarbanki. This would, he reckoned, become his crowning achievement. The Icelanders were to be freed from their cramped island existence by a financial sector capable of acting on global markets. This was more than popular capitalism; it was about ending centuries of provincialism.

The privatization of a state-run bank is never an unpolitical act. It is about the transfer of influence. Oddsson and his Friedmanite friends were convinced that the financial system had to be free to grow beyond Iceland—but at the same time be bound into the political system. That meant, first of all, excluding foreign banks, even though this was against the spirit of belonging to the European Economic Area. And it meant that the two parties in power, the dominant Independents and the smaller Progressives, had to have a decisive say in the ordering of the future privately run banks. This, one banker explained to me in language so convoluted that he had to wave his hands like semaphore flags, was essential for democratic development. "Healthy banks have always been a precondition of healthy political parties." But in Iceland that grand-sounding sentiment was quickly devalued. The two banks—Landsbanki and Bunadarbanki (which would later be subsumed into Kaupthing)—became party funding machines, ensuring a lack of curiosity about their activities from the regulators, from parliament, and from government. The obverse of the banker's dictum became clear after October 2008: sick banks exposed sick political parties, and financial turmoil fast became a crisis in the governing class.

The first sign of a flawed privatization came in 1998 when the Swedish

Meltdown Iceland

bank SE Banken expressed an interest in Landsbanki—but was turned away by David Oddsson. Oddsson's credo was that ownership should be spread as widely as possible within the island. "Conditions in Iceland are such that it is unhealthy if too much power gathers in too few hands," said the prime minister. So no foreign-bank takeover. By the spring of 2002 it looked as if Oddsson was staying true to his commitment to popular capitalism. The supposedly neutral Executive Committee on Privatization announced that it was going to sell the two banks to the public in handy lumps. On June 14, 20 percent of Landsbanki was sold directly to the public on the Icelandic Stock Exchange, ICEX. The offering was supposed to last a month. Instead it was snapped up in fifteen minutes. The government was left with slightly less than 50 percent of the bank. No single investor was allowed to buy more than 4 percent. Thirty percent of Landsbanki had already been placed in a similar way in 1998 and 1999, and Bunadarbanki was sold off in the same manner.

Then came the decisive moment.

A few weeks after the Landsbanki share sales in June 2002, the leader of the coalition parties, David Oddsson, and the then foreign minister and chairman of the Progressive Party, Halldor Asgrimsson, intervened in the privatization. The controlling stakes in both Landsbanki and Bunadarbanki were put up for sale—thus taking the process out of the hands of the Executive Committee on Privatization. From that moment, three men and a woman—Oddsson's school friend and finance minister, Geir Haarde (Independence Party), Trade Minister Valgerdur Sverrisdottir (Progressives), Oddsson, and Asgrimsson—sold off the banks. An advertisement, printed only in Iceland to avoid the risk of foreign involvement, invited bids for an at least 25 percent stake in Landsbanki and Bunadarbanki. Five parties filed a bid; political undesirables were weeded out. Bunadarbanki—which would later merge with Kaupthing—fell to a group headed by Olafur Olafsson, affiliated with the Progressives. Landsbanki landed with Independence Party loyalist Bjoergólfur Gudmundsson. Sympathetic oligarchs were in control.

"It was," says Gylfi Magnusson, the man I have appointed to be my economic guru, "the Original Sin, the beginning of Iceland's fall from grace."

And so it was, on a dark Reykjavik morning, that I got my answer.

44

4 : Respect

You have managed to do the impossible! You sold to yourself your own company over and over again and the equity growth gave you billions each time! Now is the time to shift the money abroad. Move two spaces forward.

Rules of the New Viking board game

Reykjavik is a crowded village, and while it is good to have a house there, it is better by far for the multimillionaires to live discreetly outside and commute in with the chopper to the city airport. From there it is an easy five-minute drive, behind darkened windows, to one of a handful of restaurants serving fusion fish cuisine at $150 a head. Or to transfer to a corporate jet and dine at Nobu in London. Some take part in the jet-set parlor game of flying to different mountain peaks around the world with a party of twenty best friends to dine alfresco from picnic hampers prepared by five-star chefs. The thin air intoxicates, and the laughter, one can only assume, echoes across the valleys. The more modest Icelandic variation involves choppering between volcanic peaks, sometimes between courses; it is a summer pastime. Since the sun constantly shines, the body clock is disrupted; the helicopter, rapid oxygen intake, and freshly grilled fish all help one to sleep at night.

Iceland was always proud of its rough-and-ready egalitarianism. That was largely because almost everyone is interrelated; in a micro-world where a teacher has cousins working in television, in government, on a farm, in a restaurant, and on the trawler fleet, it is little wonder that ministers do their own shopping in the supermarket. Anything else would smack of arrogance—the one quality that relatives cannot forgive. But Oddsson's creeping market revolution had not only made millionaires out of fishermen, it had also created a separate financial elite by privatizing the banks. The Octopus families had grown together with the political class becoming the closest thing to a ruling elite a small island could have. Or so it seemed. They met in their homes or in the back rooms of hotels owned by clan members; the income gap between them and their turf-hutted grandfathers was huge, but somehow bridgeable. Octopus money was not put on open display.

The opening of the banks, and the opportunities this presented for entrepreneurs to fund overseas adventures, created a new mentality. Although fortunes were diminished by the 2008 crash and its aftermath, a certain esprit de corps has grown around those who made money fast over the past decade. The early years of the twenty-first century saw a surge in personal fortunes. Around the world the number of financial millionaires—that is, those with liquid assets—rose to more than ten million. In the United States alone, 227,000 new financial millionaires were created in the year 2005, a peak year for Richistanis.

Richistan is the term coined by the writer Robert Frank—the *Wall Street Journal*'s official richologist—for this swelling community-without-borders. They have their own travel network, their own health-care system in the form of luxury clinics catering only to their needs. "The rich weren't just getting richer," says Frank, "they were becoming financial foreigners, creating their own country within a country, their own society within a society, and their economy within an economy."

The Jon Asgeir generation, born in the late 1960s, saw themselves as mold-breakers. How could the recently liberated banks be content with the Icelandic market? The only sensible commercial logic was to expand abroad. The Octopus and the more old-fashioned custodians of wealth saw Jon Asgeir and his ilk as necessary vulgarians. Their own fortunes were based on increasingly vulnerable monopolies; their business practices, though often ruthless toward outsiders, were based on clublike principles. For the time being, it was decided over cigars in leather-padded rooms, the new businessmen with their imported Ferraris could be useful. The privatization of the banks had broken new ground; the New Vikings could go ahead, make their conquests abroad, exploit easy credit. The barons of the Octopus would wait for their moment. Because the jury was still out on whether the new Icelandic tycoons were patriots, with true roots in the country, ties that bind. Or whether they were actually citizens of Richistan, flashy and un-Icelandic in their manner. If the former, the New Vikings might be tamed, cultivated, and integrated into the power structure. If the latter, they could transfer their wealth from the island at a moment's notice.

David Oddsson, said the Octopus sages, was pursuing the wrong path by complaining that the New Vikings were hijacking his Thatcherite revolution. The young businessmen had to be anchored to Iceland—recruited as donors to the Independence Party, encouraged to behave like Icelanders. Instead of bidding in London charity auctions, they could—could they not?—be encouraged to spend their money on the island. But from the moment the banks were privatized and free to ride the crest of easy credit, this was a lost cause. The young Icelandic tycoons were on their way to becoming oligarchs. They were eager to buy political support but only to ensure that their business activities were not closely supervised. They did not need—as the Octopus clans had—to claim the prime ministership of Iceland or pick up an ambassadorship. No, the oligarchs, as in Russia, were forming their own feudal class.

In the old days, feudal lords controlled whole villages, effectively owned the inhabitants, their harvest, their fish catch. "Now we are seeing a rampant re-feudalization on a supra-territorial level that replaces ownership of land with access to privileged information, to luxury and to the political elites," says the moral philosopher Peter Sloterdijk.

Three clans of New Vikings arose out of Oddsson's rush to the market. For the most part, they merely exploited the poor crafting of the Icelandic laws. The dominance of the Independence Party and the overpowering personality of Oddsson ensured that parliamentary opposition was at best mediocre. The authority and competence of parliament—once Iceland's proudest institution, successor to the ancient Althing—ebbed away. The result was legislation that produced the diametrically opposite effect to that intended. The point of privatization was not only to push the state gradually out of everyday life, but also to diversify ownership and make Iceland a nation of shareholders. Instead the clans moved in.

Each wanted a bank; each wanted a media outlet. The interplay among the three clans—above all, the weave of cross-ownership that I will discuss in the next chapter—shows how the original Oddsson notion of a more competitive economy was replaced by competing business tribes. The first power block was made up of Baugur and the FL Group, which had stakes in such companies as Sterling Airlines, Iceland Express airline, the Glitnir bank, and eventually large chunks of British high-street fashion retailers. Two strong personalities stood behind this empire: Jon Asgeir Johannesson and Hannes Smarason, both fully paid-up members of Richistan. Jon Asgeir and his wife, Ingibjörg Pálmadottir—owner of the boutique hotel 101 in Reykjavik and daughter of a retail magnate—owned a 145-foot yacht, currently moored in Monaco, and a seven-thousand-square-foot apartment, complete with bulletproof panic room, on Gramercy Park in New York.

The second grouping had the father-and-son team of Bjoergólfur Gudmundsson and Bjoergólfur Thor Bjoergólfsson at its heart. Together with Magnús Thorsteinsson, they controlled a pharmaceuticals group, the holding company Samson, and the Landsbanki.

The third block—run by the brothers Lydur and Agust Gudmundsson—held sway over the telecommunications market, frozen-food distribution, and, through their Exista holding company, Kaupthing bank.

One businessman, Olafur Olafsson, stood outside the three blocks but managed nonetheless to capture a slice of the cake: The owner of the container-shipping company Samskip formed part of the so-called S group, which had bought Bunadarbanki. Bunadarbanki merged with Kaupthing, became the KB bank, and was then fully integrated. That left Olafsson as a major shareholder in Kaupthing—wealthy enough to pay for Elton John to sing "Candle in the Wind" at his fiftieth birthday party.

Of all the creatures in this bestiary, the most complex—and most indicative of the growth of capitalism in Iceland—were Bjoergólfur and his son, Thor. Yes, they became residents of Richistan; Thor bought a house in London's Holland Park and put together a collection of rare motorcycles. The soccer-mad father, Bjoergólfur, bought West Ham United. While the Icelandic bankers embraced the bonus system, the tycoons collected their trophies. They were vulgar and—the old guard almost spit this out—nearly Russian in their love of ostentation. But something profoundly Icelandic too was the rise and fall and rise again and fall again of these two men. Not just because they were the products of a society that keeps track of grudges and grudges-within-grudges with almost archival care. The story of Thor and his father illustrates how power, genes, and money come together in Sagaland; how red-blooded capitalism came to the island.

The older Bjoergólfur was once a promising young man, handsome, clean-cut, with reasonable English and a smooth, reassuring manner. His father—Thor's paternal grandfather—headed Shell Iceland. The family was thus intimately linked with the Octopus and the Independence Party. There was nothing of the outsider about him. So, naturally, when he was approached by one of Iceland's leading families to go on a special mission to the United States, he did not refuse. Members of the Thors family had asked him for a private meeting. The Thors were even wealthier and better established than Bjoergólfur Gudmundsson's clan. They were descended from Thor Jensen, a brilliant entrepreneur and the richest man on the island at the turn of the last century. Jensen had left Denmark at fifteen in 1878, seeking his fortune as a trader. Over two decades he set up seven successful businesses—and went bankrupt twice—before buying up swathes of land. One son, Olafur Thors, had been the prime minister who had led Iceland to independence in 1944.

Now, in 1966, Bjoergólfur was being asked a favor; and favor would beget favor. Olafur Thors's niece Thora Hallgrimsdottir was in trouble. Thora was a free spirit. At a ball in Reykjavik she had fallen for a handsome American naval officer, George Lincoln Rockwell—a war hero to boot—and abandoned her marriage to a well-connected Icelandic dentist to wed him. All harmless enough, except that Rockwell became a founder of the American Nazi Party and one of the most active racists in the United States. One of his missions was to take the Ku Klux Klan into the modern age; he coined the phrase *White Power*, organized rallies, operated a Hate Bus to stir up sentiment against African-Americans.

Bjoergólfur's task was to bring Rockwell's wife and children safely back to Iceland. All expenses would be paid. It went without saying that he could be sure of the gratitude of the Thors family.

He duly crossed the Atlantic and was surprised by Thora. She had lost some of her rebellious spirit and had become a careful housekeeper, a disciplined mother. Rockwell was broke, fanatical, and had lost his old charm, his enthusiasm for sailing.

Back in Iceland, Bjoergólfur fell in love with her and proposed marriage. Thora, twelve years senior, accepted. The Thors family elders breathed a collective sigh of relief. One more potential source of embarrassment had been brought under control. The three Rockwell children took on Bjoergólfur's name, and all was well. Thora duly gave birth to Thor—in 1967, the same year that Rockwell was gunned down in a shopping center in Arlington, Virginia.

The Octopus, however, was no longer the all-controlling force in Iceland. Bjoergólfur threw himself into the shipping business and helped make Hafskip the second-largest operator after Eimskip, the Octopus-run market leader. Initially there was more than enough business for both shipping companies, transporting supplies to the U.S. base. But when an American company started to compete on the route, Hafskip floundered. Bjoergólfur borrowed to expand, but in the early 1980s—without a bank in his pocket or sophisticated financial instruments available—he struggled to keep the cash flow going. According to Illugi Joekulsson, who has written a book about the Hafskip affair, Bjoergólfur was suddenly undermined when his bank, Utvegsbankinn, declared his company in default on its loans. Bjoergólfur argued plausibly that the company was still a going concern. After he was declared bankrupt, his assets were put on a fire sale—allowing him to settle 75 percent of his debts. The situation, in other words, was not financially critical: it was a crude act to dispose of an Eimskip rival (which later took on Hafskip's ships). More, it was an attempt by the Progressive Party to profit from the downfall of a man who was so clearly aligned with the Independence Party. Criminal charges were pressed against him—the prosecutor and the chief of police were Progressive Party nominees—on 450 separate fraud charges. He was cleared on all but twenty relatively minor infractions and was sentenced to a suspended twelve-month jail sentence. For Bjoergólfur it was a bitter experience. He had been suffocated by the interests of the Octopus, which he had once served with a real sense of duty, brought down by envy, by an intolerance of competition, by party intrigue. Joekulsson describes it as "the most humiliating incident for the Icelandic justice system in recent years."

Although the coalition system in the Icelandic parliament is supposed to generate choice and match more precisely the will of the people, it encourages single-party dominance. When the Independents finally came to power with David Oddsson in 1991, they stayed in place, shuffling partners after each election, for eighteen years. The same problems that had surfaced during the 1986 Bjoergólfur Gudmundsson trial came to light then too: a tendency for courts and newspapers to listen too carefully to guidance from the politicians.

For Thor, the arrest of his father had been a shock. He was barely nineteen, attending the economics-orientated grammar school (Verslunarskoli) rather than the classical grammar where the political class tend to be educated. The house was empty when he returned from school, and he found out the fate of his father only when he switched on the television news. Since then Thor has had a single overpowering motive to get rich. "This is about respect," he said after making his first billion dollars, "about getting the respect we are due." For respect, read revenge. Reykjavik society buzzed for five years about the failure of Hafskip—the biggest bankruptcy in Icelandic history—even as the world was changing, the Berlin Wall was tumbling, and the Communist world was opening up.

Thor returned with an undergraduate degree in business studies from NYU and set up as an events manager at the two biggest clubs in Reykjavik at the time, Tunglid (the Moon) and Skuggabarinn (the Shadow Bar). In the latter bar he met his wife, the filmmaker Kristin Olafsdottir. But he had his business eye on Russia. Thor's father, now out of the limelight, was running the brewery and soft drinks unit of Pharmaco, a pharmaceuticals group. The company decided to close down the brewery—the legalization of beer in 1989 had not led to the expected explosion in demand—and asked Bjoergólfur Gudmundsson to find a purchaser for the bottling machinery. One phone call was enough—to an old Icelandic friend, the architect Ingimar Haukur Ingimarsson, who was working as a consultant in St. Petersburg. They had met when—after the Hafskip debacle—Bjoergólfur had set up a center in Reykjavik for recovering alcoholics. The center was plainly an attempt by Bjoergólfur to rehabilitate himself in the capital, but it attracted the interest of many wealthy sponsors, either because they had a drinking problem of their own or because they knew of alcoholics in their extended families. Ingimar Haukur got involved, but so too did Jon Asgeir's father. It became yet another networking opportunity for the emerging clan of New Rich. But the project was also a piece of genuine philanthropy: more subtle recovery schemes have to be devised in a community as small as Reykjavik. Alcoholics Anonymous cannot flourish in a society where almost nobody is anonymous.

Ingimar Haukur knew, of course, about Bjoergólfur's difficulties with Hafskip, his suspended jail sentence, but they were not an obstacle to doing business in Russia in the 1990s. On the contrary, it was a time for buccaneers. Ingimar Haukur himself had gained a foothold in Russia by observing the obstacles facing businessmen trying to place international calls out of their St. Petersburg hotels. Ingimar tracked down a transportable digital exchange that the United States had used to restore communications in Kuwait during the first Gulf War. He bought it, set up a company, made a killing.

The soft drinks and beer markets presented similar opportunities in late 1992. Coca-Cola and PepsiCo were importing rather than producing and bottling locally. So Bjoergólfur's bottling plant had great potential—providing that Bjoergólfur and his son applied some of their improvisational talent. Ways had to be found around the blockades erected by the local customs and tax authorities. Thor was game for the adventure. He enlisted his friend Magnús Thorsteinsson, and together with Bjoergólfur senior, they headed for what was still very much the Wild East.

St. Petersburg in the early 1990s was barely functioning as a modern city. Factories were closing; power outages crippled whole housing projects, and Mafia families were active in almost every area of economic activity, from used cars to supplying restaurants. Alcohol was, as ever, big business, and the privatization of Russian breweries was a license to print money. Bjoergólfur and his son calculated that they had to shift from bottling soft drinks into beer. Under Communism, beer had been a breakfast drink on construction sites; in the fledgling capitalist order, drinking beer was to be a symbol of middle-class advancement, gentler and more Western than vodka. But the water had to be clean, the beer had to have a long shelf life, and it had to be efficiently distributed, had to look good. It was, however, a rough world. In the Petersburg privatization, would-be brewers found themselves thrown out of windows and shot in the kneecaps. The Icelanders hired twenty security guards and set to work dealing with rats and mold in the factory, a collapsing ruble, sugar shortages. Inside the company there was a battle for control. Ingimarsson claimed that the Icelanders had not supplied the bottling equipment on time and that it kept breaking down; the point seemed to be to get a lower price from Pharmaco. When that failed, Ingimar accused Bjoergólfur of seeking a side deal, designed to give him and his son total control. Thor and his father argued that they had purchased the firm, paid off its debts—there was no outstanding business. The bottling plant was sold to PepsiCo.

While the wrangling continued in the courts, Thor spotted a chance to move into the alco-pop company Bravo. It was successfully selling sugary, gin-based canned cocktails to Russian clubbers. Thor raised $25 million from Capital Group in L.A., combined it with the proceeds from PepsiCo, and bought into Bravo. They shifted production into a sophisticated-looking, high-priced bottled beer to be called Botchkarov. It was launched with a splash—ten thousand guests invited to the center of St. Petersburg. Within four years the Icelanders had captured a 3 percent slice of the Russian beer market—it had proven resistant to the 1998 crash in the Russian market. "Beer and recession go together," a friend of Thor's told me. "Clubbing gets more frenzied, everyone gets more thirsty and seeks out oblivion."

Thor, his father, and Magnús Thorsteinsson sold Bravo to Heineken. The Dutch company paid over the odds and made them rich. Each partner pocketed $110 million. Helped by another successful investment, a Bulgarian generic-drugs company that they merged with Pharmaco, the father-and-son team were now flush with cash. Slowly, Thor's plan was taking shape. The aim, unstated but clear, was to return to Iceland and take revenge on the establishment that had humiliated his father. It was payback time. Samson Holdings, which channeled the investments of the three men, offered to buy a 45 percent stake in the newly privatized Landsbanki. This was a highly political move. Landsbanki, with its old-fashioned wooden cubicles, its century-old traditions, was the grande dame of Icelandic commerce. So, naturally, politicians wanted to be sure that its sale would translate into influence for the appropriate party. Samson picked up the bank for $140 million, even though critics say it was not the highest bidder. Buried in the details of this sale is one of the causes of the Icelandic meltdown: political cronyism.

In September 2002, Steingrimur Ari Arason, chairman of Iceland's privatization committee, sent a protest letter to David Oddsson, the prime minister, complaining that other bidders had been excluded from the Landsbanki sale. "I have served on this committee since 1991 and have never seen such poor workmanship as during the negotiations with Samson." Steingrimur Ari's view was that two matters should have been taken into consideration before selling to Bjoergólfur Gudmundsson. First, his conviction during the Hafskip trial, even if it was for book-keeping irregularities. Second, an affair in 1980 when a senior banker was convicted of embezzling money from Landsbanki, some of which was lent to Bjoergólfur Gudmundsson. Bjoergólfur denied knowing anything about the origins of the cash; the prosecutor concluded that Bjoergólfur was in fact the victim of the crooked banker. Even so, said Steingrimur Ari, Bjoergólfur's background should have been properly examined before allowing a strategic investment in a big bank. Steingrimur Ari then resigned.

Bjoergólfur and three other Hafskip executives had formally been accused of exaggerating the financial health of the shipping company during 1984 to keep credit lines open from the bank. Accounts were massaged. There was a great deal of trivia, as Bjoergólfur's supporters quickly point out. His carpets were cleaned at company expense, for example, and Hafskip settled his parking fines. Even so, Bjoergólfur had violated the penal code on several counts of embezzlement and two of fraud.

So the Financial Supervisory Agency (FME) should have questioned Bjoergólfur when it was called, as required by law, to assess his suitability to run a bank. The Hafskip case was no secret; a cause célèbre, it should have been taken into account when Landsbanki was handed over to him. The seven criteria used by the FME include an assessment of the applicant's personal financial position and that of others linked to him; the knowledge and experience of the applicant; the possibility of conflict of interest; the size of the proposed holding; the possibility that the size of the holding could make regulation difficult; the presentation of all relevant personal data to the FME; and, finally, whether he had ever been the subject of a criminal investigation.

Well, evidently Bjoergólfur raised doubts on at least one of these tests, and grounds existed to at least question whether he was going to use the bank to feed his companies. But David Oddsson wanted Bjoergólfur in place, and so did the Independence Party hierarchy. The FME knew which way to jump and, in so doing, that should have alerted Iceland's foreign partners. A deal had been struck between the banking, political, and regulating worlds. But no one was paying attention—because strikingly similar pacts were being made across the globe.

Flawed foundations produce cracks; unsteady walls lead to collapse: the basic wisdom of construction engineers. What can happen to a bank that has been privatized with an eye to securing future political advantage?

Bjoergólfur, father and son, had maintained their St. Petersburg links—the deputy mayor Vladimir Yakovlev had been particularly helpful in the Bravo years—long after they had formally abandoned the Russian market. As they moved onto the *Forbes* list of the world's richest men, so did many of the people with whom they had done business in the early 1990s. So strong were the connections that Magnús Thorsteinsson—who ran into financial problems after the 2008 meltdown—moved back to St. Petersburg to take up his property interests there. To the surprise of some, he was made honorary Icelandic consul in the port.

The Russian connection was to bother and fascinate international bankers for years to come. And not only bankers. The British activated a secret agent in Iceland—not in the embassy or attached to it—in 2005 with a brief to watch cash flows between Russia and Iceland. They feared that the banks were so poorly regulated that they could theoretically be used to launder not just the cash of Russians but also, perhaps, terrorists. Various newspaper investigations have failed to nail down the laundering suspicions, and the banks, old and new, have always denied the accusations. But it remained a concern for the British and Danish governments and a constant source of rumor in the banking world. And when Iceland went into meltdown in 2008, it prompted new questions about Moscow's hidden relationship with the island.

Bjoergólfur settled into his new role as the owner of a bank—not just any bank, but one that had been a national institution, which sheltered the deposits of one in three Icelanders—with astonishing ease. He wanted the bank to generate more profits, he said, to study overseas markets, to attract foreign clients. He was intrigued by the possibilities of Heritable Bank, a London-based bank specializing in property— Landsbanki had a 95 percent stake—and wanted to use it as a vehicle for buying into Britain and Scandinavia. And it was important to use Landsbanki's foothold in Guernsey so that it could offer its clients even more discretion.

Bjoergólfur was comfortable at last, after his difficult, lucrative years in Russia. He was again at the heart of Icelandic power. His right-hand man in the bank, the vice chairman of Landsbanki, was to be Kjartan Gunnarsson, a member of David Oddsson's clique of Friedman fans, and a force to be reckoned with in the Independence Party. Steadily, more and more young members of the party found jobs in the bank. Bjoergólfur had, after all, many years earlier been an organizer of the Independence Party youth wing.

That was the Icelandic deal: the bank became family. Bjoergólfur had, it seemed, served his penance. He was rich again and therefore entitled to return with honor. Both he and his son had brought money back into Iceland, were about to enter the *Forbes* list of dollar billionaires. So, no hard feelings.

The purchase of a bank may buy respect—supposedly Thor's goal— but it doesn't constitute revenge. The pharmaceuticals empire was rapidly growing, through strategic mergers, and becoming a leading European manufacturer of generic drugs. For a while Thor's 36 percent stake in the company, now named Actavis, was worth $700 million. Yet this was not about joining the Billionaires' Club, getting the passport to Richistan. Nor, frankly, was it part of a patriotic mission to create full employment in Iceland. No, Thor was after Eimskip, the tentacle of the Octopus, which had so traumatized him as a schoolboy and had so shaken his father. By September 2003, Thor and his partners had paid $35 million for a 9 percent stake in the steamship company. But Landsbanki—Bjoergólfur and Thor's bank—was also buying up a 19 percent holding. By 2004, Thor had achieved his goal: he was in charge of the company that had been instrumental in humiliating his family. Only then did he feel fully at ease; Iceland had paid its debts to his father. To celebrate, Bjoergólfur went out and bought a soccer team.

The Bjoergólfur tale is a kind of Nordic version of *The Count of Monte Cristo*, at least in the version according to Thor. Wrongfully accused, subjected to a flawed trial, sent into exile, offered access to a fortune, then the triumphant return. All that was missing was the element of redemption.

For a time, in the rabid 1990s privatization of Russia, the local Russian oligarchs functioned as the country's unofficial politburo. They understood the economy and ran it; politicians became marginal. The spread of the global economy prompted similar developments elsewhere: the slickest of business elites found they often carried more weight than simple elected ministers, who were corseted by national problems and obligations. Davos Man, the corporate jet-setter, came to the annual mountaintop talk shop at the World Economic Forum and year after year announced the primacy of financial innovation. Yes, change of regime could come through revolution or war. But lasting change comes, the elites argued, only through the persuasive power of commercial competition. Politicians were judged not on right- or left-wing credentials, but only on the criterion of whether they were good for business. These were the articulated views of a global oligarchy that had fused wealth and political power. Not as crudely, perhaps, as the Russian oligarchs, who were able, through their control of an often crooked privatization process, to dictate terms to a confused political class. But strong enough to suspend disbelief, to convince national leaders and central bankers that the elites had tamed risk, that they had debt under control, and that their way could guarantee national as well as personal prosperity. Politicians had somehow, over a decade, come to believe in the infallibility of bankers, the new hero class.

Thus the Icelandic nation half fell in love with its businessmen. Bjoergólfur had craved acceptance from the establishment that had expelled him. His son Thor, though, understood that readmitting his father was a sign of the weakness of the Independence Party and its intricate architecture of power. David Oddsson wanted to complete a capitalist revolution in Iceland. But what was capitalism without capital? Without people who knew how to accumulate wealth? In a photograph of the prime minister and Bjoergólfur from this time, the businessman seems to be laughing at Oddsson; the prime minister, in turn, seems to be both smiling and biting his lip. Bjoergólfur is the alpha male in this picture.

Politicians became paid staff, as surely as the gardeners and cooks who tended to the properties of the oligarchs. The politicians were supposed to maintain not the flowerbeds, but the krona; for Bjoergólfur, Oddsson had become a currency steward.

When the Icelandic economy came crashing down, the first response of the local oligarchs was to go undercover. Why else, after all, does one have a house in leafy, exclusive Holland Park if not to cushion oneself from the angry outside world. But then Thor and Jon Asgeir Johannesson started to hit back at their critics. Why had the central bank not been more active internationally? Why had the government not asserted itself? Why had the state failed? Naturally, this was an attempt to shift blame from their own recklessness. The oligarchs, after all, owned the banks; they had concocted a system whereby they lent themselves cash. But the questions posed by the Icelandic tycoons were legitimate. Why had the weak state allowed itself to be mesmerized by the moneymakers? The Davos conceit is that big business is ready to accept responsibility for its actions providing that governments recognize and protect its special needs. This compact existed in Iceland too, and it survived just as long as the country turned in high growth rates, just as long as everyone could pretend that the country was Cool.

5 : Duel

Islands are places apart where Europe is absent.
W. H. Auden to Christopher Isherwood

Were the Vikings barbarians and pagans? Or were they adventurers and the pioneers of an aggressively entrepreneurial culture? Or, perhaps, a bit of both? These questions became more than a mildly interesting discussion topic among archaeologists when a group of young Icelandic entrepreneurs started to make their mark on international business. Bjoergólfur Thor was named after Thor the Thunderer, the Norse god who watched over seamen and farmers; god of the skies, Thor protected the world with his powerful hammer, Mjöllnir, against threatening ogres. You take your given name seriously indeed in Iceland. The hammer duly became Bjoergólfur Thor's corporate symbol, the logo on the tail fin of his black jet; a tribute to the mythic Thunderer. His holding company was Novator—new Thor. Jon Asgeir Johannesson was even less subtle: a ten-foot-tall statue of a Viking, with a Fender Stratocaster guitar strapped to his back, adorned his London office. When he eventually bought a bank, it was named Glitnir, the hall in heaven where all disputes are reconciled.

> There's a hall called Glitnir
> with pillars of gold
> it's also roofed with silver . . .

according to a passage in the *Prose Edda*, Snorri Sturluson's thirteenth-century masterpiece, telling the tales of the gods and heroes in modern idiom.

No wonder that Jon Asgeir started to see himself in heroic terms as he approached his goal of owning his own finance house to bankroll his adventures. A pity that he didn't finish reading the Snorri Sturluson text about Glitnir, which goes on to say that Forseti, Nordic god of justice . . .

> spends all day long
> settling all suits-at-law.

Jon Asgeir, pursued by a hostile prime minister, found himself as much in the courtroom as in the boardroom. The sagas matter not just because all Icelandic children grow up with them. They form part of the vocabulary, part of the thought pattern, of young men as soon as they start thinking about power. Odin, the chief god in Norse mythology, has two ravens perched on his shoulders, Hugin and Munin—Mind and Memory. They are his constant advisers, spying out and scavenging on battlefields. So when Jon Asgeir became chief of Baugur—which means "ring of steel"—he made sure that he too had two key advisers, two human ravens, ready to feed him intelligence about future acquisitions. It is what chiefs did; it was a quintessential post-Viking organization.

When Jon Asgeir fell into an extraordinary decade-long duel with David Oddsson, his talk in private was of final reckonings, the Last Battle, which would usher in the Twilight of the Gods: Ragnarok.

If all this seemed a little archaic for a breed of entrepreneurs who wore black designer jeans and Armani sunglasses and who had the abrupt manner of rock stars, well, that was only part of the story. Many thinkers, but in particular the Austrian economist Joseph Schumpeter, had predicted that the entrepreneurial class would become the avantgarde of "creative destruction," the process whereby capitalism reinvents itself and constantly innovates. The entrepreneur, says Schumpeter, is no intellectual. "He compensates for inadequate information and experience with strong intuition and an eye for the essential." These new heroes have willpower and physical energy; they are motivated, he says, by "the dream and will to establish a private empire." But they also regard "business life as sport" and are driven by a love of risk. The Thors and Jon

Asgeirs may have resurrected the Viking brand, might even have been motivated by the primal passions of their forebears—for conquest and revenge—but they fit too into a vision of modern capitalism that seems to need a caste of warrior-businessmen. Capitalism, it appears, requires both kinds of Viking: the barbarian destroyer and the adventurer.

Jon Asgeir's father, Johannes Jonsson, was not part of the Reykjavik elite, having no prime minister in his bloodline, no link to one of the well-cushioned Octopus families. He had trained in a slaughterhouse and was a grocer in a supermarket chain. His son, Jon Asgeir, never pretended otherwise. Indeed, in a society as small as Iceland's it is difficult to deny one's roots. So, later, Jon Asgeir, over a bottle of wine in the bar of his wife's boutique hotel, would quote Margaret Thatcher: "Anyone who wants to know the value of money should have a grocer as a father." Indeed, there is something special about being brought up by a grocer. Of Margaret Thatcher, the historian David Cannadine writes, "She got to know people, not as manufacturing producers, nor as collective aggregates, but as individual consumers. 'We lived,' she recalls, 'by serving the customer.' "

At the age of thirteen Jon Asgeir noticed that his father's supermarket was getting rid of a broken amusement ride—a brown monkey with a saddle on its back—and took it on. He had it repaired and rented it out, and within two years he had twenty rides (whales, fire engines, elephants) and a regular cash flow. He sold popcorn too and stacked shelves in his father's shop. It was not the normal schoolboy pattern in Reykjavik. He attended the business-studies college, Verslunarskoli, seen as a peg down from the classical grammar school of Menntaskolinn, though it still had pretensions to being a serious center of learning. Its graduates had included Bjoergólfur Gudmundsson. None of this bothered or overawed Jon Asgeir; he was interested in the mechanics of making money; in Blur, in Oasis; in girls; in English soccer. Until his father lost his job. Jon Asgeir was angry—angry on behalf of his father. This was the late 1980s, and the Icelandic economy was still dominated by the state; the societal ethic was egalitarian. To be laid off was to be let down by the government and the authorities. In Jon Asgeir's eyes, his father had been stripped of his manhood. And so, in 1989—as Eastern

Europe overthrew its leaders, rejected socialism for capitalism—Jon Asgeir persuaded his father to challenge the island's retail monopolies by opening up a cheap food supermarket close to Reykjavik harbor. The logo was a cheerful porker, a piggy bank, and their business plan was simple: drive hard bargains with importers and sell in bulk with the smallest of profit margins. Reykjavikers flocked to the shop. Inflation had been high for decades, food inflation particularly so.

The business went well; the shop became a nationwide chain named Bonus. Within three years, the Hagkaup supermarket group—the established food retailers—decided to buy into its upstart rival and took a 50 percent stake. Bonus and Hagkaup then established a common supply company under the name Baugur. Jon Asgeir had three business principles. First, he had to develop strong enough clout to keep down the price of goods brought onto the island. This was an indirect challenge to the power of the Octopus. Second, to compensate for narrow margins, he had to expand fast, to keep moving. Third, he had to reach an international market because the Icelandic market would always be too small to turn a serious profit. By 1994 Jon Asgeir had opened his first Bonus store in the neighboring—and even smaller—Faroe Islands. Hardly a commercial breakthrough: the islanders were easily outnumbered by sheep. But it raised the issue of how Baugur should function internationally, with Iceland 603 miles from Norway; 1,118 miles from Denmark, the former colonial power; 2,734 miles from the United States; and 808 miles from Britain. The first step, though, was to cement Baugur's position in Iceland. By 1998, Baugur had swallowed up not only Bonus and Hagkaup but also the Nykaup chain, as well as the supply and distribution company Adfong, and shortly afterward the sporting goods store Utilif. Studying the buying patterns of the GIs and American families in Keflavik, Jon Asgeir decided to move on America first. In 2001, he acquired Bill's Dollar Stores and Bonus Dollar Stores. It was a modest debut, but it signaled to the Oddsson team, ensconced in government since 1991, that something was changing. Octopus companies had always toyed with the idea of operating in the U.S. market but—advised by their still-conservative bankers—prefered to operate within the Nordic area. Almost a century of trading patterns connected Octopus families with Danish and Norwegian mercantile dynasties. America, for many, was a risk too great. This was not, however, the way of the New Vikings.

David Oddsson, prime minister until 2004, pioneer of privatization, torchbearer for the New Iceland, watched Jon Asgeir's rise with vinegary disdain. The exile and prodigal return of Bjoergólfur Thor and his father could be understood, forgiven at a certain level. Yes, father and son were acquisitive capitalists, were buying up chunks of the economy. But at least Bjoergólfur senior was on Oddsson's side; Bjoergólfur may have had his differences with the Octopus, but he was from a good family, had strong links with the Independence Party, and indeed was—after the privatization of Landsbanki—willing to put his bank at the disposal of the Oddsson machine. A wrong had been done to Bjoergólfur; the wrong had been put right. That was the Icelandic way. Besides, Thor and his father had actually brought money into Iceland—from their dealings in Russia—not taken it out. The same, in Oddsson's view, could not be said of Jon Asgeir and his proletarian father. "These barrow boys, they even speak a different Icelandic, more crude," said a former ideological fellow traveler of Oddsson. "They inhabited a different world." And they seemed set on hijacking the market revolution, an attitude more akin to the cowboy ruthlessness of the Russian privatization than the Reagan and Thatcher models so cherished by David.

Oddsson's nature, though, was to make this into a personal rather than a political contest; Jon Asgeir's challenge was not just to the established supermarket chains, but to the Octopus, the Independence Party, and the whole superstructure of Icelandic power. Oddsson had a talent for maneuver. In Oddsson's campaign to be elected chief school prefect, he had let the left-leaning students believe that he was their man, gathered their votes, then betrayed them. The same skills had propelled him to the peak of power, and he became determined to first outflank Jon Asgeir, then crush him. More: Oddsson ruled through fiercely loyal henchmen who could be expected to anticipate their boss's wishes—and make life difficult for the entrepreneur. "If Jon Asgeir was really challenging the system," said one Independence Party insider, regarding the idea that Jon Asgeir, Thor, and the other oligarchs were the advance guard of a new order, "then all of David's defensive instincts will have been activated." Oddsson's inner circle was largely made up of men of a certain age, educated abroad—unlike Oddsson himself, who studied law in Iceland—who mirrored their leader's arrogance, his absolute conviction that he knew what was best for the island. Few women took part in his late-night counseling sessions, though many women admired him. And only one animal was on the team—Toothie (Tanni, in Icelandic), his German shepherd, who, say Oddsson friends, may have saved him from physical assault. A deranged stranger, so the story goes, rang the politician's doorbell one night. David Oddsson's wife, Astridur, was about to let him in, following Icelandic hospitality rules, but Toothie went for the stranger and he fled. Later that night, the man committed a horrific murder. "Since then," says a family friend, "Oddsson has always sought out allies who are human equivalents of Toothie—men with bite."

When Jon Asgeir decided to enter the media world, Oddsson's pack started to growl. Jon Asgeir's target was *Frettabladid*, a free paper widely circulated in Reykjavik and southwest Iceland. Entirely dependent on advertising, it was plagued with cash-flow problems. But with fast, quality journalism, it posed a real challenge to the established daily *Morgunbladid*, which was a mouthpiece for David Oddsson's Independence Party. *Morgunbladid* had been founded in 1913 and was the grande dame of the Icelandic press, so grand, and enjoying such a powerful monopoly, it chose not to publish on Mondays so that its editors could go for long weekends. Parliamentary reporters often sat in on—and contributed to—internal sessions of the Independence Party. During the Cold War, speeches by Independence Party politicians were routinely converted into articles; editorials rarely wavered from the party line, though an abortive attempt was made to question the policy of awarding quotas to fishing magnates. The editor, Styrmir Gunnarsson, was soon called to order by the bosses of the Independence Party and indeed Landsbanki.

So when *Frettabladid* ran into financial trouble in 2002, there was general glee not only at *Morgunbladid* but also within the Oddsson clique. Which turned to dismay when the newspaper was bought up by the businessman Gunnar Smari Egilsson, who turned out to be a front man for Jon Asgeir Johannesson. Oddsson immediately understood this to be a threat: a rich man was reaching for political influence at the expense of the Independence Party. At the very least, it would entail massive investment in *Morgunbladid* to beat off the challenge. Jon Asgeir had first flickered onto Oddsson's screen when he joined—and led—the attempt to take over the FBA investment bank in 1999. That had involved a direct showdown with the interests of the Octopus. Now Jon Asgeir was set for a fresh confrontation. He was eleven years younger than Oddsson, too young to have experienced the years of Cold War policies when it was enough to brand a critic "a Communist" to silence debate. Jon Asgeir was a different kind of opponent and, most galling of all, was coming to prominence by exploiting the market-liberalizing reforms introduced by Oddsson himself. Now Oddsson saw him as Enemy Number One.

The battle for media outlets was a proxy conflict. Buying *Frettabladid* was a coded way for Jon Asgeir to demand a seat at the political table. Oddsson, though, was determined that he alone should set the placement. Money for *Morgunbladid* was channeled through Bjoergólfur Gudmundsson, the Independence Party's favorite oligarch. Little wonder that the media failed to spot the approaching crisis, the catastrophic meltdown of 2008: objective analysis was not the name of the game, only tribal fealty. The inability of the media to warn of or even comprehend the approaching breakdown fed into the crisis. Not just in Iceland, but across Western societies, the fourth estate was blinded by its own problems. As in Iceland, many newspapers found themselves inhibited by owners who expected their organs to be, if not directly politically engaged, then at least "pro-business." That is, talking up the boom, pleading for deregulation and more open markets. This was not just an intellectual commitment. Financially struggling local newspapers became dependent on real estate agencies buying up advertising space. "The newspaper industry is the marketing arm of the real estate industry," says media expert Danny Schechter. Yet local newspapers in particular should have been listening to the warnings coming out of community housing organizations about subprime mortgage funding. National newspapers meanwhile focused their business coverage toward the business community, rather than trying to explain developments to ordinary readers. Increasingly business sections became a closed world, with reporters reproducing rather than questioning the views of corporate leaders. In part, says Daniel Bogler of the *Financial Times*, this was because of poor accountancy skills on the part of journalists. "They go to a briefing and a company gives them a story, and they don't really have a counternarrative." This absence of a counternarrative helped scuttle Iceland, but was a general problem that blighted coverage across the world. The failure of the financial system was also a failure of journalism.

"In Iceland we are a split nation," said Reynir Traustason, editor of the tabloid *DV*, which also had connections with Jon Asgeir's Baugur. "There are those who follow David Oddsson, and those who are against him. The same goes for Baugur's Jon Asgeir Johannesson." Followers of Jon Asgeir were known as Baugsmidlar (Baugurites). "The sugar daddy behind *Morgunbladid* was Bjoergólfur Gudmundsson." This created a pattern of dependency that was by no means unique to Iceland: financial investigation was deemed not only unnecessary but also dangerous, for it could harm the interests of the financial backer, be it Jon Asgeir or Bjoergólfur. Cross-ownership of the media essentially dulled the press and television as an instrument of democratic control. Instead, they became cheerleaders for rival teams. The only theme that everyone could agree on—Oddsson and the Independence Party machine on the one hand, Jon Asgeir and his allies on the other—was that Iceland was rich, Cool, and a premium brand. Any scratch on the veneer would harm all the players.

Jon Asgeir's start-up of Bonus had made him a popular figure in Iceland. Discounting in a country where high food prices were perhaps the main source of complaint, along with his slightly roguish appearance (long hair tucked behind his ears, black jeans, rock music blaring from his SUV), had turned him into a kind of Robin Hood figure, a guerrilla businessman. Inflation had come down in the first few years of Oddsson's rule, partly thanks to an agreement with the labor unions and an economic downturn. But food prices had stayed unremittingly high, and most people blamed this on the established supermarket barons, on the unusually powerful officials in the import and customs and excise offices (almost all food had to be imported), and on insensitive politicians. Jon Asgeir showed that bargain discounting—a central feature of shopping in the rest of Europe and in the United States—could be brought to Iceland. That is, smart business practices could allow Iceland to escape its fate as a high-cost island.

Oddsson did not object to competition—how could he, as a disciple of Hayek's and Friedman's?—but he was unhappy with Jon Asgeir's relentless grab for companies. The Jon Asgeir business model in Iceland was to expand quickly and increase his bargaining power with importers, but that meant moving toward a monopoly position and, in Oddsson's eyes, distorting competition. So when, in January 2002, David Oddsson urged intervention in the grocery market, it reflected both ideological confusion and personal resentment. Confusion, because Oddsson believed that he could steer the market economy that he had himself liberalized. The correct way forward would have been to build strong, independent regulatory institutions that could monitor the evolution of the market. But too much of Oddsson's governing style depended on his personality, his striding into a room of civil servants and barking, "Something must be done!" His adherence to a political clan, the long ledger of unpaid political debts, meant that supposedly independent state institutions became offshoots of his Independence Party. It was a system of favors received and dispensed. Institutions such as Landsbanki and *Morgunbladid* became party loyalists. That was the way it worked. So when David Oddsson insisted that no single company should have more than a 60 percent market share in the food retail business—the threat was a breakup of companies—he was clearly referring to only one company, and only one person: Jon Asgeir.

Not only Oddsson was worried about the rise of Jon Asgeir; the Octopus families understood that gaining a dominant hold on the Icelandic food chain was not going to satisfy him. The Octopus clans had developed their power network because of the ease with which one could cross-own chunks of the economy. Now Jon Asgeir—and the other would-be oligarchs—would use exactly the same methods to destroy the influence of the Octopus. New wealth was about to drive out old wealth. It soon became plain that the new oligarchs had their sights set on Icelandair. The airline was potentially a license to print money. Icelanders with the travel bug had only one way off the island: by air. The privatization of the banks between 1999 and 2002—in particular the handing over of a majority share in Landsbanki to the Samson group, owned by Bjoergólfur Gudmundsson and his son Thor—had shaken up Iceland; in theory, everything in Iceland was for sale. The oligarchs regarded Icelandair as the prize and, with David Oddsson's blessing, were determined to keep at out of the hands of their colleague Jon Asgeir.

The New Vikings grasped that Iceland had fundamentally changed since the freeing of the banks. First, old established companies—the preserve of the oligarchs—could be hollowed out and turned into investment holdings with a bit of deft share trading. Second, the banks themselves were now players. And, crucially, no one was paying attention: not the government, not parliament, not the press, and not the financial supervisory authority. What followed was a fast shuffling of the cards—a technique that was to become the trademark of the Icelandic tycoons as they amassed their paper fortunes.

Eimskip, the venerable shipping company—a vehicle of the Octopus families—was looking vulnerable in 2003. Two banks, Landsbanki and Islandsbanki (later to become Glitnir), joined forces with the Fjarfar group, controlled by Jon Asgeir Johannesson. Together they formed the Straumur investment fund—and targeted Eimskip. Throughout 2003 they bought up Eimskip shares. By the autumn they were able to impose their conditions on Eimskip. It would have to sell its investment division, Burdaras. Who took the spoils? Landsbanki, owned by Bjoergólfur Gudmundsson and Thor, got a big chunk of Burdaras—and as far as Thor was concerned, the beginning of a sweet revenge for the humiliation of his father by the Octopus. Burdaras meanwhile sold its shares in Icelandair to Straumur.

Straumur and Islandsbanki then sold all their Icelandair shares to a group called Oddaflug. This intricate, intense share-dealing was a successful attempt by Jon Asgeir's rivals in the retail business to freeze him out of Icelandair. Jon Asgeir was left with only a small, meaningless parcel of shares in the airline. The move pleased Oddsson and the Independence Party grandees. Oddaflug, which by January 2004 had a 38.5 percent share of Icelandair, was owned by Hannes Smarason—one of the fastest thinking of the young oligarchs—and his then father-in-law,

Jon Helgi Gudmundsson, who controlled the food retailers Byko and Norvik. Hannes Smarason was at the same time vice president of the DNA testing company Decode—and a close associate of the company's boss, Kari Stefansson, who in turn was a close friend of David Oddsson's.

Such was the tangle of commercial networking, politics, and personal friendship. Oddsson was not pulling the strings in these multilayered deals. But he had set the terms and had made no secret of his distaste for Jon Asgeir. Understanding Icelandic capitalism was akin to listening for the underlying musical themes flowing through the Wagnerian Ring cycle. Jon Asgeir's Baugur sold its shares in Icelandair, apparently admitting defeat. He had been outwitted by his fellow oligarchs and it was time to bail out. But the Icelandic business world moved at breakneck speed. Within a few months, in October 2004, the terms changed again—Hannes Smarason had broken up with his wife and was therefore no longer beholden to her father. Some of the ill feeling was thus removed. Smarason was no longer the instrument of a grudge match between his retail magnate father-in-law and Jon Asgeir. Suddenly, Jon Asgeir was back in favor, buying up shares again in Icelandair, forging a new alliance with Smarason.

Inevitably, the duel between Jon Asgeir and David Oddsson turned personal. On state television Oddsson accused Jon Asgeir of offering him a bribe. The accusation was hedged to prevent Jon Asgeir from launching a libel action—the bribe offer, said Oddsson, had come through a reliable middleman: 300 million Icelandic kronas to be transferred to an untraceable account. In return, Oddsson was supposed to stop interfering with Jon Asgeir's business. The next day Jon Asgeir denied that he had made any such offer. The middleman started to backtrack, saying that perhaps the whole thing was said in jest. With his claim, Oddsson—who only went on television to send one, specific message—had demonstrated that Jon Asgeir was no Robin Hood, and far from being a champion of the man in the street. In taking an intimate feud into the public domain, Oddsson was betraying one of the principles that he and his fellow members of the libertarian Mont Pelerin Society had learned at the feet of Friedman and Hayek. As the leader of a market revolution, he had to accept some kind of accommodation with wealth creators, however much he disliked their manners and motives. "Who will deny that a world in which the wealthy are powerful is still a better world than one in which only the already powerful can acquire wealth," wrote Hayek in *The Road to Serfdom*. "The power which a multi-millionaire, who may be my neighbor and perhaps my employer, has over one is very much less than that which the smallest function-aire possesses who wields the coercive power of the state and on whose discretion it depends whether and how I am to be allowed to live or to work." Oddsson was the political product of the "already powerful"; that was his lot as the promising product of the Independence Party with its strong linkages to the Octopus. The fact is, he was unable to modernize Iceland without first modernizing his party; Tony Blair had understood this in Britain, while Margaret Thatcher and Ronald Reagan had tried to dodge the problem by creating a personalized style of government. Oddsson could not square the circle. That was part of his individual failure, and every time that he heard of a new, triumphant acquisition by Jon Asgeir—carried out by stealth, using market instruments that Oddsson himself had put into the world—part of him died. A choleric, he could be gripped by such an apoplectic rage that he would fall off his chair. No one triggered these fits more effectively than Jon Asgeir: undereducated, amoral, that was the World According to David.

Jon Asgeir, and the other tycoons, introduced the American busi-ness model to Iceland. Its underpinning credo appeared to be that greed can be a benign and sustainable force. In 1971, long before asset-stripping—the filleting of companies for their most profitable slices—became standard business practice, the economists Ken Arrow and Frank Hahn asked, "What will an economy motivated by greed and controlled by a very large number of different agents look like?" Their answer: "There will be chaos." For Oddsson, the New Vikings were short-termists, committed to nothing. The opaque nature of their holdings was supposed to blur the responsibility of private ownership; they were on their way to owning everything in Iceland, but only to generate a quick profit. Oddsson had let the genie out of the bottle. And Oddsson, sensing his increasing irrelevance as the prime minister of a community whose pace and rhythm was being set by others, responded by consolidating the old power structures.

By the time he left the political stage in 2009, he and his Independence Party tribal loyalists had controlled Iceland for eighteen years. In that time the Independence Party had developed something akin to the nomenklatura system practiced by the East European Communists during the Cold War. All power derived from the party, which handed out rewards and took them away again. That is why the Independence Party bosses appeared to be willing to allow control over Landsbanki, the bank that had become a party fiefdom, to pass to Bjoergólfur Gudmundsson: he had paid his dues to the nomenklatura. And Bjoergólfur returned the favor again and again, subsidizing careers and filling party coffers. Landsbanki was a huge donor to the Independence Party.

The concept of state power is shaky in Iceland. How could it be otherwise? The country has no army; the police force is tiny, overstretched; the individualistic culture dislikes swagger in the country's civil service; and an informal system of favors within families and clans keeps the place moving. In a society of three hundred thousand, something is slightly top-heavy about the trappings of power: a president, a prime minister, a cabinet, a national health service, a central bank. All that makes for imbalance, a feeling that there are more chiefs than Indians, and it stirs skepticism about the true clout of institutions. So the will of the state can easily be replaced by the will of political clans.

David Oddsson's dearest wish was to rein in Jon Asgeir and abolish (as he told friends) the "law of the jungle." But Jon Asgeir was not in any profound way breaking the laws of the state. It would be complicated to throw the book at him. Not impossible, though, to make his life difficult, to trim his wings by presenting his methods, his lifestyle, as morally dubious. All one needed was a complaisant prosecutor's office, political friends at the helm of the police, a press that was in cahoots with the Independence Party—and enough people who felt slighted by Jon Asgeir and his family to turn publically against them.

From 2002 to 2008—the six years that charted Jon Asgeir's transformation into a global player and then his fall from grace—he was bombarded with investigations into his business practices. Sometimes the timing was more significant than the charges. A police raid on his offices in 2002 effectively knocked him out of the bidding for Arcadia, the British high-street shopping group that owns Topshop and other fashion outlets. When an indictment was drawn up—detailing forty charges against him—in the summer of 2005, he was bounced out of the running for the Somerfield supermarket chain in Britain. Even though many of the charges of embezzlement and fraud had been three years in the making—twenty thousand boxes of evidence were accumulated—they were surprisingly weakly formulated. In fact, Jon Asgeir's mastery of cross-ownership and rapid turnover in shareholdings made the prosecutor's job a nightmare. Some of the accusations were, at best, petty: the use of a company credit card to buy a cheeseburger in the United States, for example. In the end, Jon Asgeir was sentenced to three months in jail, suspended.

The aim seemed to be social embarrassment at home, and the hope that his business partners abroad would take him less seriously. One case pitted Gaumur—the company that represented the interests of Jon Asgeir, his father, and his sister—against Jon Gerald Sullenberger. Sullenberger was the boss of a company called Nordica, which owned warehouses in the United States that supplied the Baugur group. Gaumur claimed to have transferred $465,000 to Sullenberger to strengthen his company. Sullenberger argued that the money was in fact payment toward the upkeep of Jon Asgeir's yacht, *Thee Viking*, moored in Florida. Jon Asgeir was not keen to be seen as a yacht owner—it did not fit with his discount-supermarket image—so the yacht was put in Sullenberger's name. Then Jon Asgeir held up payments, and Sullenberger, who had known Jon Asgeir and his father for twelve years, started to protest. The trial documents were leaked and, according to Sullenberger's lawyers, showed that Jon Asgeir had used the *Thee Viking* for some extravagant corporate entertaining. To celebrate the acquisition of Vifilfell, which distributes Coke in Iceland, in November 2001 Jon Asgeir had allegedly decided to treat some of the executives involved in the deal. Sullenberger got *Thee Viking* ready, but was in London at the time of the party. When he returned to Miami, he found the yacht a mess and had it repaired and cleaned. Shortly afterward, the head of a local escort agency called—he had supplied women to the tune of more than $19,000. The payments were made in installments of $2,500 by swiping a Visa card made out to Baugur. But the card had been reported stolen and all payments were canceled. Now the escort agency boss wanted the cash from Sullenberger as the owner, on paper at least, of *Thee Viking*. Sullenberger approached Jon Asgeir, who said that all bills would be settled through his Luxembourg account. As tensions grew between Jon Asgeir and Sullenberger and they headed for trial in both Reykjavik and Miami, Sullenberger's defense team suggested that everyone who had been on the yacht at the time of the party should be summoned as material witnesses. This would have profoundly embarrassed a significant chunk of the Icelandic business class and made Jon Asgeir look foolish indeed. So a settlement was reached out of court; Baugur paid up.

Now, none of this is exactly groundbreaking in the checkered history of corporate entertainment. *Thee Viking* was worth $1.1 million, was sixty-two feet long—but was hardly in the league of some of the boats used by Russian oligarchs for their networking parties. The sums were not huge, and it wasn't the first or last time that company credit cards would be used for dubious pleasures. But one detail was significant: Sullenberger's lawyer, who had stuck the pin through the butterfly that was Jon Asgier, was Jon Steinar Gunnlaugsson, a former member of the Milton Friedman fan club, a future chief justice of Iceland—and a close friend of David Oddsson's.

It is difficult to see the *Thee Viking* affair in any context apart from a continuation of the duel between Jon Asgeir and David Oddsson. "That's just the paranoia of the Baugsmidlar," says an associate of Oddson's, using the slightly contemptuous term for employees of Baugur. "David was prime minister and this was an extraordinary time in the world—remember 9/11? Do you think he would have got involved with anything so trivial?" Well, no, perhaps not. The web of loyalties around Oddsson, though, was such that plenty of courtiers were ready to please him. "Jon Asgeir's head on a platter, that would have put a spring in Oddsson's step," says another former colleague.

The arrival of Jon Asgeir in the land of Richistan became obvious to all when he strode into the Reykjavik courthouse wearing a black

Armani suit and a white Make Poverty History bracelet. This was the summer of 2005, and the charges that had swirled around him three years earlier and that had seemed to dissolve had now been firmed up. Jon Asgeir was still in no doubt that he was the target of a political conspiracy. "They, the police, would never have gone into a company of this size in Iceland without authority from above," said Jon Asgeir. Most of the charges related to business between 1998 to 2002 involved share transfers and loans made from his private holdings to his publicly listed company Baugur. A warehouse to store Jon Asgeir's car collection; a riding lawn mower for the estate of Baugur vice president Trygvvi Jonsson.

The real reason for Jon Asgeir to worry was not the prospect of being sent to jail but, again, the bad publicity eroding his credibility abroad. Well before the trial was being prepared, a former mistress of his father's was making it plain that she was willing to dish the dirt on the family. Jonina Benediktsdottir was forty-five, blonde, suntanned, and, for Icelandic tastes, a little too fond of costume jewelry, a little too loud. But she was a sharp businesswoman, educated at McGill, who had set up her own highly profitable fitness center. As the wealthy wife of a wealthy surgeon from a well-connected Reykjavik dynasty, she was part of the capital's bridge-playing, chattering elite. Then, in early 1999, she found herself sitting next to Jon Asgeir's father, big, bluff Johannes Jonsson, on a flight from Iceland to Copenhagen. "Within a short time he had proposed that he and my husband should open a private hospital together." She was apparently impressed by his hands: strong butcher's hands with spatulate thumbs. Soon enough, he was exercising at her gym, making jokes about the nonalcoholic drinks available, asking her out for supper. Her husband discovered the affair—Reykjavik, capital of a fishing nation, loves gossip as much as a fisherman's wife. Jonina divorced and moved into Johannes's apartment in the swanky Grafarvogur district. Before long she discovered one of Johannes's secrets: his tightness with money. The renovation of the apartment, she says, came out of her pocket; she subsidized too their shopping trips to Denmark (Johannes, who could barely speak English, preferred Copenhagen to the oligarchs' more usual weekend destination of London). Johannes's suits began to fit better thanks to Jonina's advice and to her credit cards. The quid pro quo was that Johannes, or some part of the Baugur empire, would chip into Jonina's pet project: Planet Pulse, a one-stop health club for the emerging superrich or those who would like to bump into them in the changing room. The plan was to offer ayurveda treatments, and personal fitness trainers, to make it into a meeting place, congeal the political-business class with those who served them, the architects and interior designers. Deals in Iceland had always been made in steamy hot tubs; Jonina wanted to modernize the concept. But the flagship club—a chain had been planned—cost more than $1 million to set up. Johannes's interest began to wander, and when the debts began to mount, he found himself less than enthralled with Planet Pulse, and with Jonina. The relationship crashed, Jonina applied for bankruptcy. Her gripe: Baugur should have bailed her out.

Jonina was more than a woman scorned. She had inside information—albeit mainly hearsay—about how Baugur was managed, about the relationship between Jon Asgier's family and Baugur at a critical time in its development. The chance of publicly humiliating Jon Asgeir, even feeding the state prosecutors, was too tempting for the Oddsson fan club. Yes, it was a faintly tacky, even sad story of thwarted love, but not ultimately anything very unusual in Richistan. For those targeting Jon Asgeir, however, the story of Jonina, suitably packaged, was useful ammunition. Styrmir Gunnarsson, former editor of *Morgunbladid* and staunch ally of David Oddsson's, says that both Jonina and Jon Gerald Sullenberger approached him, explaining their problems with Baugur. The editor suggested that they turn to Jon Steinar Gunnlaugsson. Jon Steinar, said the journalist, was *innvigdur og innmuradur*—"one of us," one of the closed Oddsson group. When it became clear that Jonina was throwing in her lot with the Oddssonites, *Morgunbladid*'s main competitor, *Frettabladid*, owned by Baugur, published private e-mails between Jonina and Styrmir.

Iceland is not just a country with Viking roots. It is also an island of chess players. Fishermen typically used the off-season to carve chess pieces out of whalebone, wood being too valuable. The game is part of everyday life, played in cafés and in midsummer on the dockside. Even the older generation does not dwell on the supposedly groundbreaking summit between Ronald Reagan and Mikhail Gorbachev in Reykjavik in 1986. But everyone has a memory of the 1972 world chess championship in Reykjavik between Bobby Fischer—who in 2005 received asylum to protect him from U.S. charges of violating the economic boycott of Yugoslavia—and Boris Spassky; their games were televised in the schools. At least nine Icelanders have since gone on to become grand masters.

The principles of chess were carried over to the domestic political game, as the prime minister and the country's most combative tycoon fought to position themselves. Their game, so often played to a pointless stalemate, was about how a small state could flourish in a globalized world economy. For Jon Asgeir, the aim was to transcend the island and its tiny market. Although he had made forays into the Faroe Islands and Denmark, it was obvious to him that expansion had to be into the Anglo-American sphere. The easiness of credit, the new financial instruments, the freshly privatized, ambitious banks, all pointed to the need for raw capitalism, which rewarded speed of decision-making, high calculated risk, and an eye on short-term profitability. The so-called American business model was what Jon Asgeir so much admired. In fact, though, many big U.S. corporations do not make much use of this supposed business model; generating the largest possible profits in the shortest time at the expense of wrecking long-term market positioning was not the model of choice for most business strategists. Oddsson's supporters, in deploying their shotgun approach to blasting Jon Asgeir, may accidentally have hit on the entrepreneur's true weakness: he did not understand how to build up and integrate an organization capable of planning a three-year strategy. He did not have to: the banks were ready to lend to him anyway on his past performance as a brilliant, intuitive player. When his intuition failed him, as it increasingly did, he borrowed more money. "And when the banks were less cooperative, he bought himself his own bank," says Katrin Olafsdottir, professor at Reykjavik University's Business School. That bank was Glitnir, which the professor is now trying to unravel, separating its myriad debts from what could still become a going concern, sifting through the rubble left by Jon Asgeir and his creative destroyers.

If Jon Asgeir was the Bobby Fischer of commerce—shy, impulsive, with a sharp eye for openings—then David Oddsson was its Boris Spassky. Well-meaning—nobody has suggested that Oddsson ever sought personal profit—vain, slightly troubled, not averse to risky gambits, but ultimately overcautious. Why was he so passionately opposed to Jon Asgeir? Why was he so embittered that he was willing to compromise the integrity of his historical mission to modernize Iceland by resorting to cronyism, to install his placemen everywhere? Margaret Thatcher had understood that the first step in a market revolution that deregulates and disperses initiative must be to centralize political power. Oddsson did the same, but in so doing created a siege mentality in his Independence Party, which developed a constant need for enemies. Jon Asgeir annoyed him because he gave the impression that he had no emotional need for, or connection to, the island. "I have gone cold on Iceland," Jon Asgeir told a reporter after the police, the prosecutors, and the political class had turned on him in 2005. If Jon Asgeir had any ambition for Iceland, it was to lift it out of its drab provincialism, to turn it into a glamorous place to take his international friends—often the only ones he could trust—for a weekend. Oddsson's heart beat for provincial Iceland. The role of a small country was not (as Jon Asgeir would have it) to deny its smallness, but to encourage the big players in the world to take it seriously. It was a question of the island finding its voice. And so David Oddsson talked a small state big: it was to be a country with a strong currency, capable of defending and promoting its national interests. That, believed Oddsson, should be the new, up-to-date mission of the Independence Party, which had given him a political home. The other way, the Jon Asgeir way, would only enmesh Iceland in other forms of dependency, create new forms of feudal or colonial rule.

Who won the game? Nobody. In the end, both men, in their stubbornness, their pettiness, steered Iceland toward the edge of a cliff.

6 : Bonus

Every man loves the smell of his own fart.
Icelandic proverb

Avaritia was, for Christians in the second century A.D., one of the seven mortal sins. The word meant both greed and miserliness. Plainly, what bothered the moralists was excess: an exaggerated drive for possessions was unacceptable greed; an exaggerated thrift was unacceptable mean-ness. When Iceland started to fall apart in the autumn of 2008, the questions raised were universal ones: Did we get greedy, catch it like a virus? Or was greed thrust upon us? Equally, when the financial crisis became, with astonishing speed, a deep global recession, governments everywhere urged their citizens to spend, spend, spend. The concern with greed had been replaced by the other meaning of *avaritia*—the fear that excessive thrift, a shunning of consumption, would propel the world toward a great depression; its vital juices would dry up.

Iceland, which had always commuted between boom and bust—the cycle dictated by the movement of fish in the Atlantic and the erratic weather—found something familiar about this crisis, this sudden, aggressive downturn in its fortunes. Yet it could not quite get its head around that fundamental question of individual greed and collective euphoria. "I would come back from abroad," says the diplomat Urdur Gunnarsdottir, "to a homeland that had become strange, with its big cars and posh shops and everyone buying things they couldn't afford."

Iceland had been a poor country for as long as anyone could remember, even with the influx of cash that came with the American base in Keflavik. Although the U.S. base commanders were obliged to pay wages equivalent to the national norm, overtime and black-market dealing ensured that any Icelander on the American payroll was significantly better off than when employed elsewhere. This led to an inflationary spiral, with workers from all sectors playing catch-up. For most of Iceland's postwar history the island has been a captive of high inflation—only David Oddsson managed to bring it under control in the early 1990s. The island, heavily dependent on imports, was hit hard by the oil crisis of the 1970s: inflation rose to a shocking 43 percent in 1974. Even in 1980, 59 percent inflation ate into the currency. Inflation, says the writer Kristof Magnusson, made a mockery out of saving. The old wisdom of the fishing families—to save in good times for bad times ahead—and the finger-wagging of Lutheran priests did nothing to brake or change Icelandic spending patterns during the 1970s and 1980s. Magnusson says, "In the '80s double-digit inflation rates were simply normal. This was the time when my father asked me: 'Why don't you take out a loan and buy a house—inflation will pay.' Everyone tried to spend their money as quickly as possible and did what every other Icelander did, which was to accumulate as much debt as possible." Icelanders, then, were imprudent spenders even before the ascent of David Oddsson and the privatization of the economy.

In a country with a cultural memory of impoverishment and colonial subjugation, the sense of money to spend was liberating. It was irrational, since the money was worth little, but enchanting nonetheless. "Every five years a new suburban outpost of Reykjavik was blown into the lava to make way for even bigger houses. All first-time buyers were entitled to a loan of ninety percent of the cost price," says Magnusson. "When I returned to Iceland in 1991 and asked a friend what had gone on in my absence, he proudly replied, 'We now have more cars per capita than the Americans!' " This behavior had an element of hysterical recklessness, but it couldn't really be described as greed. The popular logic was straightforward: "Why save? I've got my house."

Iceland was, in the 1980s, still a controlled, almost socialist society with strange, old-fashioned customs. The sale of beer was banned until 1989 for fear that it would introduce young people to the "hard stuff," and the state invested heavily in hospitals, schools, and pensions. Most of the welfare legislation had been influenced by the Depression of the 1930s. By 1968, Iceland could boast one doctor for every 750 inhabitants; infant mortality was the lowest in the world. "Welfare in Iceland has not grown from the charitable patronage of the rich but has always been a collective activity," wrote the British author John Griffiths in 1969. "There is therefore neither shame nor greed associated with the taking of benefits." This combination of a security net, a free-spending lifestyle, full employment, and hard work created a special kind of freedom of spirit.

By the end of the 1980s, Iceland had become a state of young people, highly educated—literacy levels were among the highest in the world—and ready to party. True, no one quite understood how the island was supporting itself. It called itself a bumblebee economy: the puzzling aerodynamics of a bee applied too to this top-heavy country. With a population of three hundred thousand—less than that of Hull, the grim British port where it used to unload its fish—and barely any industry apart from an aluminum smelter, it nevertheless supported its own national currency, prime minister, president, a central bank, and in the 1960s at least a dozen daily national newspapers and forty bookshops in the capital alone. So, when Iceland nudged its way onto the world stage by winning international song contests, or with the strangely out-of-focus, in-focus singer Björk, or the postrock group Sigur Rós—who performed in the Hollywood Bowl—it dawned on outsiders that the island perhaps was not just lava and sheep droppings, but actually Cool. Even before the Icelanders embarked on the Gold Rush, it seemed—in the wide-eyed perception of (initially) the Scots and the Nordics, then later the English, the Irish, and younger Wall Street traders—to be a kind of playground for the new era. The nightless summers, the easiness with which the evening would begin with drinks at home (so much cheaper than reaching the early stages of drunkenness at a club), then the cheerful lining up at one A.M. in front of the bars, the forced intimacy of loud music, followed by an invitation to party with someone who did not live with his or her mother. Dawn was registered not by the rising of the sun but, in summer at least, by the activity on the docks, the loading and unloading of tackle. It was, for outsiders, an enchanting place.

Björk Gudmundsdottir, who appeared to share the Icelandic countryman's belief in the "hidden people," elves who could make life difficult if not shown respect, mixed jazz and electronic and alternative rock to produce an Icelandic sound. In 1992 she broke from her group the Sugarcubes, and by 1994 she had won two Brit awards. In 2001 she caused a sensation at the Oscar ceremonies by appearing in a typically eccentric costume made out of swan feathers. Although she opposed everything that David Oddsson stood for—above all, his determination to expand aluminum production on the island—her clear, high voice provided the musical backdrop to what was beginning to seem like a new era. Life under high inflation had a kind of dreamy irresponsibility to it; the Oddsson revolution—aimed at stabilizing the currency and encouraging private enterprise—was a way of telling young people that they could determine their own lives. The Oddsson 1990s were not in the first instance about getting rich, but about becoming free. Björk played her part in this by promoting the image of Iceland as a place where the young respected their traditions, their language, their elders, and where, nonetheless, they were in constant, innovative rebellion. In her wistful song "Modern Things," she reflects that the newfangled consumer objects flooding Iceland had just been biding their time, "in a mountain/for the right moment"; the mountain being Esja, the battered old volcano that Björk could see from the window of her apartment on the Reykjavik dockside.

No, Icelanders were not ravaged by greed, not at first, but rather gripped by a sense of their time having come. Insofar as David Oddsson could explain away his Friedman-esque mission as a breakout, the destruction of an old order, he could capture the popular mood. In the early 1990s Oddsson represented creative change rather than tired cronyism. That gave him some political credit. A deal with the trade unions, in which they promised to restrain wage demands, gave him and the country some breathing room. "There had never been such wage restraint before, it was a unique deal," says the economist Katrin Olafsdottir. Even the economic slowdown of those years allowed him to address the central question of leadership in Iceland: how to reach economic security, how to transcend the sea and the soil, how to build a modern society.

In 1991 David Oddsson had inherited an economy with three pillars: fish, which were Iceland's main export; geothermal power, which could not be exported; and a U.S. Army base that generated jobs and sales. His problem was how to make these elements into a source of stable growth. The retention of the U.S. base was a priority, but that decision was almost entirely out of his hands; he was a supplicant, his being the only government in the world that, after the end of the Cold War, was begging Washington to keep its troops in place.

The government was limited too in how much impact it could make on fishing; the quota system had been streamlined under Oddsson, and the fishing industry would plainly undergo gentrification. That is, fish finance, the funding of expansion by borrowing against future catches, was gradually supplanting the gritty business of netting the cod and cleaning them, packaging them onshore. The fish futures traders were increasingly sophisticated young graduates from U.S. and Canadian universities, with the dirty work done by Eastern Europeans, especially Poles.

"In the old days," Kristjan tells me at the dockside, "we ate haddock and cods' heads. Everything else went for export." The old days being the 1960s, when Kristjan, who later bought a van and went into the delivery business, was a resentful teenager. "The whole island worked towards fish, it was like a religion, with the skippers of boats being priests and the boat owners being bishops. We were supposed to sacrifice everything to the fish—our families, our free time." It was a world of absent fathers; of cottages reeking of fish; of part-time jobs in the smokeries; of fish flapping outside the house to dry. Nowadays, you can eat cod at afford-able prices in Iceland, but the sense that fish—by being the only real livelihood—distorted society, held it back in some way, is still heard, at least in the southwest of the island.

Oddsson tried to break away from the tyranny of fish by tapping geothermal power. Charles Babbage, the inventor of an early version of the computer, had seen the possibilities of the hot, high-pressure water pushing its way toward the surface. "In a future age," wrote Babbage in 1832, "power may become the staple commodity of the Icelanders, and of the inhabitants of other volcanic districts; and possibly the very process by which they will procure this article of exchange for the luxuries of happier climates, may in some measure tame the tremendous element which occasionally devastates their provinces." It was precisely this calculation—that volcanic force could somehow be harnessed to the good of the country—that inspired the Icelandic government of the 1960s. Geothermal power already supplied the bulk of the island's energy needs; it appeared to be an endless resource. Electric power, offered cheaply enough, was valuable. All one had to do was find an industry that needed huge amounts of energy—the smelting, for example, of aluminum.

The first project was to build a hydroelectric power plant, financed partly by the U.S. bond market. By May 1965, the Althing, the Icelandic parliament, had created the National Power Company to run the power station just below Mount Hekla, two hours out of the capital, to fuel Reykjavik and provide the electricity for a smelter at nearby Straumsvik bay. It was to be the first of several smelters, and aluminum under the Oddsson government would soon rival fish as the prime export. In the six years between 1997 and 2003, Iceland became the largest producer per capita of primary aluminum in the world. The Icelanders naturally play a great deal with the "per capita" calculations; with such a tiny population, they can, and frequently do, pose as world-beaters; from Nobel Prize laureates to Olympic medal winners, the mathematics is on their side. But in fact aluminum smelting—and therefore aluminum exporting—expanded massively under the stewardship of Oddsson, making up 10 percent of exports in 1995, and 37 percent in 2008.

The promotion of an industrial Iceland by Oddsson involved social upheaval and spawned a new protest movement that took up the mantle of the anti-NATO demonstrations of the 1940s and 1950s. It also entailed a large-scale diversion of water, a confrontation with nature. Thousands protested against new smelters, among them Björk. Her mother even went on a hunger strike, but survived. Alumina is extracted from bauxite by electrolysis—requiring vast amounts of electricity. Hydroelectric power is the most economical. Hence the need for dams. An Alcoa smelter was erected in 2006 in eastern Iceland, but not before the gigantic Karahnjukar dams had been constructed in a highland valley on the edge of the Vatnajökull glacier: nine dams and accompanying dikes blocked two rivers, robbing the rare pink-footed goose of its summer breeding ground.

Aluminum ensured full employment in hard-up eastern Iceland. But the fear was that Oddsson was trying to do two things at once: to industrialize Iceland and to privatize it. In the late nineteenth century, progressive thinkers such as Einar Benediktsson had dreamed of an

Iceland with factories and railways. But it never happened; Iceland missed out on the industrial revolution. When Oddsson accelerated the aluminum deals, he was therefore regarded with suspicion. Smelting, after all, was a fairly primitive industrial process—the bauxite was shipped to the island, the primary aluminum shipped out—and was not going to make Iceland into a knowledge culture.

The outsider finds it difficult to understand the passion. Iceland may have a small population, but has a relatively big landmass—almost as large as England. The chances of its air and waters being irreversibly polluted by four smelters are not that big. The danger was, and is, that Icelanders tend to grasp for a single solution—the one fix that will save them from poverty and economic chaos—then pump it up like a pneumatic tire until it either bursts or becomes unusable. The writer and polemicist Andri Snaer Magnason suggests that is one of the founding myths of modern Iceland: "The war saved us from the Depression, and then came the Marshall Plan once the war was over; then it was the herring that saved us, and when that disappeared, we had the aluminum plant and the Burfell hydro scheme to save us." So the Americans were milked for every last cent; the herring were overfished; the world's aluminum companies courted and encouraged to expand endlessly within the island. The idea of modernization was so appealing that it could not tolerate restraint. "The other Nordic cultures have the concept of *lagom*—of moderation in all things," says Urdur Gunnarsdottir. "We never had that." The opposition to the aluminization of Iceland was not just about protecting nature. It also reflected the fear that the Icelandic temperament for extremes— nothing exceeds like excess—would take over, that one smelter would follow another until the sky turned black over Iceland.

Would it be any different when Icelanders turned to financial adventurism? Who would set the boundaries, define the limits of zeal?

J. K. Galbraith was right: bubbles can occur anywhere. They are not tied to any particular society or culture. There was the tulip mania of the seventeenth century (when a single bulb could be traded for the equivalent of $30,000), the South Sea bubble of the eighteenth century, the manipulation of U.S. railroad stock in the nineteenth century. These periods of hysteria grip whole societies. The South Sea Company lent money to the British government to finance a war against France. In return, Parliament in 1720 gave the company a monopoly in trade with South America. The company then underwrote the English national debt, on a promise of 5 percent interest from the government. Shares immediately rose to ten times their value, and speculators set up companies to milk profits from ordinary people who believed they could become rich by investing in the Next Big Thing. One company was floated to buy the Irish bogs; another said it would revolutionize warfare with square cannonballs. When the bubble burst, porters and ladies' maids—who had bought their own horses and carriages with their supposed new wealth—were ruined, bishops lost their life savings, and the powerful postmaster general poisoned himself.

No society is immune from speculative madness. But Iceland, driven by its enthusiasms, its cyclical bouts of depression, and its informal information network, does seem to be Bubble-land.

So when Oddsson pushed ahead with the privatization of the banks, few voices in the academic tundra suggested that this might be the route to disaster. Most Icelanders had an extraordinary sense of catching up with the rest of the world. The financial-services industry was the Next Big Thing. David Oddsson and the other Icelandic Friedmanites had seen how the 1980s deregulation of the banking system had transformed bankers from passive guardians of deposited wealth to active players who, in their ability to change spending habits and encourage investment, were doing their bit to rebrand nations. Although Oddsson was the antithesis of Cool—being both a reflective writer of fiction and poetry, and a man of provincial cultural tastes, a supporter of the local theater—he understood the importance of national image-making. The Coolness, the steady flow of rock stars in search perhaps of an uncorrupted society free of sycophancy and easy on taxes, could be transformed into something more substantial. The privatized banks could trade up on an internationally attractive Iceland, profit from, develop, and export the island's new, enhanced self-image. And so they were given carte blanche; bankers became ambassadors abroad, and at home, new, slick fast-laners.

When the United States responded to the Great Depression by passing the Glass-Steagall Act of 1933, it took a major step toward protecting ordinary investors. The act required bankers to decide whether to be commercial banks—that is, closely supervised parts of the monetary system, subject to reserve requirements, with deposit insurance—or investment banks, without government guarantees. As long as these categories were blurred, investors could be misled into believing that their cash investments were in safe hands, secured by law. Glass-Steagall reduced the risk of conflict of interest, with bankers selling financial products to customers for their own gain. The following year the Securities and Exchange Commission was set up to monitor Wall Street. By the 1980s, leaders could believe that the specter of a new depression had been banished forever. Holding back the financial services industry, as it was coming to be known, was seen as irresponsible governance. The world had changed. Glass-Steagall was repealed—not by Oddsson's hero Ronald Reagan, but by the Democrat Bill Clinton—and the bankers entered the vanguard of social change.

In Britain, Margaret Thatcher had made the capitalist revolution popular by selling government-subsidized housing to tenants at reduced prices. Freeing the banks would allow those on low incomes to enter the homeownership market, to shift them subtly away from proletarianism. Financial deregulation, in other words, was a step toward making society more democratic, introducing new choices for individuals and not just padding the salaries of the bankers. Until privatization, Icelandic bankers had been viewed as stolid, unimaginative, risk-averse, but nonetheless in possession of a kind of schoolmasterly integrity. "If you wanted to borrow even a piffling sum, you would put on your best suit and rehearse your lines in front of the mirror," says the Reykjavik real estate broker Högni "Huck" Kjartan Thorkelsson. "Then, after making you wait, he would cut thirty percent off your requested loan simply to demonstrate his power, or maybe to protect the assets of the bank." That changed. "By 2003, you could ring up and extend your credit line by millions. Just like that, no face contact."

Icelandic banks had the same essential problems as banks everywhere: their traditional business was barely profitable. The economics of taking in deposits and lending money out again earns the narrowest of interest margins. This may seem a childishly obvious statement, but it helps explain the compulsive need to expand and the built-in problems of leverage. Even more so in Iceland: how were three large banks supposed to flourish in a society of three hundred thousand, fewer than two hundred thousand of them wage earners? Banking economics functions only on a large scale. Even conservative banks borrowed ten times their capital, and investment banks such as Lehman Brothers borrowed thirty times their capital. At that level of borrowing, of leverage, it takes little more than a sneeze to blow away capital and expose lenders.

Financial engineering, novelty, has been at the heart of every bubble. Little wonder that when in February 2009 I ran down the economist Gylfi Magnusson again in his office at the University of Iceland, he was reading Galbraith, grunting at the passage on the South Sea bubble. Magnusson gives a slightly nervous impression, like a pale, rich boy who has strayed into the bad part of town. The next day I discover the reason for his twitchiness: he had just accepted the post of business minister in the new Icelandic government, a job that wins ulcers rather than Oscars. "Our banks did not fall into the trap of exposing themselves to the U.S. subprime mortgage market," he says, adding that they did, however, walk into every other possible trap. For a while they could even present themselves as victims of U.S. mismanagement, of the world liquidity crisis. But in fact privatized Icelandic banks had barged their way into the global market at precisely the moment when the speculators were running wild, and the banks were unable to smell the danger.

"I would sit here," says Katrin Olafsdottir, at the University of Reykjavik Business School, "with my final-year students, trying to keep their attention at a time when they already had contracts from the banks in their pockets." During the lunch break, instead of grazing laptops or trying to master the Phillips curve, they would cruise the nearby American-style Kringlan shopping mall, planning how to spend their future bonuses. "You can imagine how we felt. They pulled in two or three times a professor's income within months of leaving the seminar rooms." Bonuses were not vast by international standards, but large enough to shock. Even the messenger boys at Landsbanki picked up a bonus of around $2,000. Inexperienced, entranced, the new recruits were given early responsibility at Landsbanki, Kaupthing, and Glitnir, blissfully unaware of their inexperience and entrancement. They had entered a world in which debt—the same debt that had been a ball and chain for their grandfathers—had become a plaything, even sexy. Farmers and fishermen understood derivatives; they took bets on their harvests, their catch. The task of young bankers across the globe was to encourage over-extended borrowing, especially but not only on homeownership, even at the serious risk of default. The whole reward structure was based on tugging customers into debt, then turning debt into a commodity.

Down south, in Britain, and to the west on Wall Street, great business brains were working on collateralized debt obligations (CDOs), the new product of the booming financial industry that lumped together different grades of debt. They were high risk, but they were high yield. The process made risk manageable by dispersal, and that took the shame out of debt. Everyone, it seemed, got a chunk of the winnings. First-time buyers found it easy to get mortgages; house prices rose, and since the new generation of bankers had no collective memory of a bust—and had probably skipped the college classes on Depression economics—they too believed in the inevitable rise in property values. The banks and real estate agents grew fat, and markets everywhere relished the charm of asset-based securities and the black art of leverage.

The Icelandic banks did not get sucked into collateralization, but they matched the new mentality in the boardrooms. Debt was no longer a problem in need of a solution, but part of the universal alchemy. For ordinary Icelanders, as for ordinary punters around the world, the sale of derivatives, the currency-futures market, and the rest of the toolbox were something that happened in Borgartún, the Reykjavik street where the banks had set up their headquarters. It was why their bright children were being paid such high salaries; an abstraction. What affected them directly was the "carry trade." The currency carry traders seemed to be on a sure bet, at least during the good years. They shifted their clients' money from low-interest countries such as Japan and parked it in Iceland, with its extraordinarily high rates. That boosted the money available to Icelandic banks for investment abroad. Borrow low, lend high: it was a simple enough concept. Speculators borrowed in Japan at 3 percent—and lent in markets such as Britain, New Zealand, or Iceland with higher interest rates. Iceland with its 15 percent rates—kept high to control inflation—was particularly attractive. There is nothing underhand about carry trading; the risks are obvious. It is vulnerable to shifting rates—and to any drying up of liquidity. Funds moved around in this way were known as hot money—they could be dropped like a hot poker if there was a risk of being burned. Hot money can flood into a country and create the illusion of wealth, boost the local currency. And it can leave just as quickly at the first sign of panic. It was a shaky basis on which to build a banking system.

Yet the bankers actively sucked ordinary Icelanders into their system. How best to guard yourself against the rising cost of personal loans, indexed to the cost of living? You borrow in foreign currencies: as long as the krona stayed strong (and as long as that hot money kept on coming into the country), you couldn't go wrong if you bought your house or car, or paid for your holiday, with a loan denominated in Japanese yen and Swiss francs. It was the surest way to beat inflation. The strength of the krona appeared to be permanent, a reward for being Icelandic. "It must have seemed like a no-brainer," says Michael Lewis, author of *Liar's Poker*, "buying these ever more valuable houses and cars with money you are, in effect, paid to borrow."

David Oddsson had laid the foundations for a consumer society, but he was not being rewarded for it politically. In 1996 his Independence Party candidacy for president lost out to that of left-leaning Olafur Ragnar Grimsson; the Independence Party—despite its big infrastructural projects, its handing out of government contracts, its control over *Morgunbladid*, the tabloid *DV*, and RUV state television—was not as radiantly popular as Oddsson had hoped. The 1990s had been for him an intense period of hard work, a heavy legislative load, and outright conflict over the building of aluminum plants. He could not understand how Icelanders could be so ungrateful, so churlish in not recognizing the genius of his leadership.

But by the 2003 general election his coalition partner, the Progressives, had come up with a plan to increase the popularity of the government: 90 percent mortgages from the state fund Ibudalanasjodur. Until then Icelanders had to pay large down payments before even being considered for a loan, a deterrent for the young, many of whom (such as the slacker hero of Hallgrimur Helgason's cult novel *101*) lived with their parents in an extended childhood. The commercial banks, now privatized and free of any serious restraint, started a bidding war for the favors of the young apartment buyer. Kaupthing, in 2004, offered competitive deals with interest rates sometimes dropping to 4 percent. Loans became 100 percent. House prices went through the roof—and the Icelanders felt they had been touched with wealth. Using their houses as security, they started to buy new furniture, new cars, trailers, motorbikes, summer cottages. At the same time salaries were growing and the Icelandic krona seemed not just muscular, it was virtually on steroids.

The Icelandic banks began issuing their own platinum cards. Bank clerks were no longer grim-faced bureaucrats, but had become a combination of salesmen and financial gurus. The value of Icelandic stock was soaring. Between 2003 and 2004, the U.S. stock market doubled. Icelandic stocks grew by a factor of nine; by 2006 the average Icelandic family was three times richer than in 2003. The sense of enrichment derived from the sudden rise of the Icelandic investment banker. The bankers urged their customers to buy banking stock. The buying spree, with Icelandic oligarchs collecting baubles across the world, infected the banking staff themselves. Kaupthing employees were offered cheap loans to buy stock in their own establishment. To be a banker in 2006—in Iceland; anywhere—was to be part of a gilded elite. "We had wings," one young (now unemployed) banker told me in b5, a club once frequented by financiers. "We could fly." When Kaupthing was nationalized in 2008, the wings fell off. The bank staff lost their jobs, their bank stock was worth nothing, and they were still saddled with the loans. Bankers became victims. But a few years earlier it seemed as if they were the new superheroes. The 2008 Icelandic television series *Manhunt* featured the murder of a banker from Glitnir; one suspect was his deputy, who was having an affair with his wife. The slack-jawed detective was shown interviewing the woman in her newly installed kitchen; her affair, she admitted, took off because her husband was constantly abroad, buying up companies. Art was imitating life. Bankers were behaving, in the words of one oligarch, like Medici princes. One banker bought a fine old house in West Reykjavik, next door to Geir Haarde (the then finance minister), and, in a display of creative destruction previously unseen in the capital, had the place ripped apart in order to install state-of-the-art technology, imported parquet teak tiles, and the sleekest of imported furniture. Before Christmas 2007—with the time bomb ticking under the international banking system—forty construction vehicles were seen outside the villa; the street had to be sealed off, a virtual state of emergency imposed on the neighborhood so that the finishing touches could be put in place before the holiday.

Eyebrows were raised, but the self-enrichment of the banking class was seen by the middle-class Icelander as little more than vulgarity, laughable excess. For, after all, they too were now aspiring members of Richistan. The banks had made it all possible. "Shopping was fulfilling an emotional need for us," says Ragna, a thirty-two-year-old architect, speaking in February 2009, shortly after becoming unemployed. She was celebrating in a pub with her friends after ritually wrapping her defunct credit cards in a children's woolen glove, tying it to a stone, and chucking it with a polite *plop!* into Reykjavik Bay. "We were playing catch-up with the rest of the world." Mobile phones, commonplace in Copenhagen in 1995, were still a rarity in Iceland and at that time absurdly expensive. It was the same across the board: furniture, fashionable clothing, the latest films. Iceland was desperate to join the modern world, and the banks seemed to offer a way of buying into progress. It was seen as a kind of human right to spend money. The rich—or even the moderately well-off, aware of the foreign buying power of the strong krona—went on weekend shopping excursions to London and Copenhagen. Christmas shopping in America began in early November; flights to Boston, New York, and Minneapolis were booked out by the summer. But this raised the question, why weren't these hot products available here in Reykjavik?

Six months into the crisis, I visited one of the few luxury shops to have survived on Bank Street, and it resembled an ancient relic, a Roman bath-house, perhaps, a hint of a lost civilization. Koi carp were still in a pool downstairs, and upstairs a tired pianist played a grand Steinway. Prada jackets were still for sale, but the zest had gone out of high-end shop-ping. "Every society gives itself scope for change and self-fulfillment, and that's what beautiful clothes do for you," said Gunilla Gudmundsson, too bright (it seemed to a non-Icelander) to be selling blouses. She used to work for the Icelandic newspaper *Morgunbladid* as a correspondent in Paris, then for a fashion magazine, now in a clothing shop that might as well be a museum. "There was nothing wrong with what the Icelanders did during the good years; they wanted something better, that's all."

In the clubs—Café Oliver, for example—it was not unusual for a table of off-duty bankers to spend $15,000 on a Saturday night. The Icelanders discovered that their fish worked well in fusion cooking, so restaurants with Nobu prices opened up downtown; as in London or New York, the waiting list for a table was long and arbitrary. The so-called Good Years, from the new millennium to 2007, saw the rise, as one jaded Icelandic journalist put it, of the "urban asshole": the pompous, obstructive maître d'; the guardian of the VIP lists in the clubs; the supercilious stockbroker. The nature of work changed. Fishermen started to worry more about currency baskets than about their nets. For the dirty work, they had Poles; the egalitarian, proudly self-sufficient islanders suddenly had a servant class. The obsessive dusting of the house-proud housewife, the competitive cult of cleanliness in provincial homes, gave way to coffee mornings where one could loudly complain about the sloppiness of one's cleaning lady, Magda from Kielce.

Carpenters converted their workshops into private limited companies, hired Eastern Europeans, and stopped planing wood, as the surest way to riches was to start an import company and rent or buy a shop downtown. Or to take out a 100 percent loan to buy a property, install a power shower and a shiny steel kitchen, then rent it out to foreign bankers stationed in Iceland. The assumption, as in New York or London, was that property prices could only go up; yes, construction was going on around the country, but with such a fundamental shortage of homes, the bubble could never bust.

Ludvik Geirsson, mayor of Hafnarfjördhur, south of the capital, spreads out a map of his township. With twenty-six thousand inhabitants it is the third-largest settlement on the island, and since 2002 it has grown at the rate of a thousand people a year, part of the urbanization of Iceland. The map shows pink patches close to the town center. "New housing estates, new roads, four hundred houses, half of them detached houses, enough for a thousand residents." Now it is a ghost town. "Instead of a thousand new residents, we have twelve hundred unemployed." Housing loans, indexed to inflation, have become toxic.

It used to be the ambition of every Icelander to own his or her own house by the age of forty. The banking revolution accelerated this trend, made people think that homeownership did not entail sacrifice but could rather be the basis of a completely new lifestyle. All one had to do was trust the bank. So every day Icelanders tuned in to the radio, not to hear the weather forecast, but to see how the Dow Jones and the FTSE were faring. The outside world had started to matter, to be central to daily existence, and the doorkeepers to that world were the clever young graduates working in the banks, the same wunderkinder who played hooky from Katrin Olafsdottir's classes. The nature of debt had changed and so had the social relationship between ordinary people and their banks.

The banks, and their supposed understanding of global capital, were the modernizers of Iceland; everything and everyone followed in their wake. Lenders and borrowers, debtors and creditors, had become fused in the passion for profit; in their willingness to ignore bad news; in their joint determination to support the branding of the New Cool Iceland. Samuel Johnson, writing of eighteenth-century debtors' prison, warned against piling the guilt on the debtor. "The truth is, that the creditor always shares the act and often more than shares the guilt, of improper trust . . . There is no reason, why one should punish the other for a contract in which both concurred." The popular mood in 2009 was to set up prisons for greedy, irresponsible lenders, rather than for risk-taking borrowers, who saw themselves as victims. But the compact between creditor and debtor, always complex, has become even more nuanced. Banks, on the whole, are not criminal organizations even if they are sometimes guilty of criminal negligence. They have had to take extraordinary risks to survive, and in a way repugnant to many, they celebrate their survival by raiding the cookie jar of bonuses. But their sin is not so much avarice as the nonmortal misdemeanor of losing control. Their clients, at least in Iceland, had a similar problem. Both debtors and creditors believed in an Iceland that could never exist, a society that could talk its way out of poverty into prosperity, not in a generation but in a decade. Was that a ridiculous dream? Yes, it was.

7 : Delusion

Margur verdur af aurum api.
"Money makes monkeys out of men."
The *Hávamál*

The Icelandic salmon is conceived in cold river water as clear as gin.
When it puts on a bit of weight, it swims to the Atlantic in search of
food. It returns with uncanny accuracy to its original river bigger and
ready to mate; a busy commuter's life. As Thorstein tells it, you can learn
a great deal about the Icelandic oligarchs from this complex, sensitive
fish: Like salmon, they have a sharp eye for movement and an acute
sense of smell, which steers them back home after their feeding forays
on the open seas. "And," says Thorstein, who surely knows, "their lack
of taste, their readiness, if the time and temperature is right, to swallow
anything that is put in front of them."

Thorstein is a gillie, a fishing guide who during the summer season made
a steady living out of connecting rich anglers with their prey. The Icelandic
banks and the big companies rented out stretches of the Laxa I Kjos,
the Langa, and Nordura rivers, for up to $5,000 a day. Although almost
everyone was an incompetent angler, the gillies did their work well, and
there was usually some kind of catch to boast about. Later, in the fishing
lodges, the anglers would have a dinner served by Iceland's celebrity chefs,
complemented by French wine, port, and lava-filtered Icelandic vodka.

For prominent anglers—Prince Charles and Eric Clapton have been
entertained on the Icelandic riverbank—the purpose was little more than
innocent networking. When the banks were at their height (and yet only
a few short years from collapse), they would make a point of inviting top-
dollar international celebrities to Iceland: John Cleese of Monty Python

fame was hired for a television commercial on behalf of Kaupthing. As one banking executive remembered it, the discussion would go "Let's have Bill Clinton for the annual party. No, we can't have him, everybody has him." The country seemed to be driven by an almost deranged desire to be taken seriously by the world. An Icelandic intermediary was ordered to sound out the Vatican as to whether the Polish pope could be persuaded to visit the island, not, of course, to Catholicize society, but to reinforce its international brand. Salmon fishing was part of this lobbying; favored anglers were being softened up for deals or sized up for viceroyships in the expanding Icelandic empires abroad.

European nobility had started to fish for Icelandic salmon at the beginning of the twentieth century, and even after independence the best rivers were the preserve of the state banks and ministers. Ordinary anglers were chased away by gamekeepers. To have power in Iceland means to have privileged access to nature. "This was not about fishing, most of them couldn't cast a line," says Thorstein. Jon Asgeir booked the whole of the Langa River for a week in the prime season, August, with a gillie for each guest. In August 2006, Baugur top management took executives from British retail chains such as House of Fraser for a week on the river. The following year Baugur invited a group of politicians on a salmonfishing trip on one of Iceland's most spectacular rivers. All were board members of Reykjavik Energy. The plan apparently was to merge Geysir Green Energy, owned by the FL Group of Hannes Smarason, with Reykjavik Energy Invest. The politicians stood to gain share options; Baugur and FL were set to win control over the city's energy. Just to make sure, the FL Group donated thirty million Icelandic krona to the Independence Party in 2006. Unusually, news leaked out from the riverside, and the mayor of Reykjavik, Vilhjalmur Vilhjalmsson, one of the happy anglers, resigned, and the government wobbled. The leakage showed that the power of the oligarchs was beginning to weaken; that the time for sweetheart deals with politicians in hot tubs after a hard day's angling and picnicking were coming to a close. But before that, after the privatization of the banks, between their steep rise and deep fall, there was to be half a decade of rampant acquisition.

Thorstein is a red-haired man in his thirties, smooth-faced and university-trained and not at all the typically closefisted gillie, conforming to the stereotype only in that he has a flask of vodka in the inside pocket of his flak jacket. From his point of view, as an itinerant servant of the oligarchical class, the years on the riverside, the quiet tuition, helped inform the business practices of the New Icelanders. It didn't make them better anglers—"their bloody BlackBerrys would tinkle and throb the whole time"—but it might have made them better empire-builders. "Fly-fishing is deception, like any form of hunting," says Thorstein. "You have to observe, exploit its habits, offer the fish something. And you can't take anything for granted with a salmon, you have to respect him. They say, 'Running fish don't take,' but they can be caught. You have to watch the weather, smell it."

Those, it seems, were the skills deployed by the oligarchs when they started fishing in Britain and Scandinavia. "Jon Asgeir would come back from some charity do with Phil Green [the owner of British Home Stores (BHS), a major fashion chain] or Tom Hunter [the Scottish magnate], and he would say the name of a shop, something that he had picked up in conversation, and we would spend the next ten hours number crunching." This from a Baugur scout, a young, British-educated Icelander, paid to spy out lucrative takeover targets. The acquisition strategy was simple enough: to spot undervalued UK stock, preferably with property assets, and create a presence on the British high street.

The Baugur scouts were the gillies, but Jon Asgeir was not a bungling angler. Typically he would pick up British franchises for Nordic countries and test the products, smell out the markets. After taking on the Topshop franchise, he bought his first shares in the Arcadia group (controlling not only Topshop but also such outlets as Miss Selfridge) at thirty-nine pence a share. That was in 2001, and Jon Asgeir was thirty-three. Within two years he had made almost $160 million by buying up chunks of Britain's undervalued shopping centers. Jon Asgeir's instinct was to reel in the whole Arcadia group—"a mere porpoise attempting to swallow a whale," he admitted later—but the politically motivated Icelandic police raid on his headquarters tripped him up. Phil Green moved in instead with a rival offer, but Jon Asgeir sold his Arcadia stock for a $104 million profit—enough to fund the invasion of Britain.

Jon Asgeir felt most at ease in the purchase of a 22.8 percent stake in the

Big Food Group, which included the retail company Iceland, the whole-saler Booker Cash and Carry, and other food-delivery services. It was a $523 million takeover and announced Baugur's arrival as a major player in Britain. Jon Asgeir, uneasy with words but fast with numbers, calculated in his head the margins not just on individual supermarkets but also on products. On the whole, though, he would delegate management to loyal locals, some of them vetted on the Icelandic riverside, others in his favorite London West End watering hole, the bar in the Sanderson Hotel. As his group ballooned in Britain, he instituted traffic-light management—healthy companies would be graded "green" and would have to report only once a week; those on his watch list were graded "yellow"; while "red" companies had to send in a daily sheet of analysis. In the early years of the expansion, most had the yellow dot stuck to the report cards. The British high street had been poorly managed since the 1990s.

"Jon is a nice guy," said Stuart Rose in 2002. At the time Rose was head of Arcadia; subsequently he went on to manage Marks & Spencer, another dream target of the Icelanders. "He's very determined and he gets twelve out of ten for persistence. Baugur was the first to spot the fact that Arcadia was not going bust, and it has read the UK retail scene very cannily." Jon Asgeir could turn round his acquisitions, halt a decline—as in the Danish Magasin du Nord. He understood that in an age of easy credit, he could become the Prince of the Shopping Mall. The British were spending, spending, spending—and putting the bills on their credit cards. Meanwhile the value of prime-location real estate was rocketing. The saloon wisdom—"with bricks and mortar you can't go wrong"—became a business plan for the Icelanders. They found sympathetic bankers—Peter Cummings, the HBOS strategist, was particularly receptive—and borrowed heavily, using their property assets as security.

Tom Hunter, who brought Baugur into LXB, a private property company, was á fan. "They look at companies, think they are under-valued, and say, 'We'll buy some of that.' It might be simplistic, but it has paid off for them." Hunter and Jon Asgeir got along: the Scot came, like Jon Asgeir, from a grocer's family. Hunter was at the time Scotland's richest man, having made his initial fortune building the Sports Division retail chain, which he sold for $481 million in 1998. He then set up the holding company West Coast Capital in 2001 and invested across the retail spectrum—including in several of Jon Asgeir and Baugur's ventures. Hunter shared the view of Alex Salmond, the first minister of Scotland, that Iceland and Scotland belonged in a new Arc of Prosperity, that the two countries were wealth generators in a way that some other Nordic countries failed to be. Hunter introduced Jon Asgeir to philanthropy—the world of charity dinners and auctions—which was an essential entry point into the world of the retailing superrich. Ironically, though, Hunter, who had promised to invest $1.6 billion in charities over his lifetime, found his philanthropic goals thwarted when he lost money in the meltdown—not least because of his stakes in Jon Asgeir's companies.

Sir Phil Green, though both partner and rival to Jon Asgeir, was more skeptical. When the Icelandic police raided Baugur's offices in 2002 as part of a Reykjavik fraud probe, Green was furious and confused. The Icelanders were new to him, and he needed to know that he was not about to go into business with a crook. A reporter rang him at two thirty P.M. on the day of the raid.

"I was screaming blue murder," recalled Green. "I tried to contact Jon, but he had gone fishing in Iceland. I was not amused. We found one of his men and an Icelandic banker."

That evening in the cafeteria of the BHS shop on Oxford Street, Green and his advisers summoned the Icelanders for a showdown. The shop was shut, the chairs already stacked on the tables so that the cleaners could get on with their work. According to one participant in the meeting, the conversation went as follows:

Icelander: Hello, Philip—

Green: How dare you talk to me like that! How dare you f**cking lie to me!

Icelander: Sorry, Philip—

Green: Don't you sorry me! How dare you talk to me! You have left me standing on a ladder that is getting kicked over.

I wish I had never met you. I don't know where Iceland is and I don't care. So far as I know, there are not that many people in Iceland. How unlucky can I be that of the four that I meet, three are under a fraud investigation. While I was finalizing a deal with you, you were in the other room talking to the Icelandic fraud squad.

That pretty much set the tone for Green's relations with the Icelandic invaders. He came to recognize that Jon Asgeir could muster the resources to buy up fashion chains that he coveted, but nagging questions were constant.

"Where's the money coming from, that's what Phil would ask," says an executive who worked with Green at the time of the Arcadia takeover. "They don't bloody produce anything up there." Green had a point; Baugur was, perhaps, a mirage. If Jon Asgeir's partners had ever visited him in his office in Reykjavik—rather than helicopter to the salmon lodge or camp out in his wife's hotel—they would have seen that corporate headquarters resembled nothing so much as an ocher-painted Boy Scouts' hut. His New Bond Street office was, despite the flashy London address, modest and was shared with the Kaupthing bank. Jon Asgeir preferred doing business on the move, in hotel lounges. "His central weakness was that he had no understanding of how to integrate an organization," said the ex-Baugur scout (now unemployed). "That didn't matter at first, but it became important when we started to expand aggressively abroad."

When skating over thin ice, it is best to skate quickly. So Jon Asgeir stepped up the pace. By the summer of 2003, after barely eighteen months in the British market, he had not only his 22.8 percent holding in the Big Food Group, but also 10 percent of House of Fraser, 3.6 percent of the Somerfield supermarkets, a small stake in JJB Sports, and he had bought and sold a stake in the pregnancy- and postnatal-clothing group Mothercare for 785,000 GBP profit. In the next five years, until 2008, Icelanders shaped the way that the British ate and drank and influenced the way that they dressed. Baugur alone had substantial stakes in French Connection, Oasis, Karen Millen, and Whistles—all part of the essential wardrobe of young Englishwomen. House of Fraser fell into Baugur's hands and Debenhams too, the grazing pastures of the middle-aged, middle-class department-store shopper. Baugur bought up Goldsmiths, the jewelry chain and supplier of Rolex watches, as well as Iceland, the frozen-foods shop. The group became the second-biggest shareholder in Woolworths, the bargain store that had been part of small-town Britain (and indeed the United States) since the 1930s. And it held a big stake in Moss Bros., the first port of call for those in urgent need of a dinner jacket for a black-tie event. With the average cost of a wedding in Britain having risen, by 2008, to 20,000 GBP, the Icelanders made sure that they supplied the morning coats.

And it was not just Jon Asgeir. The brothers Lydur and Agust Gudmundsson took over Geest and supplied the sandwiches, retailed by Marks & Spencer and Tesco, that fed the busy office worker. Hannes Smarason of the FL Group bought and sold a 16 percent share in EasyJet, the bargain airline carrier. And Bjoergólfur Gudmundsson followed in the footsteps of the Russian oligarchs by sealing the classic trophy acquisition: a mediocre soccer club that could be improved, cosseted, and sold on. The purchase, in 2006, was true to form for the New Vikings. Conducted at extraordinarily high speed, it was, by most objective measures, overpriced. The Icelandic oligarch—alerted by his friend Eggert Magnusson, chairman of the Icelandic Football Association— offered 85 million GBP for a club that had only recently been promoted back to the Premier League. West Ham had grown on Premier League cash but slipped into an inferior division after a string of bad games in 2003. Top players—David James, Rio Ferdinand, Joe Cole—were sold to balance the books. But a promotion in October 2003 and a lucrative television deal made West Ham interesting for Bjoergólfur's scouts.

The result: Iceland captured mainstream England. The British were phlegmatic about this sudden shift of ownership. Were they not living in a globalized world? Had they not seen the car industry, once their national pride, shift from their shores? If it had been the Germans on a spending spree, the British would have reacted more strongly. The sense of the Germans trying somehow to reorder Europe on their terms nagged at the English, and German purchases of British national treasures usually led to an allergic, tabloid-induced reaction. But since the

City of London's Big Bang of 1986—when the boundaries between merchant banks, brokers, and market makers had been abolished—both company ownership and the survival of large-scale manufacturing had become less important. The U.S. investment banks had taken over the city and no one much cared. If the Icelanders wanted to sell tank tops to the Londoners' teenage daughters, that was just fine too.

True, the Icelanders seemed a little shifty, but that had become the nature of the business. Take the battle for Somerfield, with its network of convenience stores: the place to go for headache pills and a pint of milk on a hungover Sunday morning. Not exactly a great British institution, but filling a useful niche, and of interest to the bidders, with a commercial-property portfolio of 1 billion GBP. Jon Asgeir, who already had a small stake in the Somerfield chain, put his marker down. Who was he pitted against? The brothers Ian and Richard Livingstone, running a 4 billion GBP property portfolio through London and Regional Group Holdings. Their wealth was even more opaque than that of Jon Asgeir. The parent company, Nutmeg Ltd., was incorporated in Guernsey; London and Regional had stakes in ten companies, most of which were holding companies themselves. Ultimately, decisions were made by the brothers: fast, cold-nosed, without schmoozing.

The other contender for Somerfield was the Tchenguiz brothers, Robert and Vincent. The family had left Iraq for Iran in the 1950s, before fleeing to Britain when the shah was toppled in 1979. The brothers are depicted in the British tabloids as classic, old-fashioned playboys indulging in Saint-Tropez, clubbing, gambling, and soccer tournaments, more visible on the dance floor than the trading floor. Robert dated the singer Caprice. But their talent, or so it seemed before the 2008 credit crunch, was to behave more like financiers than property magnates. They securitized their future rental income, rather than borrow against the value of the property. Vincent Tchenguiz, through his company Consensus, typically struck a 366 million GBP sale and leaseback deal with the Tesco supermarket chain. Robert built up a stable of pub portfolios through his company RZO.

In other words, Jon Asgeir may have seemed like an extravagant character, but he was in fact something of a small-town hick compared to his rivals.

At the time of the 2005 Somerfield bid—the Icelander eventually abandoned his independent offer and teamed up with Robert Tchenguiz—Jon Asgeir was not much younger than the Livingstones or the Tchenguiz brothers, yet he was a little in awe of them. He was a fast decision-maker, but not as fast as the Livingstones. He was a risk-taker, but not a gambler in the manner of the Tchenguiz brothers. The idea that the New Vikings were somehow unique in their campaign to buy up Britain was misplaced. Across the world, but in particular in London and New York, the axis between retail, property, and banking drew in some of capitalism's most piratical practitioners. The very uniformity of the British high street, with its chain stores Tesco, Marks & Spencer, WH Smith, its McDonald's and KFC—and the ensuing death of the mom-and-pop shop and distinctive town centers—attracted the fleet-of-foot investor. Chain stores were in effect commercial-property empires. If the stores could be made to work, if competition could be squeezed, the value of those prime-location buildings would rise faster even than the soaring values of residential property. The loans that could be engineered on the back of these property assets fed breakneck expansion. For the likes of Jon Asgeir, nothing was worse than standing still.

Jon Asgeir was not much of a strategist. Rather, he followed his instincts in the manner of a salmon fisherman: teasing, deceiving, and sometimes landing the fish, sometimes letting it slip away in the current. "Emotionally, what was important was a sense of the chase," said a City analyst who tracked Baugur for the best part of a decade. And a sense of freedom. John Ruskin had the measure of the Icelanders: "No human being, however great or powerful, was ever so free as a fish." Jon Asgeir understood three things: the axis of retail, property, and banking could only function in his favor if the retail outlets were consistently profitable (a dead shop destroyed property values), if credit remained easy, and if the banks were willing to share his risks. That was not strategic thought; merely survival skills. On the retail side, he understood how to sell food, how it should be presented, and how product selection could be adapted to differing tastes. Icelanders, with their traditional dishes of ram's testicles, grilled puffin, and whale sushi (all, admittedly, rarely eaten delicacies in recent times), did not seem a natural barometer for European food preferences. But since building up his Bonus chain on the island and beyond, Jon Asgeir had developed a good grasp of how tastes were becoming more sophisticated, how the demand for a whole range of cheeses had expanded throughout the 1990s. And the American presence on Iceland had made an impact too. At the Reykjavik bus-station café, one can eat *kjammi og kok*—flattened sheep's head with Coke. The food retail business was subtle; successful managers were chroniclers of how their local communities were modernizing, how ready they were to experiment, to try Australian rather than Californian wine, and how sensitive they were to price fluctuation.

But the fashion business was more complex. Jon Asgeir knew the basics: Young women—in Britain in particular—had money to spend and were ready to go into debt to buy an outfit that would make them feel attractive at next Saturday night's party. And Iceland's clubbing revolution had changed the way that young Icelandic women presented themselves; the party began on Friday midnight and ended on Sunday morning. That entailed three changes of fashionable clothing, eye-catching but robust enough to survive crowded, sticky all-night dancing. By the time the Baugur group was sidling into the British disco scene, Thursday night had become the new Friday. Young women were celebrating three nights of the week, and since they were partying with the same people, they needed four changes of clothes. At the same time work environment had also become an arena for competitive dressing. All this meant a national growth market for fashion retailers. Yet Jon Asgeir—who preferred to dress all in black or, at a push, in a style that mimicked the faux elegance of Bryan Ferry—had little idea about female fashion. His long-term girlfriend, later wife, however, knew exactly how women wanted to dress. Ingibjörg Pálmadottir was the daughter of another Icelandic retail magnate, Palmi Jonasson, founder of Hagkaup. Her father got rich on selling clothes, Jon Asgeir's selling food; a match made in retail heaven.

The decisive factor in Jon Asgeir's move into Britain was emotional rather than strategic. How did the Iceland and Booker stores—pit stops for the busy mother loading up on Alaskan cod and frozen french fries—fit in with the going-to-the-office suits and non-iron blouses on offer at Karen Millen? Fish sticks and high-street fashion, how was that supposed to work? "It was simple," says a former Baugur adviser. "Jon Asgeir understood the British woman, she had disposable income, used more than one credit card; she worked, wanted to look attractive, but didn't have time—she bought clothes on her lunch break, and her dinner on the way home." That was a picture, more precisely a marketing caricature, of modern young women. And Jon Asgeir knew it to be true not only because the same process was happening in Iceland, but because his wife, Ingibjörg Pálmadottir, was telling him as much. She and her coterie of female friends spent more time in London and Copenhagen than in Reykjavik, not only shopping for themselves but for their teenage daughters. Sleek, high-cheekboned, Ingibjörg was taller than the chunky Jon Asgeir, bright, and multilingual. "She and her friends laughed at the Icelandic taste for woolly cardigans, the beige and the gray," said a former Ingibjörg pal. "If Iceland was to join the modern world, then it had to look the part. So naturally she steered Jon Asgeir into fashion, though she never succeeded into getting him to a proper hairdresser."

Ingibjörg, independently wealthy, with an educated eye—she was trained at Parsons School for Design in New York—set up the 101 hotel. It was just down the hill from the central bank, two minutes' walk from the cabinet office, three minutes away from Glitnir, around the corner from Café Oliver, a stone's throw from Björk's dockside apartment, and, though this only later became relevant, a short stroll from the Salvation Army home for the destitute. It was at the hub of the square mile that controls a country of 39,770 square miles.

The logic of owning a chic hotel seemed overwhelming to Jon Asgeir and his wife. Across the world, high-priced, expense-account-driven restaurants were booming because the unspoken consensus in the globalized business community was that deals were not made in the office; only contracts were signed there. The warm-up, the positioning— the hors d'oeuvres and the main courses of a business deal were served up at a restaurant table. This was the hour of the celebrity chef, brought in to add glamour and a sense of privilege to gritty negotiations. The private bankers preferred the Seafood Cellar; the central bankers the Fish Market; but for tycoons such as Jon Asgeir these were all too public. Every restaurant had its spy, and the village was global. Better by far to put up guests at 101—named after the postal district rather than

George Orwell's terrifying Room 101—and feed them salmon sashimi in the alcoves of a bugproof, underlit eating zone.

Ingibjörg did well; the place, loosely modeled on the couple's favorite hotel, the Philippe Starck–designed Sanderson in London, became the hangout of choice for Jon Asgeir's English, Scottish, and U.S. business friends. His decision to buy a small chunk of Saks Fifth Avenue was made in the 101 bar with a scout from the United States. What did Jon Asgeir expect to do with a 3 percent stake in the U.S. retailer? The truth is that he probably did not know; it was a chip on the poker table. But Ingibjörg liked the place, and Ingibjörg was Jon Asgeir's ambassador to Richistan. She understood that Jon Asgeir would never be accepted by the old guard of the Octopus; there were thus only two ways forward: to make Iceland more open and more attractive to successful business elites in Europe; and to help define popular taste abroad, because that was the path toward high-profile, cutting-edge power. "Well, you know, she's not Lady Macbeth or anything," says her former friend, "but she understood right from the beginning the power of clothes, that universal brands and global tastes give you a kind of authority. If Jon Asgeir had stuck to fish fingers and the Big Food Group, who would have cared about him, who would have given a damn?"

Around 101, around Ingibjörg, a clique of clever, ambitious women took shape. There were the fashion designer Steinunn Sigurd; the aluminum-smelting chief Rannveig Rist; Tinna Gunnlaugsdottir, director of the National Theater; various artists and actresses. It was possible, within the 101 consensus, to be both patriotic and aware that they were living in the deep provinces. Their conversation came to resemble a never-ending Chekhov play with the women yearning not for Moscow but for New York or London. Then Dorrit Moussaieff joined their clique.

"Dotty but charming" (in the words of a NATO diplomat), Dorrit Moussaieff came from a dynasty of Bukharan jewelers who reputedly embedded the robe of Genghis Khan with gems. Born in Jerusalem, she moved to London at the age of thirteen with her family and started selling jewels at the family shop in the London Hilton. An early marriage with a designer, Neil Zarak, gave her a British passport and allowed her to duck out of Israeli military service. The marriage collapsed eleven years later, and Dorrit concentrated on building up an international web of celebrity friends, partly through her jewelry designing and selling, partly through a passion for networking. She counts Shakira Caine (wife of actor Michael Caine) as her best friend, was a regular guest of art collector Charles "Charlie" Saatchi, and developed an unusual talent for befriending people whose careers were about to hit a glitch. Lifestyle expert Martha Stewart (jailed for insider trading) is a friend; so too is disgraced newspaper magnate Conrad Black (currently serving six and a half years for fraud). Denise Rich, ex-wife of U.S. businessman Marc Rich (the fugitive who was pardoned by President Bill Clinton just before he left office), buys Dorrit's gems and is also a friend.

So when Dorrit fell in love with and, in 2003, married the president of Iceland, Olafur Ragnar Grimsson, there was a buzz of anticipation in what was to become Ingibjörg's 101 set. Dorrit operated in a kind of benign daze, believing for a while that she was dating a Finnish diplomat rather than the president of Iceland. But she set about integrating 101 with her own extraordinary circle. She was the most glamorous woman on the island: a contributing editor to the British society magazine *Tatler* and, according to the magazine *Harper's Bazaar*, the Third Most Connected person in Britain. Olafur Ragnar, meanwhile, was baffling the island. Many assumed him to be going through a midlife crisis; his wife, popular and down-to-earth, had died two years earlier of leukemia.

Dorrit frothed with ideas; most of them seemed absurd to her new best friends; they had not previously been exposed to such social exuberance. This, after all, was a woman of the world who wore not one but three diamond necklaces; who, when she went down to the docks, wore a dark green moghul emerald. Why not get her friend Sean (Connery) to help out Icelandic actors? The director of the National Theater nodded skeptically. Why should Dorrit not get her friends in the Moroccan royal court to strike a deal between Moroccan and Icelandic fishermen? Well, yes, why not? Even after the collapse of the Icelandic economy, Dorrit was scattergunning ideas: converting, for example, an old air base into a huge burglarproof, temperature-controlled warehouse for the world's private art collectors. The plan was hatched with her friend Francesca von Habsburg, who knows about art. "We are four and a half hours from America. Three and a half hours from Europe, and very close to Russia," said Dorrit. "People are paying astronomical fees to store their work in England or Switzerland. We'd offer storage at half these rates. People can come, look at the art, have massages, go to a spa, and eat unbelievable food." The concept—check up on your Warhol while munching whale-meat sushi—has yet to catch on. But maybe the timing had something to do with it.

The buzz surrounding the opening of 101, and the arrival of Dorrit in 2003, were more than society chitchat. It was part of the fusion between one section of the wealth class and the grandees of the political class. Something changed in Iceland's political chemistry at this point. Olafur Ragnar Grimsson had been a vocal, often crude left-winger. The presidency, politically marginal in the manner of Queen Elizabeth or other constitutional monarchs, requires that the officeholder be above party politics. So, naturally, Grimsson was set to move from the left to the center. At the same time, the death of his first wife had softened him, aged him a little. But something more radical was at work. "Grimsson spent his career fighting for low-income families, and then he turned around completely," says journalist Sveinn Birkir Bjoernsson. "He went from being a leftist politician to being the spokesperson for the corporation and the banks."

The chemistry of this transformation is complicated but comprehensible if one remembers the Lilliputian geography of Reykjavik and the social anthropology of its competing tribes. David Oddsson disliked and was contemptuous of Grimsson. For Oddsson, the silvery-haired former leftist was representative of the slow-moving, antimodernist tendency in the island culture that Oddsson so much despised. The contempt was mutual. Speaking in parliament, Grimsson had once accused Oddsson of having *skitlegt edli*—literally, a "shitty character." Oddsson also hated, with an almost irrational fury, Jon Asgeir Johannesson. Ingibjörg, meanwhile, was friends with Dorrit. Dorrit was in turn encouraging Jon Asgeir to expand abroad, to internationalize Iceland. The lunchers at 101 had firm ideas of which fashion outlets in London were worth snapping up. And more, the president's daughter was given a job at Baugur. Yet more: Jon Asgeir offered Dorrit a lift from London to Reykjavik in his corporate jet. Some in Iceland felt it was acceptable for the president's wife to hitch a ride; it saved money and reduced the possibility of the first lady making another gaffe, such as the one she had made on an intercontinental flight from Reykjavik sitting next to a tensely coiled young girl who plainly hated flying.

"What do you do?" asked the president's wife.

"I'm a singer," said the girl.

"Oh, poor you," said Dorrit. "Well, if you ever want to use the spare room in my London place, let me know."

"Yeah, thanks," said the singer, who was, of course, Björk.

The meshing of interests between Jon Asgeir and President Grimsson became more and more obvious. David Oddsson was concerned that Jon Asgeir was coming to dominate the media scene, that Baugur could in effect become a state within a state. "Baugur held fifty to sixty percent of the Icelandic grocery market," said Illugi Gunnarsson, adviser to Oddsson at the time. "They owned a large stake in Icelandair, dominated the distribution of medicine, petrol, the insurance and the construction market." Baugur's subsidiary the Northern Lights media group could, Oddsson believed, break the power of the Independence Party. The banks were swelling up, and their connections with the business world, and indeed with the expansion into Britain, were at best obscure. If they took over the media, parliament—the proudest, the oldest in the world—would become a mere afterthought, a museum sponsored by Baugur. Northern Lights in fact owned two of Iceland's three national papers—*Frettabladid* and the tabloid *DV*—four radio stations, and a television station. Oddsson's law, duly passed by parliament in 2004, stated that a company whose main business interest was not in the field of the media would be denied a broadcasting license. Nor could it get a license if more than 5 percent of its shares belonged to a company or a business bloc that had a dominant position in another sector. And it had no chance of a license if it was already a newspaper publisher.

"These laws were not general," said Skarpheddin Berg Steinarsson, who was head of Northern Lights. "They were solely intended to damage Northern Lights and its owners." Oddsson was, in other words, trying to break the power of Jon Asgeir at home, at the moment when he was becoming an international presence. Other Icelandic oligarchs had kept a lower profile; Jon Asgeir was supposed to be punished. "Oddsson had already called Jon Asgeir a street urchin and said Baugur had a stranglehold on Icelandic consumers," says Skarpheddin Berg, "plus our media had been very critical of the ruling parties. They found that uncomfortable."

Grimsson was aghast at the vote in parliament. In his view it was not aimed at breaking up media concentration but rather at bolstering the personal power of Prime Minister David Oddsson and the Independence Party, which had become his own kingdom. So the president canceled a trip to attend the royal wedding of Crown Prince Frederik of Denmark to his Australian fiancée Mary Donaldson and stayed in his palace—actually little more than an elongated eighteenth-century schoolhouse—to veto the media law. It was the first use of the presidential veto in sixty years. For the Oddsson camp this was proof positive that the president had fallen under the influence of buccaneering Icelandic businessmen. Yet Oddsson himself had liberated the businessmen to do exactly what Jon Asgeir was now doing: setting out to conquer foreign markets and burst out of the tight corset of a society that had barely more than two hundred thousand consumers. That was the paradox: the businessmen were David's creations, "his bastard children," as one Oddsson sympathizer put it. For much of the rest of the Icelandic estab-lishment—and not just the ladies who lunched at 101—David Oddsson had gone too far, tipped into a kind of megalomaniac excess, an apparent need to crush Jon Asgeir, the upstart who was poisoning his revolution.

The outside world did not really register the rift: a small dustup in a community the size of a small Midwestern U.S. city or one of the smaller London suburbs. It wouldn't have mattered anyway because the whole of Iceland's elite, whatever its internal quarrels, was singing the praises of their Cool community. From president to prime minister, from ambassador to entrepreneur, Iceland was being branded as the Nordic Tiger; a model for those who believed in the magic of numbers. While Jon Asgeir was taking his favorite British investors for a few days of expensively bungled fly-fishing, financial observers would have done well to keep their gaze fixed on the eccen-tric activities of the presidential couple. Dorrit went in search of the perfect birthday present for her billionaire friend Stephen Schwarzman, chairman of the Blackstone Group. She came up with a nude portrait of Schwarzman's wife, Christine, a collage made up of bits of the *Financial Times*—in salmon pink, of course. There was no better use, said Dorrit, for financial information.

8 : Bubble

The lava dust can be very tiresome to the eyes,
and it is a good thing to take a pair of tinted glasses.
W. H. Auden, writing from Iceland

David Oddsson developed a problem with swallowing. For weeks in the summer of 2004 it became so difficult to eat anything without clogging his throat that he virtually lived on mashed potatoes, explaining to others around the restaurant table that he was on a diet. Stress, he must have thought, constricting his passages. The battle with Baugur and the president over the media bill—the veto meant that Oddsson would have had to seek a national referendum, but he decided instead just to drop it—and the sheer slog of fourteen years as prime minister had taken their toll. His face was beginning to sag, and even the shortest walks with his wife, Astridur, seemed to tire him. Astridur, a trained nurse, urged him to have a checkup. The diagnosis was thyroid cancer. But the tumor was treatable, and Oddsson's passion for combat was revived, this time not against wayward entrepreneurs or crypto-socialists or the numskull (i.e., non–Independent Party–controlled) press, but against disease. He responded well to treatment, looking almost rested, and that should by rights have been the moment for him to retreat to his country home with Toothie and write his memoirs.

And why not? He had presided over an astonishing period of growth; he had changed the structure of Icelandic society. Farming and fishing, though still the emotional heart of Iceland, were no longer major employers. That role was now filled by the service sector—mainly private banking. Iceland's population was even smaller than that of tiny Luxembourg's, but the country was on its way to becoming a financial powerhouse. And it was above all a balanced economy. Luxembourg had steel foundries as well as tax-efficient banks; thanks to Oddsson, Iceland could match that with aluminum. Its low-cost geothermal energy used so hugely in smelting had in effect become an export good, almost as lucrative as fish. Now, this had not been achieved in a single-handed effort of will by supernatural powers. Nor was it uncontroversial—Björk and the aluminum resisters blamed Oddsson for selling Iceland's birthright, of committing the original sin of nature-defacing industrialization. But he had come close to winning economic security for Iceland. In doing so he had made society less egalitarian, but that appeared to be an acceptable price. A thoughtful report in 1960, drawn up by the economists Jonas Haralz and Arni Vilhjalmsson, had suggested economic independence in Iceland would have to entail more concentrated political power: "The dilution of executive power makes it difficult to formulate and carry out coherent economic policies. The prevailing egalitarianism has, through its shaping of tax policy and wage structure, stifled capital accumulation and reduced economic incentives." Oddsson had—like Thatcher in Britain of the 1980s—duly concluded that freeing the market had to be combined with the centralization of political authority. Under Oddsson, power shifted from the rural communities to Reykjavik; state institutions became more, not less, dependent on his political whim.

What, then, was supposed to happen if Oddsson retired to concentrate on writing his amusing stories and walking the dog? A vacuum would open up. Geir Haarde—his former finance minister and amiable crown prince—would be in place, but he was hardly the man to stop the unraveling of the Oddsson legacy. David knew his British history: he did not want Geir to be the equivalent of John Major to Margaret Thatcher, a fumbling heir. After so many years with Oddsson at the helm, the fundamentals of his Iceland looked all right: per capita GDP was $40,000 in 2004, putting it fifth in the OECD (the Organization for Economic Cooperation and Development); there were a fully funded pension system, a fiscal surplus, and rising exports. Wherever one looked, Iceland was at the top internationally: for health care, literacy, economic freedom, lack of corruption, press freedom, and political stability.

Oddsson's transformation of Iceland had been based on three

pillars—Liberalization, Stabilization, and Privatization, LSP for short. First, during his initial term came stabilization. He had brought inflation under control, helped by a national accord with the trade unions in 1990, and slow economic growth until the mid-1990s. That one could live without big annual wage hikes was a new idea for Icelanders. "Economic policy until 1990 was aimed at keeping the peace in the labor market and employment high," says the economist Katrin Olafsdottir, "so you would have collective agreements for high wage hikes and then shortly afterwards the government would step in and devalue the krona. That meant high inflation rates and widely fluctuating real wages." Inflation topped 85 percent in 1983 and came crashing down to single digits only after Oddsson took over in 1991 (admittedly helped by recession). His gurus Margaret Thatcher and Ronald Reagan had both made the taming of inflation their priority. Oddsson, however, had won his battle without a bitter confrontation with the unions. His market revolution had no equivalent to the British coal miners' strike; on the contrary, workers were persuaded by the logic of the situation. If Oddsson could deliver low inflation, higher growth, and secure jobs, they were willing to go without major pay hikes. "It was unique and very Icelandic," says Ms. Olafsdottir. By 2004, however, the teachers were on strike, inflation was on the rise again, and everybody was scrambling to get a slice of the cake.

The liberalization and the privatization of the Icelandic economy was accelerated by Oddsson's program to Europeanize Iceland without actually joining the European Union. Joining the European Economic Area in 1994 gave Iceland access to European markets, and it in turn broadly adopted European trading norms. It continued to subsidize and protect its farmers, clamping high tariffs on imported food and using hygiene regulations to keep out uncooked meat. Above all, it stayed out of the euro and kept its distance from Brussels. Iceland became more competitive. But by 2004 it was beginning to look as if Iceland had opened itself up too much to the outside world. "Membership of the EEA," says economist Gylfi Zoega, "involving market integration and free mobility but without the participation in a common currency and joint decision-making, made economic policy in Iceland difficult, even impossible. The local central bank was no match for the vast flows of funds that came into the country." Simply put, it had become too easy for Iceland to fool itself that it was no longer a small country but a global player. That had been David Oddsson's aim: it was possible, as Luxembourg had, to box above one's weight if one developed financial muscle. But as early as 2001, while David Oddsson was at the height of his power as prime minister, the central bank of Iceland had commissioned and published a critical report by U.S. economist Joseph Stiglitz on the dangers of smallness. It was not legitimate to compare Iceland with Luxembourg, which was a fully fledged member of the European Union, was intimately linked with Belgium and Holland, had developed banking traditions over centuries, enjoyed a common border with Germany, Europe's largest economy, and which, when all was said and done, was still significantly larger than Iceland. Iceland was the smallest economy with its own monetary policy within the OECD. Its GDP ($14.5 billion in 2007) was little more than one thousandth of the U.S. economy, one twentieth of the Danish economy—and one third of Luxembourg's.

"The global financial crisis of 1998–99 brought to the fore the problems faced by small open economies," warned Stiglitz (who went on to win a Nobel Prize in 2001). "Sudden changes in investor sentiment can impose destabilizing capital flows and high interest rates even on countries that have followed prudent macroeconomic policies." Iceland, he said, was particularly vulnerable as "a foreign exchange market with an average daily turnover of only 40 million U.S. dollars, and a stock market capitalization that is roughly one-tenth the market capitalization of a moderate-sized U.S. company." Oddsson was, of course, aware of all this. The idea that smallness, when coupled with flexibility, could be turned into an asset in a globalized world—that size really did not matter—was attractive, the premise of so much that had happened on his watch during the 1990s. But smallness at a time of global crisis, that was dangerous. As Oddsson left office in 2004 and underwent treatment on his tumor, he began to lose some of his confidence. He had launched Iceland on a great Thatcherite experiment, changed the attitude of his party, helped raise Iceland's standing in the world. But the Asian financial crisis in 1997 had underlined some of the island's vulnerabilities. The case against David Oddsson is not that he was unaware of the risks mounting up against Iceland—he had registered them, albeit with some years' delay when he stepped off the government carousel—but that he dealt with them dilettantishly. In his eagerness to protect his historical legacy as the creator of the Nordic Tiger, he ignored and mismanaged some of the key threats.

So, after recovering from his cancer with astonishing speed, he moved first from the prime ministership to the foreign ministry, then in October 2005 took over as central-bank governor. There was no choice, he told friends; he had to keep his hand on the tiller. If that were really the case, David Oddsson would surely go down in history as a national hero, a man weakened by sickness who, sensing that his country needed him, stayed in public service. A more likely explanation is that Oddsson was addicted to power, could not cope with its withdrawal, and moved into a highly political job. Nowhere else in Europe is monetary policy so emphatically in the hands of the political machine: the Icelandic central bank has three governors, at least two of whom are political appointees. By the time that Oddsson arrived there—the Black Fort, as some call it—he was bored by independent economists' harping about the Icelandic parallels with the Asian meltdown of 1997–98. This was 2005! And Iceland was far, far away. "When I raised these issues with top central-bank managers," remembers Thorvaldur Gylfasson, "I was told firmly, 'Iceland is not Thailand.' " Gylfasson's office at the University of Iceland does not resemble the clinical clean-desk-at-the-end-of-the-day orderliness of other dissident economists. It is a pleasing clutter of scholarship, and buried under documents in the in-box are three paper-weight monkeys. "Here," he says after unearthing them, "See-no-evil, Hear-no-evil, Say-no-evil—the three directors of the Icelandic central bank."

Oddsson arrived at the Black Fort in 2005 determined to talk up the krona and enforce inflation targeting. The whole establishment was selling Iceland hard by then; it was not a time for public doubts. In May of that year President Grimsson gave a speech at the Walbrook Club in London and did not allow any shadow of doubt to creep in. He sang the praises of Iceland's financial miracle. To an audience of British businessmen and politicians, the president said it was time for U.S. and

British corporations to overhaul their business model. The Icelanders were revolutionizing the very idea of corporate expansion. "How has it been possible to achieve such success in so many different fields and in such a short time, in areas where we definitely had no prior competitive advantage, areas such as pharmaceuticals and prosthetics, banking and finance, retail and fashion—to name only a few?" Pay attention to Iceland, he said, the Viking way was the future! "We are succeeding because we are different, and our track record should inspire the business establishment in other countries to reexamine their previous beliefs and the norms that they think will guarantee results."

The secret of the Icelandic miracle, said the president, came down to creative risk-taking, a secure home base, the lack of bureaucracy, the element of personal trust, the speed of decision-making—but most of all, the country's strong work ethic. The president, who had spent his political career as a fiery leftist, thus artfully ignored that Iceland's market revolution was ideologically driven. Rather, he seemed to suggest, the changes reflected qualities inherent in Icelandic character. "This is a heritage from the old society of farmers and fishermen, where necessity dictated that the fish catch had to be brought ashore and processed immediately when the boats came into harbor, and that they had to be turned and collected when the weather was favorable. When Kaupthing bank beat the other bidders for the Danish FIH Erhvervsbank, the disappointed English representative returned to London and informed his boss that the Icelanders had won because, as he put it, 'When we go home, these guys are still working.' " Grimsson ended with a phrase apparently supplied by Dorrit: "You ain't seen nothing yet!"

Oddsson was not such an extravagant cheerleader as the president. But abroad at least he avoided even the slightest criticism of the banks or the oligarchs since that would have been tantamount to sabotaging the krona. At home, though, Oddsson had made plain he was unhappy about the way that bank privatization—*his* privatization—was turning the financial institutions into cash machines for the tycoons, and how the banks themselves were becoming self-rewarding high-risk-takers. While he was still prime minister, in November 2003, Oddsson had announced on Icelandic state radio that he was so outraged by Kaupthing's commercial practices, he was going to withdraw his own savings. He then did just that, stomping to the main branch of Kaupthing and tucking his savings into a large brown envelope. It is not clear what he did with the money, but it was an extraordinary act for a national leader. Now the gesture forms part of his defense portfolio, proof that he had always been critical of the bonus culture and the new banking culture.

Oddsson's dissatisfaction could be traced back to a share deal that had been clinched between the two senior executives of Kaupthing bank, Sigurdur Einarsson and Hreidar Mar Sigurdsson, just before Bunadarbanki had fully been swallowed by Kaupthing. Both bosses had somehow made 300–400 million Icelandic krona out of the merger, as well as generously padded salaries. They then led Kaupthing Bunadarbanki into an alliance with Oddsson's archenemy, Baugur. Together, Kaupthing and Jon Asgeir bought up all the assets owned by Jon Olafsson, formerly of the Orca group, which had opposed the Octopus families. That is what shifted the Northern Lights media group into Jon Asgeir's empire. At the end of his prime ministership, then, David Oddsson was confronted by one of his foes, Jon Olafsson—under investigation for tax fraud at the time—being helped out by another of his foes, Jon Asgeir, with the active collaboration of a bank that the Oddsson team had privatized.

Thus when David Oddsson took over at the central bank, he did so with an ambiguous attitude toward the banks and the financial system he was supposed to be supporting. The essential problem, which would defeat Oddsson and ultimately torpedo the whole nation, was the mystification of capital—that is, the extraordinary web of cross-ownership, with holdings exchanging hands at such a dizzy pace it was almost impossible to pin down who had responsibility for what. This lack of transparency was not unique to Iceland—indeed, it had been a feature of the Asian crisis and the collapse of the Russian stock market in 1998—but it was played out here among a uniquely small group of actors. The way that Jon Asgeir captured a controlling stake in Glitnir—"He needed a bank so he went out and bought himself one," as Katrin Olafsdottir put it—resembled an anthropological case study. Financial clans feuded, traded, and tried to ouwit each other.

The interplay between Jon Asgeir and MIT Sloan School–educated Hannes Smarason gave Baugur the key to Glitnir's safe. Smarason was of the same generation (born 1967–68) as Jon Asgeir and Thor and had the same instincts—that old, established companies need not stick slavishly to their brand but could be turned into all-purpose investment vehicles. At a time of easy credit you could pick up chunks of high-performing companies, make some improvements, and sell fast at a significant profit. The mistake was to hang on for too long, or—God forbid— to become emotionally committed to a company. That may be why Smarason currently lives in Kensington, not in Reykjavik: Icelanders do not like the way that Icelandair was chewed up by Smarason's adventures. Smarason was McKinsey-trained, and its cost-cutting consultants were dubbed Mack the Knife for good reason—but none of the Icelandic oligarchs really cared about popularity.

In September 2003 Smarason and his father-in-law, with a controlling interest in Icelandair, had blocked Jon Asgeir's attempts to gain a foot-hold in the airline. But when Hannes changed sides just over a year later, the terms changed. Just before David Oddsson entered the Black Fort in 2005, Jon Asgeir bought 3 percent of Icelandair shares, and another 3 percent behind the scenes. By March, Smarason had founded a holding group, the FL Group, and Icelandair became one of its subsidiaries. Inga Jona Thordardottir—wife of Geir Haarde, the Oddsson ally and soon-to-be prime minister—was invited onto the board. She resigned, along with most of the board, two months later. Why? Because Hannes had demon-strated the equivalent of the three-card monte, a use of cross-ownership and personal contacts to transform a fortune of 5 billion Icelandic krona, about 57 million euros, into a somewhat sturdier sum of 20 billion krona.

It was a particularly dazzling sleight of hand even by the standards of the Icelandic oligarchs. Hannes's friend Palmi Haraldsson bought the no-frills airline Sterling as well as the indebted Danish airline Maersk Air for 5 billion Icelandic krona in March 2005. By October, Palmi's invest-ment company, Fons, had sold it to Hannes and his FL Group for 14.6 billion Icelandic krona. Hannes and Palmi then set up a new company, Northern Travel Holiday (NTH), controlled by Fons (44 percent) and the FL Group (34 percent). Hannes and his FL company then sold

Sterling to NTH for 20 billion krona. The board did not like it, and the maneuvering befuddled shareholders, but since FL reported profits of 6.6 billion Icelandic krona for 2005, everyone seemed happy to let Hannes do what he wanted. The FL Group now held 16.2 percent of EasyJet, the British-based bargain flier. Only the economist—and chairman of the Icelandic Shareholders Association—Vilhjalmur Bjarnason openly raised questions about the strange transactions. "Why didn't FL just buy Sterling in the first place?" he asked at the FL shareholders meeting. "He didn't get a straight answer," recalls one participant at the session, "and the general consensus was that he was weird. Profits were up, we were all winners, who cares?" Both Kaupthing and Landsbanki had been involved in the share-trading and picked up their commissions, so they too were happy. Even the government was not complaining: both the oligarchs and the banks were paying large amounts of taxes; treasury coffers had rarely been so full.

By 2006 Jon Asgeir was getting closer to his goal of owning a bank. Hannes sold off parts of Icelandair, sometimes to his friends. The Icelandair car-rental business went to a pal who had the Toyota franchise. And Hannes started to buy and buy: 10 percent of Finnair; 10.7 percent of Bang & Olufsen, the high-end, design-conscious Danish sound-system specialist; 16.4 percent of the Danish beer-maker Royal Unibrew. As far as Jon Asgeir was concerned, though, the key transaction during this period was Hannes's purchase of 16.4 percent of Islandsbanki (soon to become Glitnir). Hannes bought and sold like a merchant in the Istanbul souk. His most profitable deal was the sale of his EasyJet stake, which brought him a profit of 145 million euros. In June 2006 he bought a 24.2 percent stake in the Straumur Burdaras investment bank—from Bjoergólfur Gudmundsson and his son Bjoergólfur Thor—and sold it again in October. But it was the relationship between Jon Asgeir and Hannes that flourished most.

The FL Group, Jon Asgeir's Baugur, and the British retail investor Kevin Stanford set up Unity Investment, bringing them a 20 percent stake in the fashion chain French Connection, 28.5 percent in Moss Bros., and 12 percent in Woolworths. And by that summer the FL Group had a 24.4 percent stake in Glitnir. At this point the FL Group declared itself to be solely an investment company. Its portfolio was unorthodox, to say the least: airlines (Hannes added a 6 percent stake in American Airlines), breweries, high-tech audio equipment, banks. But no matter, Jon Asgeir and Hannes were bonding.

They were seen together in 101 that summer shaping plans to take part in Gumball 3000, the celebrity rally that sometimes sees reckless racing along public roads and whose registration fee alone was more than the average annual salary of an Icelander. In Europe, Gumball was viewed as a sign of rich people's contempt for the ordinary citizen; the cars were high-powered, expensive, and wildly driven. But Hannes was at the crest of his success; nothing, it seemed, could hold him back. After all, this was the same man who, in the swankiest part of Reykjavik, had bought two grand houses, linked them with a bridge, and spent thousands of dollars on getting the perfect front door. So, naturally, he put an Icelandair Boeing 707 at the disposal of the Gumball drivers (the cars themselves were transported between continents on three heavily insured Antonov cargo planes) and souped up his own Porsche Cayenne Gemballa for the race. The starting line was Pall Mall in London, the finishing line the Playboy Mansion in L.A. In between, the millionaires from around the world would be speeding toward Vienna and Belgrade, between Phuket and Bangkok, between Salt Lake City and L.A.: three thousand miles, eight cities. Hannes, who tried to persuade Jon Asgeir and his wife, Ingibjörg, to take part in their Ferrari, plainly felt like one of the modern mythical heroes, a Master of the Universe. A newspaper declared him to be Businessman of the Year. The newspaper was owned by his friend Jon Asgeir.

By the beginning of 2007, FL had acquired a 30.4 percent stake in Glitnir (and 3 percent in Commerzbank, 22.4 percent in Finnair), but the tide was starting to turn against Hannes. Airline industry shares were dropping worldwide; his investment portfolio began to look chaotic rather than interestingly different. Baugur bought a controlling stake, reshuffled FL—and Jon Asgeir at last won his bank.

These developments did not, needless to say, please David Oddsson, two hundred yards away at the central bank. The banks were swelling, and nobody really had an idea what was going on inside. The total assets of the banking sector were 96 percent of GDP in 2000—before privatization was even halfway complete—and eight times GDP in 2006. By the time the blister popped in 2008, bank assets amounted to almost ten times GDP. The speed of the development had taken everyone aback, Oddsson included. Suddenly, it seemed as if every young graduate—in math, chemistry, even in history—every member of the local chess club, every other slacker in the late-night line outside Café Oliver, wanted to be a banker. It was partly the allure of the bonus culture, of course. In Britain and the United States large bonuses at banks first became common in the 1980s, in a different age. Iceland's Big Bang came almost two decades later. Some derivatives selling went on in Iceland, some attempts to play the game of splicing up and packaging debt, but the young entrants were more likely to be enticed by the promise of picking up bonuses for investing in an overseas purchase. Mergers and Acquisitions was the "sexy" department. Parents spoke proudly of having a son or a daughter working in a bank.

Iceland had built its wealth on long, often badly organized, working hours (even after joining the EEA, which should have cut down the fifty-hour weeks). But the young bankers seemed to outsiders to be manifestly efficient. As the invasion of foreign markets stampeded ahead—as output surged by 25 percent from 2003 to 2006—bankers really seemed to be supermen. True, the big bonuses were being picked up by senior staff, who took pension-fund managers on all-expenses-paid flights to the VIP boxes of British Premier League soccer games, golfing and skiing, on salmon-fishing expeditions in Russia. In one deal-brokering trip orga-nized by the Icelandic banks, fund managers and private investors were helicoptered from a yacht moored in Greek waters to watch the Euro Cup final in Athens between AC Milan and Liverpool in 2007. But some of the glitter reached the younger bankers too, providing they were energetic enough. When Kaupthing partly financed Baugur's takeover of Big Food just before Christmas 2004, the cash rained down even on those who did the photocopying. The bank backed Robert Tchenguiz's 151 million GBP bid for Laurel Pub company; it had an equity holding in Karen Millen and Oasis, alongside Baugur; it bought FIH, a Danish bank, for 700 million GBP. Landsbanki, meanwhile, paid 43 million

GBP for the British stockbroker Feather and Greenwood. For David Oddsson and his central-bank economists it must have been clear—at the very latest by 2006—that the surge in Iceland came not just via aluminum smelting but also via bank borrowing. Growth was largely debt-financed, with the borrowed money trickling into the domestic economy through taxes and loans to domestic companies. If you throw free money at it, any economy can grow by 25 percent.

When Kaupthing bought a 9.5 percent stake in the traditional small British investment bank Singer & Friedlander, the head of the bank, Tony Shearer, was surprised by the way Kaupthing representatives had behaved. "None of us had ever heard of them," recalled Shearer, "so we met them for a social lunch. But at no stage did we ever have discussions about the business; they didn't say, 'Look, we just bought nine and a half percent, tell us how it works.' " The normal practice at S+F, indeed at most small investment banks, was to give a presentation to major share-holders. Even when Kaupthing raised its stake to 19.5 percent, however, it did not show any interest in learning financial details. Shearer traveled to Reykjavik to find out more about the bank's investors.

"Everybody there was incredibly young, all pretty similar, a board of directors who, I think, except for one person who was either Danish or Swedish, were all people from the same community within Reykjavik." After a while he decided, "These are not the sort of people I want to work with." An examination of the bank's books showed that half its profits came from investing in the financial markets—even though it had no experience of international banking—and only 10 percent from conventional banking. That was an astonishing level of risk. "We simply did not trust them." The takeover went through anyway—for cash—but Shearer exposed his doubts to the British Financial Services Authority. "As the home regulator, the Icelandic regulator confirmed there was no reason why the transaction could not go ahead," said an FSA spokes-woman. "We required Kaupthing to take a number of actions to address governance issues in London, including the appointment of independent nonexecutive directors."

This pattern of shedding responsibility became familiar as the global crisis unfolded: 1. Icelandic bank with dubious credentials bids for established foreign bank using borrowed money. 2. Targeted bank eagerly takes the offered cash, claiming to be acting in the interest of shareholders. Registers doubts with FSA or other regulatory body. 3. FSA contacts Icelandic regulator, who offers reassurance. 4. Icelandic regulator attends school reunion with Icelandic banker.

The frailty of the system is obvious—indeed, it is no "system" at all—but was particularly glaring in Iceland, where the oversight agency (the FME) comprised barely forty-five people in 2006, only fourteen of them economists. Over a quarter of the staff were lawyers without business experience. The employees were overstretched and underpaid, no match for the financial clout of the banks. "I remember meetings where one sat at the end of a long table in meeting rooms," says Elin Jonsdottir, a former lawyer in the share-trading department of FME, "and in front of you sat a panel of lawyers and senior bankers, all red-faced with anger about the supposed interference of the FME." David Oddsson would later complain that the central bank was unable to peer into the dealings of the regulator because it had—shortly before he took over as governor—been declared independent, a formally separate institution. He could therefore pass on his misgivings but not directly criticize Kaupthing, Landsbanki, and Glitnir. In this strange state of affairs, the banks were swelling under his very eyes. If he opened his tinted window on a Friday night, he could hear the chirruping of younger bankers as they set out for a night of clubbing at b5.

But then, Oddsson was rarely in the office on a Friday afternoon. That was the time he liked to think about his writing.

The banks were growing and growing, and even the most elementary economic knowledge could have told Oddsson that this was pushing him into an extraordinarily difficult position. The central bank was in no position to be the lender of last resort. But David Oddsson was a lawyer, not an economist. As prime minister he had freed the banks; interference would break the very independence that he had given them. For him, it remained a mystery as to whether the banks were investing in good assets or bad.

Instead, he focused on what he considered to be the central bank's top priority: bringing inflation under control and guarding the krona. Interest rates shot up from 5.3 percent in 2003 to 15.25 percent in 2007. Yet these drastic increases did not prevent the bubble; indeed, they fed it. And they failed to harness inflation. Central-bank interest rates can target inflation in two ways. Either through standard commercial-bank interest rates, since most commercial banks are dependent on central-bank loans, or through the currency exchange rate, especially in countries such as Iceland that are heavily dependent on imports. A strong domestic currency normally leads to lower domestic prices on imported goods—and despite the sheep and the fish, most of Iceland's foodstuff is brought in by ferry and plane—and hence lower inflation. But David Oddsson's reliance on the interest-rate instrument failed, partly because so much domestic debt was linked to the retail-price index. When the RPI rose, many loans and mortgages rose accordingly.

The privatized banks had begun to aggressively market loans in foreign currencies, in Swiss francs and yen. "We would get cold calls from the bank," says Yrsa, a now unemployed architect, "banks who hadn't previously bothered even to register our presence or recognize our faces, and a young voice would offer us the possibility of buying a new car in a parcel of currencies from countries we had never visited. The car dealers and the banks were working hand in hand." Sell more than your quota of yen-denominated loans, and your bonus was secure. The trend heated up the economy—and made a nonsense out of monetary policy. The high policy rates merely provided profit opportunities for the carry trade—whereby speculators borrow at low rates in Asia and park the money in a high-interest country—which magnified the rate of credit expansion, the stock market bubble, and the housing boom.

Inflation targeting failed. David Oddsson was too slow to realize this, but he was not the only central banker in the world to fail to grasp that targeting was putting the economy on a dangerous track. As late as 2007, Columbia University's Frederic Mishkin—commissioned by the Icelandic authorities to write a positive account of the country's monetary and growth policies—was still arguing that inflation targeting was an "information-inclusive strategy for the conduct of monetary policy." Meaning that it took into account all relevant variables—exchange rates, stock prices, housing prices, and long-term bond prices—via their impact on active and future inflation. It appeared to be the final stage in an evolution from the nineteenth-century gold standard, the restored gold-exchange standard of the 1920s, the Bretton Woods system of adjustable exchange rates, and the termination of dollar convertibility into gold in 1971. Mishkin, a former governor of the Federal Reserve, was convinced that "it is highly presumptuous to think that government officials, even if they are central bankers, know better than private markets what the asset prices should be." Decoded: Although Oddsson was aware of the asset price bubble, it was not for him to prick it in advance. The role of the central bank was to control the aftermath.

The central banks lost the plot. In the United States, the Fed kept interest rates too low in the early 2000s and thus contributed in a major way to the housing boom and bust. By pulling rates down too low, the Fed caused other central banks to set too low rates: the bubble was reproduced across many of the developed economies.

The chaos facing Oddsson was thus generated from outside—by poor calls from the Fed—and from inside, by a rigid adherence to inflation targeting. It was above all a failure of central banks. By allowing asset bubbles, central banks lost control of their economies.

But none of this diminished Oddsson's individual responsibility, his slowness of response when it was obvious that the Icelandic economy was coming unstuck.

The British credit-rating agency Fitch spotted, in February 2006, that the Icelandic boiler was about to explode. The rapid credit growth, the steep current-account deficit, the escalating external debt—it all seemed to point to trouble, and Fitch changed its outlook for Iceland from "stable" to "negative." "Credit growth of over 30 per cent per annum continued unabated, the current account deficit expanded to 15 per cent of GDP in 2005, and net external debt has climbed to well over 400 per cent of current external receipts," said the report. Paul Rawkins, its main author, told reporters laconically, "The risks of a hard landing have increased." It got worse. A few weeks later Denmark's Den Danske Bank produced a damning analysis of Iceland's "geyser economy." GDP, it said, was set to contract by between 5 and 10 percent; the good times were over. It was, the Danes warned, brewing up for a repeat of the Asian crisis of the 1990s.

The similarities with the Thai crash in 1997 were clear: a huge flow of capital into the country, a sudden fall in confidence, and a massive outflow, leading to a mutually reenforcing triad of economic slow-down, asset-price collapse, and banking crisis. The Thai events exposed the "crony capitalism" of the region—the ease with which developers could get cash from local banks to build unnecessary office blocks—and other Asian economies were sucked in. It all sounded familiar. The other Nordic economies in particular were getting nervous. Landsbanki issued a detailed rebuttal; so did the other Icelandic banks and most of the political class. One of the report's authors flew to Reykjavik to defend the analysis and found himself booed. "They took it really personally; we were being threatened with lawsuits." Nobody wanted to hear that the party was about to end. Least of all from a Dane, a representative of the former colonial masters. But Iceland was indeed approaching the end of the bubble, and it was lucky to struggle through the next thirty months with its credibility more or less intact.

All the warning signs were blinking red; the sirens were blaring. Early in 2006, the Bank of Japan indicated that it would raise interest rates. Investors sold positions in Iceland; they canceled their bets. It was as simple as that. Iceland, which had thought itself rich and on top of the world, found itself uniquely vulnerable. All the ingredients were in place for a major meltdown long before the global liquidity crisis. Those who spotted the danger were shouted down. The other credit-rating agencies were persuaded to keep their assessment of Iceland unchanged. The buying spree in Britain continued unabated. Agust Gudmundsson announced in April 2006 that he was going to take out a 155 million GBP loan to finance the purchase of Laurens Patisseries and thus provide chilled desserts for the British dining table. Business, then, as usual. And David Oddsson? "As far as I can tell," he said in April 2006, "the banks are acting responsibly on the good foundations that they have built. It's absurd to talk about a crisis."

9 : Invasion

The only thing I have to do is look each day and see how much money came in. Fifty million pounds came in, just last Friday!
Sigurjon Arnason, CEO Landsbanki, 2006

In the rolling greenness of southern England nestles the village of Sutton Scotney, where the thwack of a leather ball colliding against a cricket bat is heard more often than the urban howl of police sirens. Past thatched cottages, a low-ceilinged pub, and a Norman church you reach Naomi House, the bequest of Mrs. Cornelius Reid, who in return for fourteen freshly plucked roses payable each year on the summer solstice, allowed a new charity to use 2.2 acres of her grounds. Inside the house, its walls covered by soft-focused photographs of strained-looking parents with their children, is the Butterfly Suite, where the temperature can be reduced to 24.8°F, allowing the bodies of dead children to be kept for a fortnight. It is the basement room of a hospice. On the edge of the bed in this room that struggles to be cheerful, Professor Khalid Aziz rails against Iceland.

Or more precisely, a system that failed to protect his and other charities, that was unable to shield mainstream England from foolish investments. "We were hoping to open all six beds [for teenage patients], but will probably now only be able to afford half that number. We started off putting our money into what was then Singer & Friedlander in 2004— an old, established British bank regulated by the FSA. It was taken over by Kaupthing in 2005. We had no reason to believe there was anything untoward. People said, 'Why did you put your money into Iceland?' We didn't, we put our money into London. Okay, it was owned by an Icelandic bank. It was 5.7 million GBP, a third of our asset base."

In 2006, the New Vikings needed cash to expand and to plug the holes of their leaking longboats. And the Icelandic government, worried about critical assessments from the credit-rating agencies, needed the banks to at least appear more stable. So a scheme was hatched to set up competitive online banking services that would lure cash from Britain, from the Dutch, from the Germans. The British in particular responded to the bait. Landsbanki's Icesave offered higher interest rates than were available at home, and the image of Iceland fitted the popular mood: the banks were Cool, fleet of foot, and yet somehow reliable. The Icelanders benefited from the high name recognition of British brands—which English child could resist a visit to the Jon Asgeir–owned Hamleys toy shop in London?—and, however undeserved, the presumption of Nordic caution.

Barely any British institution was untouched by the Icelandic financial system. Oxford University deposited 30 million GBP into Landsbanki, Glitnir, and KSF. The Metropolitan Police—the authority that controls Scotland Yard—invested another 30 million GBP; the Sussex Police Authority, 6.8 million GBP. Transit for London, 40 million GBP; Cambridge University, 11 million GBP; the National Cat Protection League, 11.2 million GBP; 116 local governments poured 858 million GBP into Icelandic banks. Three hundred thousand individual British were Icesave depositors. Gordon Ramsay, the foulmouthed master chef, turned to Kaupthing to refinance a loan. Fire departments and churches put their trust in Icelandic investment funds. So, embarrassingly, did the Audit Commission, the body monitoring public spending, which was later called on to investigate what went wrong with the British. Just like the prospectors who loaded up their spades, water barrels, wives, and children into covered wagons to seek their future in the American West, the British abandoned their normal caution and headed north. It was bubble behavior. Iceland went bust and Britain lost its savings.

As a result, moral boundaries blurred when the crisis unfolded. Who was villain and who was victim? How negligent was the government, were the controllers; how far did greed—or narrow institutional "performance targets"—drive irresponsible public investment? For

Khalid Aziz, who led a consortium of thirty British charities fighting to reclaim 50 million GBP lost in Icelandic banks, there was little doubt about the victims. His hospice caters to an uneasy mix of ages, with a pit full of plastic balls, fluffy toys, and a music room for the smaller children, and behind the ball pit, Xboxes and PlayStations for teenagers. The aim of Naomi House is to provide respite care for the families of seriously ill children. "We need somewhere for the older teenagers," said Professor Aziz. "So that they can have facilities appropriate for their age." The charity began putting money into Singer & Friedlander, and when Kaupthing took it over, turning the bank into KSF, Naomi House saw no cause to move its funds. Construction began on a 12 million GBP six-bedroom complex—complete with soccer pitch for children in wheelchairs—when KSF went broke and the charity effectively lost a third of its capital. The hospice extension is unfinished.

It is not difficult, visiting a hospice that has been left in the lurch, to share the common British view of the Icelanders as amoral plunderers. The Icelandic banks, and the oligarchs who stood behind them, were desperate to suck up cash. British officials believe a conscious decision was made by a handful of the Icelandic superrich to target Britain in an attempt to rescue their lost position. Some stories, repeated in Reykjavik and London, have a group of New Vikings sitting together in a house in the so-called West End of the Icelandic capital, plotting the launch of Icesave as a way not only of filling their coffers but also of taking the British down a peg or two. The mood was said to be impassioned, more than just commercially calculating. According to one version of this story, a businessman ended the meeting by standing up and declaring, "Let the British pay!"

Pay for what exactly? For Icesave, of course. But Kaupthing bank tried a similar scheme with its online service Kaupthing Edge—and drew in many hapless German investors; so this could not be accused of being an anti-British sting. Both Icesave and Kaupthing Edge were orthodox, registered savings programs. The accusation of deception came from the way that the overseas deposits were secured. Had Landsbanki and its backers anticipated its collapse when they launched Icesave in 2006, then it could be said that the oligarchs had criminal intent to defraud the British and other savers. But the evidence seems to suggest that they were merely living in hope, that they were scooping up new money to buy breathing space for further profitable adventures. That was the fatal flaw of the Icelandic oligarchs—not that they were pirates, for that was the whole nature of global mergers and acquisitions, of the hedge-fund culture, but rather that they continued to believe in the certainty of their own success, the Croesus touch. Yet by the time that Icesave was launched, the magic had long since gone.

The Icelandic businessman's alleged comment about making the British pay was probably not so much about loosening British purse strings as settling a historical score. Every Icelandic male in his early forties with a close relationship to his father—both Thor and Jon Asgeir being prime examples—had experienced the British as a rival, enemy, and warily observed friend. The three Cod Wars, in 1958, 1972–73, and 1975–76, had seen the Royal Navy attack Iceland in the name of British national interests. Or at least that is how the Icelanders saw these conflicts. From the beginning of the modern Anglo-Icelandic relationship, when British forces landed in Iceland during the Second World War, the Icelanders had detected a trace of imperial swagger in London. The relationship was not quite as strained as with the old colonial masters, the Danes, but it was nonetheless complex. "We prefer the Scots," a flush-faced former banker tells me as we tuck into a cholesterol-boosting shellfish lunch in Reykjavik. "They're modest, thoughtful, stubborn, and discreet—just like us." The English, said the graduate of St. Andrews, regarded the Icelanders as a remote island people with nothing to offer civilization apart from fish. And even that the English wanted to take away.

No wonder that the English seemed to walk around with a permanent sneer: Iceland was, for them, at the bottom of the pecking order. ("Why else do they keep saying we have the population of Bromley? Does Bromley have its own literature, the world's oldest democracy? I don't think so.") It had become the task of red-blooded Icelanders to show that Britain was an imperial bluffer; that did not exclude an edgy friendship in between flare-ups, but it remained a historical mission, something one guzzled in with one's mother's milk. The focus may have shifted, with the years, from fish to finance, but the passion to outwit the British was a constant. Thus it was that Thor Thors—the hero, the role model, for the family of Bjoergólfur Gudmundsson's wife, Thora—stood up in the United Nations during the first Cod War to declare, "Swarms of British trawlers have scraped the bottom of the sea almost up to the door of our poor fishermen's homes."

The first Cod War, which so colored the hostile Icelandic image of Britain, had not been particularly violent. The most tense confrontation of the war—which pitted seven tiny Icelandic patrol vessels against fifty-three Royal Navy vessels and scores of trawlers—was when the patrol boat *Thor* tried to stop the British trawler *Hackness* by firing four blank shots across its bow and then a live shell. A few minutes later a Royal Navy warship appeared and the commander declared, "If you open fire on the trawler, we will sink you!" The Icelandic vessel withdrew, but in Reykjavik the anger spilled into the streets. A crowd gathered outside the British ambassador's residence and threw first stones, then smoke bombs, and finally slingshot objects at the house.

This, in 1958, was an almost unprecedented outburst against British power. The ambassador, Sir Andrew Gilchrist, responded by playing at full blast a record of the Edinburgh City Police Pipe Band and their rendition of "The Barren Rocks of Aden." For those outside the house this conjured up the image of the ambassador, a Scot, defiantly playing the bagpipes and marching up and down within the beleaguered residence. The world press praised his stiff upper lip and condemned the Icelanders for their breach of etiquette. But Gilchrist's superiors at the Foreign Office were upset—they didn't approve of public eccentricity—and sent him to the Djibouti embassy. And Iceland nutured its grudge.

The generation of Jon Asgeir and Thor was influenced meanwhile by the Third Cod War of 1975–76. The first clashes with Britain were essentially about British overfishing in what Reykjavik considered to be its territorial waters and what London saw as the high seas. In 1975 Iceland declared that the ocean up to two hundred nautical miles from its coast fell under Icelandic authority: British trawlers within this exclusion zone were considered poachers. The clashes that ensued were more violent than anything that had gone before. The Icelandic patrol boats cut the nets of the British trawlers, and the two sides rammed each other in the gray, choppy seas. In one clash, the *Thor* again shot at a vessel; in another, a British nuclear-armed warship, the HMS *Falmouth,* rammed the *Tyr*. The *Tyr*'s captain ordered his men to man the ship's guns ready to shoot at the *Falmouth*. Anticipating a long war, Iceland asked the United States to supply Asheville-class gunboats. When the U.S. administration refused, Reykjavik asked Moscow for Soviet Mirka-class frigates and threatened to close down the NATO air base at Keflavik.

The assumption then—as it was later in October 2008—was that playing the Moscow card always concentrated minds in NATO. But even though these Icelandic threats were largely bluff, they sapped Iceland's reputation as a reliable ally.

Iceland won all three of the Cod Wars; that is, it fought for and defended its expanded fishing limits, and by embarrassing Britain in various diplomatic forums, it won some international support. It was a simple enough argument: fish were its livelihood and national survival demanded it protect its waters. Britain emerged looking like a bully. "We are probably the only country that has ever defeated the British empire at sea," says Olafur Hardarsson, professor of politics at Reykjavik University. Victory was won by making the British military operation hopelessly expensive; Iceland swelled with pride and a whole generation of school-children—Jon Asgeir and Thor among them—grew up thinking they were unbeatable, that a tiny country could defeat an empire. But another calculation too was that the British would inevitably hold a grudge against Icelanders. How long would that grudge last? Generations? That is what the sagas taught.

A visit to Hull in the north of England suggests that the Icelanders were not far off the mark: the experience of the Cod Wars has trans-lated into a deep distrust. The fishing industry in Hull was based at St. Andrew's dock, part of which was dubbed the Iceland market. Boom time for Hull was the 1950s, before the first Cod War, because Atlantic waters, unfished during the Second World War, were brimming not only with cod but with halibut. Those were the days when 150 trawlers left regularly from Hull; now only three are still registered. "It's hard for everyone to forget and for other people to forgive," says Carl Minns, head of the local government. In 2006, Hull unveiled a green-tinged statue in the harbor area—the dockside Iceland market has long since lost its name and is now the site of a shopping mall—called *Voyage*. A plaque says that it marks a bond between Iceland and Britain "created by more than 1,000 years of sea-trading." One man who refused to attend the ceremony was Jimmy Williams, now eighty-one, who used to be a mate on the *Arctic Corsair* trawler. "You can understand our bitterness," he says. "It was a dangerous game they were playing. They destroyed an industry, but not just that, a whole community. There was never any love lost between us."

The Icelanders did not fully understand that they had made victims out of the British. During the Second World War, Iceland had become prosperous; some Icelanders call it the "blessed war." The same war, though, had seriously strained the British economy. By the time of the first Cod War, the value of the UK fishing industry's catch was equivalent to a saving in foreign exchange big enough to pay for the entire fifty-five-thousand strong British force in Germany. Cod might have been existential for Iceland; but it was not a trivial matter for Britain. When Iceland first tackled Britain, in 1958, the British were suffering from a profound balance-of-payments crisis. Somehow Iceland succeeded in making the British feel like victims.

Kids of Jon Asgeir's generation played Icelanders vs. the British in the schoolyard; almost everyone in his class wanted to be a trawlerman or in the coast guard. These were the national heroes, the true descendants of the Vikings. But in adulthood the schoolchildren-turned-bankers were content to fish in English pockets. That too was a kind of victory.

The British were angry not just because they had lost their savings, but because they felt that online banking should not get tangled up in ancient grudge matches. Icesave was set up in the UK in October 2006 (and from May 2008, only months away from the meltdown, in Holland). The scheme appealed to the British, who had been shifting in large numbers to online banking. High street banks, which used to be proud temples with pseudo-Doric columns and leather-topped desks to write out deposit slips, were now places for losers—customers with too much time on their hands and inadequate computer skills—and the social standing of the branch-bank manager had slumped to the level of a cell-phone salesman. The middle-class customer was online and had no particular brand loyalty.

Icesave's marketing slogan was "We make a clear difference." Clear, as in ice: honest, transparent, Nordically solid. Different, as in interest rates of over 6 percent, outstripping anything that British competitors had to offer. Three types of savings account were on offer: an immediate-access savings account, a cash Individual Savings Account (ISA), and a range of fixed-rate bonds. These bonds were the most attractive for the British saver, and the lifeline for the Icelanders. Icesave caught the popular imagination, especially of young, single professionals. After buying one's ready-made frozen dinner in the UK from the Icelandic supermarket (and having snacked at lunch on Marks & Spencer sandwiches prepared by another Icelandic firm), one could withdraw money from one's Icesave account to buy a new dress at Icelandic-owned Whistles or Oasis. The consumers did not catch the whiff of desperation, and why should they? Icesave was slick, intelligent, modern. More than 300,000 customers signed up in the UK, with deposits of over 5 billion euros. In Holland, in five short months, Icesave drew in 1.7 billion euros from 125,000 customers. An Icesave account was an account with Landsbanki's branches in London and Amsterdam.

Kaupthing Edge came into operation in 2007 and scooped up funds from across Europe, offering personal savings accounts in eleven countries. Unlike Icesave, Kaupthing Edge accounts were usually held with Kaupthing subsidiaries outside Iceland, rather than with branches of the parent bank. The exceptions were Finland, Norway, Austria, and Germany. This became a problem above all for the Germans: some thirty thousand savers had difficulties with deposit insurance, similar to that experienced by Icesave clients, when the Icelandic banks collapsed.

The British, however, bore the brunt of Iceland's financial collapse. Not for the first time in history, they proved to be slow-witted investors.

But one problem went beyond Anglo-Icelandic rivalry or the clumsiness of British investors. Since the 1990s more and more money had accumulated with local authorities in the United States and Britain—billions of dollars were put at their disposal. The Thatcher/Reagan market revolution had also forced individuals to become market players, if only to maximize their pensions. Yet these new financial administrators were not particularly competent. They relied too heavily on middlemen, and their trust was often abused. This phenomenon applied especially in the use of new financial instruments such as the collateralized debt obligations (CDOs).

In the United States, municipalities, even schools, were encouraged to act as hedge funds. To plug budget shortfalls, administrations were encouraged to "get creative" with their funds. They quickly found themselves in the hands of enablers who were eager to sell them dubious financial products. The motivation on the part of local officials was not greed but a misplaced sense of duty toward their clientele, i.e., their constituents, both to maximize funds and minimize risks. This was self-delusion.

The school board in Whitefish Bay, Wisconsin, found that it had a yawning gap in its teachers' retirement plan. A local investment banker proposed that Whitefish Bay join together with four other school districts and borrow from overseas. The money would then be put into complex investments that would haul in modest profits to be paid out every three months. The schools stuck $200 million into the deal, involving CDOs from the respectable Royal Bank of Canada. "We're being very conservative," said their adviser. It was, he said, a responsible way of spreading and thus reducing risk. "In order for the school district to lose money," said the adviser, "there would need to be fifteen Enrons." At the time, 2006, Enron was regarded as a once-in-a-lifetime coagulation of incompetence, corruption, and breakdown of control. So the schools went ahead—and unbeknownst to them, or indeed to their ill-informed investment adviser, the $200 million had become part of the collateral for $20 billion of corporate bonds; the "success" of CDOs was based on the duping of those bondholders at the bottom of the repayment heap. The Wisconsin schools, which did indeed lose their money, were not infected by a global delirium. They made seemingly rational decisions spurred by the fear that they were somehow falling behind; shun financial innovations and you betray, so it seemed at the time, a trust to the people whose money you were managing.

A similar reasoning was responsible for the extraordinary willingness of the British to put their funds into Icelandic banks. Plainly, some of the 127 British local governments with Icelandic deposits regarded yield as more important than financial security and liquidity. Built-in pressures, performance benchmarks, were set by bureaucrats. "A key indicator is investment returns in comparison with an average interest rate," says the British Audit Commission's post-meltdown analysis "Risk and Return," "and treasury teams are encouraged to outperform the benchmark where possible." The Audit Commission, analyzing how so many local governments could have got it so wrong, found staff who said they could not afford to place deposits of less than three months, which generally offer lower rates of return. And the Icelandic banks were offering competitively high interest rates.

It is natural to believe that those who invested in Iceland were risk-takers, that high-risk, high-yield investment somehow unleashed the gambling instinct. In fact, the Audit Commission, having analyzed the mechanics of how public money moved to Iceland, found a different pattern. Those who opted against Iceland were cautious, not just about the country's banks but about the information and guidance coming from throughout the financial system; they were alert rather than conservative. The big enthusiasts for Iceland in the UK—Kent County government, for example, which deposited 48.9 million GBP in the flawed banks—were anything but risk-takers. They locked in their investment for over one year, making it difficult to take advantage of fluctuating interest rates and credit ratings, and waited passively for the guidance of the rating agencies. This often turned out to be their sole source of information. Even then, the agencies were sometimes ignored. The following table, prepared by the Audit Commission, shows how different management styles influenced local governments and charities, a dozen police authorities, universities, and transport authorities in the UK. And to what degree they were responsible for their own victimhood.

Characteristic	Noninvestors in Iceland	Investors in Iceland
Attitude to risk	Cautious. Recognize the need to own all risk-reward decisions and the need to maintain a questioning, challenging mind-set.	Reactive. Conduct little research into the risks being taken.
Approach to risk management	Manage risk proactively: —invest funds with riskier counterparties only for short periods of time; —consider the possibility of breaking a deposit before maturity; —manage the counterparty list without waiting for a rating downgrade; and —consider country limits for counterparties.	Manage risk reactively: —wait for rating agencies to change a rating before amending limits; and —regard policy as only relevant for new investments, not existing ones.
Use of credit ratings	Recognize that credit ratings and comments from advisers are merely one source of information that can be used to build an understanding of risks in the markets and with counterparties.	Rely on a single short-term or long-term credit rating. Highly dependent on information provided by treasury advisers. Have gaps in understanding regarding the use of credit-rating agencies, including: —which one(s) to use; —the measures to use (long-term/short-term and so on); and —what to do when a counterparty has different ratings with different credit rating agencies.

Governance and scrutiny	Elected member oversees finance function, takes an interest in the treasury policy, and challenges assumptions built into the limits and minimum credit criteria. Finance staff proactively approach elected members and provide briefings on key issues relevant to the treasury policy, including risk limits. Elected members are able to provide robust challenge to the key policy parameters.	Elected members do not engage in the treasury policy and, instead, leave it to the experts in finance. Failure to question policies year-on-year and mechanistically use their adviser's policy template.
Use of information	Extensive. Includes actively researching counterparties and the markets.	Limited. Overly reliant on a single information source —for example, e-mails from a treasury adviser. Reliant on benchmarking information that focuses on using lowest rate achieved on borrowings and highest rate achieved on cash investments, which encourages local authorities to take on more risk to show an improved placing in the benchmarks.
Relationship with counterparties	Know the bankers that they are investing with.	Excessive reliance on brokers means that some local authorities do not have direct contact with their banking counterparties.

Reliance on yield	Prioritize security and liquidity above yield. Maintain a balance between security, liquidity, and yield by investing short term where risk dictates. For some, it is rare to invest for longer than three months.	Highest returns available in marketplace are sought. Some (overt or covert) pressure to maximize returns to balance budgets.

For local government treasurers, the only real advice came from the credit-rating agencies. This was their taste of international finance. The world of small-town financing had been transformed since 1997; the innovative government of Tony Blair, the New Labour ethos, and above all his chancellor of the exchequer, Gordon Brown, had freed the City, allowing and encouraging London to become a metropolis that danced to the tune of the financial-services culture. The trickle-down effect had been felt not only in urban culture, but outside the city, in the provinces too. Spending on local government services in the UK had increased from 51 billion GBP in 1998 to 112 billion GBP in April 2009. The amount deposited in Iceland by local governments had doubled from 15 billion GBP in March 2000 to around 31 billion GBP on October 7, 2008. A great deal of money was in a small number of hands; these financial managers were inexperienced, having risen through local politics —perhaps by making a name for themselves in opposing the cutting down of a few cherished oak trees, or closing a noisy youth center—and were dependent on outside advice for ambitious offshore investment.

Ultimately investing in Icelandic banks did not generate that much better a reward. "On average, local authorities received an extra 0.065 per cent interest when they invested in Iceland in comparison with other similarly rated institutions," says the "Risk and Return" report; "equivalent to an extra 650 GBP per year per million deposited." The Kent County government, identified as one of seven "neglectful" investors, has defended its record as reasonable conduct at a time when Iceland was seen as a dominant force on the British high street. In fact, though, it was both overly dependent on the judgment of credit-rating agencies and capable of ignoring them when they predicted trouble ahead. Local government, in other words, blundered into the global financial crisis and did its bit toward betraying the taxpayers. The credit agencies had admittedly sown confusion over Iceland in 2006, downgrading the country's banks, voicing doubt, but then announcing renewed confidence in the island. And the rating agencies had made a substantial contribution to the subprime mortgage crisis as it began to unfold in 2007, having unwittingly misled investors with their high gradings of CDOs. But the Fitch report of May 22, 2008, was damning, entirely unambiguous.

Even the central bank of Iceland could not put much of a spin on it. "The risks of a hard landing for the Icelandic economy have increased, in Fitch's opinion, and this would likely lead to increased loan impairments and pressure on profitability from domestic operations," said Iceland's central bank bulletin glumly. Fitch also saw profitability weakening in "businesses most closely aligned to capital markets and investment banking"—that is, Jon Asgeir with his controlling stake in Glitnir, Thor and his father with their stake in Landsbanki, and the Gudmundsson brothers in Kaupthing. In other words, Fitch was warning not only of an Icelandic banking crisis, but one that would drag in all of Iceland's players. "In 2007, all three banks generated around 35 per cent of their operating income from capital markets and investment banking activities," said Fitch. "The banks' capital ratios—a strength in recent years—have been eroded to varying degrees by ongoing expansion, leaving less of a cushion to absorb problems and maintain confidence." The report continued in this vein. It was, to put it mildly, a clear signal to disentangle oneself from Iceland.

That was certainly the reading in Iceland itself as oligarchs and bankers began to make their dispositions. But not to the treasury departments of British local governments, despite their supposed dependence on the rating agencies. Between October 1 and October 3, 2008—that is, after the Icelandic central bank had clearly signaled the demise of Glitnir as an independent institution, after the Lehman collapse, and amid swirling rumors of national bankruptcy in Iceland—seven local governments in the UK breached their own accountancy procedures and deposited 32.8 million GBP in Glitnir and Landsbanki. Some of that cash may eventually be recovered, but for the most part it was flushed down the drain. One local government made its deposit twenty minutes before the rating agencies sent out an alert and further downgraded the Icelandic banks. In Kent, a local official failed to open an e-mail announcing the downgrading before going ahead with the transfer. These were last-minute errors. But throughout the troubled summer of 2008, deep into September, dozens of local governments in the UK were still blithely transferring money to Iceland.

"Had all local authorities stopped placing deposits in the Icelandic banks in April 2008, the total amount of funds at risk when the banks collapsed in October would have been 389 million GBP instead of close to a billion pounds," said the Audit Commission. "We talk about the Icelandic banking system being run by the mediocre and incompetent," an accountant from a northern English authority told me. He had tried to persuade his local treasury department to change tack on Iceland as early as January 2008 and, at the time of our meeting in March 2009, was under pressure to take premature retirement to cover up the council's tracks. "But the truth is, most of our budget people just plodded on like First World War soldiers led to slaughter at the front. I asked one of them about it and she just shrugged. 'It's not your money, don't get excited.' That's what she said."

It was a failure both of control and of guidance. Richard Kemp, deputy chairman of the Local Government Association in the UK, was asked at a parliamentary hearing if he had advised local governments to invest public money offshore. "Let me put it this way," said the councilor, "there was no advice not to." This was the hub of the problem. Globalization had the effect of bringing small players—with control over significant public funds—into the game even though they were ill-prepared and often naïve. They were the greenhorns, the patsies in the poker school. Ultimately, said a House of Commons inquiry, they had to depend on their common sense, their prudence, and that was not enough. "Local authorities are required to take their own decisions on the level of prudent, affordable capital investment," said the school-masterly author of the House of Commons report. "They have a duty to the taxpayer diligently to protect the money they are investing on their behalf." So the national government, it continued, should not bail out those local councils who were unable to manage properly their resources: that would be rewarding imprudence. This reference to an old-fashioned virtue is not just a reflection of the average age of those who sit in parliamentary committees. It is a way of separating the responsibilities and obligations of the individual from that of the state. Decision-making in a fast-moving global marketplace is akin to that on a battlefield: even relatively low-ranking officers have to be able to identify danger and respond accordingly.

At the time of the great British sellout to Iceland in 2006, former banker Catherine Cowley was publishing a book, *The Value of Money: Ethics and the World of Finance*, in which she pointed out the potential of derivatives to destroy whole economies. Cowley, now a nun with the Congregation of the Religious of the Assumption, argued then that some derivatives were too dangerous to be sold and that the obscuring of risk had upset the moral compass. It was time, she argued, for the financial world to reward integrity. The starting point was understanding prudence, which meant more than good housekeeping or maximizing profit. "When Aristotle wanted to give an example of the prudent person he chose a successful general, because prudence involves looking at all your options and working out what the most effective means are to what one wants to achieve." This, she makes clear, is the antidote to bubble-thinking, to the herd behavior that led to irrational investment on Iceland. "The good general will marshal his troops in an effective way. It's got nothing to do with overcautious bean-counting. That is not prudence. I think we have lost sight of its original meaning."

10 : Denial

Day after day the battle went on,
In such a way that all who fell and all weapons lying on the battlefield,
And even the shields too,
Turned to stone.
At dawn, however,
All the dead men got up and fought and all their weapons became new.

The *Prose Edda*

Prime Minister Geir Haarde did not do pathos; he did bumbling indecision; he did wet-palmed handshakes. The Icelanders created a neologism, to *haarder*, meaning to prevaricate, to put one's head in the sand. A transitive verb.

So when the prime minister made his speech to the nation on October 6, 2008—having first, he stresses in interviews, changed his tie, and interrupting state television for his announcement—there was a real sense of shock. The words seemed too big for him, like borrowed clothing. "Fellow countrymen . . . If there was ever a time when the Icelandic nation needed to stand together and show fortitude in the face of adversity, then this is the moment. I urge you all to guard that which is most important in the life of every one of us, to protect those values which will survive the storm now beginning. I urge families to talk together and not to allow anxiety to get the upper hand, even though the outlook is grim for many. We need to explain to our children that the world is not on the edge of a precipice, and we all need to find an inner courage to look to the future . . . Thus with Icelandic optimism, forti-tude, and solidarity as weapons, we will ride out the storm." Icelanders are understandably cautious about using storm metaphors. Too many trawlermen have been lost at sea. Then, to cap it all, Haarde uttered, "God bless the Icelandic nation!" Iceland is a Lutheran country, but an understated one. God does not, on the whole, enter public discourse or political rhetoric. "He sounded like a captain about to abandon his ship," says a translator friend. "It was a man-the-lifeboats speech."

Hildur Helga was at her bank at the time, trying to cash some checks. "Everyone was just very stunned, gathered in front of the screen, asking why he was doing this. My friend was waiting for me outside in the car; she had been listening to it on the radio, and she was clutching the steering wheel, completely pale. On the street people were walking like zombies—news percolated through almost instantly in downtown Reykjavik—and that was actually how it would continue for weeks." Robert Jackson, a British writer, remembers, "Edda, my partner, was in tears on the sofa beside me."

This, then, was what economists meant when they talked of a hard landing. Could a nation really go bankrupt? Can it really just shut down business, change its address, and switch off the lights when the bailiff comes knocking at the door? "A brand like Iceland, or for that matter the United States or Britain, isn't like Woolworths," says Norbert Walter, chief economist of Deutsche Bank. "A state can't just disappear from the map or be bought up by a bigger country or put up for auction." Haarde, by warning Iceland of impending national bankruptcy, had oversimplified a complex situation, a condition of vast indebtedness, the collapse of the financial system, of a virtually paralyzed polity, but at the same time a frozen normality, a society in which money was still being exchanged for goods and trawlers still chugged out to sea.

The expectation was that Iceland would start to resemble Argentina in 2002 when it declared itself unable to pay its bills, with $155 billion in foreign debt. The Argentinean currency collapsed (like the Icelandic krona, the peso had been hopelessly overvalued), there was a run on the banks ($1.3 billion withdrawn on a single chaotic day), food was hoarded, and the newly impoverished (about half of Argentina's 37 million people) began to beg outside restaurants. But this was not the Icelandic way. Foreign journalists visiting the island two months after Geir Haarde's speech seemed almost disappointed at the lack of social breakdown. The fact is, genuine state bankruptcy is rare, usually experienced (as Germany did twice in the twentieth century) after a lost war. Although Icelanders compared their sudden debt burden with the backbreaking reparations imposed on Germany after the First World War, in truth, default or bankruptcy is usually just the prelude to long, always humiliating rescheduling negotiations. These are not pleasant, especially for a country that had been proud of its status as the happiest nation in the world, but stop somewhat short of the apocalypse.

What hurts is the fall from grace. Countries with small populations magnify their achievements. When things go wrong, they overstate their tragedy. Judgment is distorted by per capita statistics. Thus for a short while Iceland could claim that it had higher GDP per capita than the United States. If you are a nation the size of a small town, then you will always find reasons to be proud of yourself. More Nobel Prize winners than anyone else in the world—per capita. And therefore surely, the most intelligent society. The highest number of Miss World winners—per capita. Proof positive, surely, that Icelandic women are the most beautiful. But when the absurd achievement-league tables are reversed, when misery is measured, then the per capita calculations are more accurate. The sheer amount of debt piling on Iceland amounts to over $403,000—per capita. That is, a family of four faces a bill, made up of public and private debt, of over $1.6 million. Not a statistical trick, but a statement about the generational burden resulting from a mismanaged economy; a declaration of national bankruptcy in the sense that the island's future as a wealth-producing society is over, if not forever, then for a long time indeed.

David Oddsson said later that he saw the crisis coming—a brewing perfect storm that drew into the vortex the disproportionately huge banking sector, its terrifyingly active and heavily leveraged use of borrowed money to buy abroad, the opacity of cross-ownership, the premise that credit would always be easy. All this worried Oddsson at the central bank, and according to his version, he passed on his worries to his successor as prime minister, his loyal, subservient friend Geir Haarde. In the Oddsson version of events, the central bank submitted a memorandum to Geir Haarde on the poor state of the three Icelandic banks on February 12, 2008. Haarde, in subsequent testimony to a parliamentary committee (on December 7, 2008), said he could not recall any such communication from David Oddsson—one of the few occasions that Haarde has publicly distanced himself from his former mentor. Yet three days after the memo was sent, Haarde called a meeting at his office, attended by the foreign minister (and Social Democratic leader), Ingibjorg Solrun Gisladottir; the finance minister, Arni Mathiesen; and the banking minister, Bjorgvin Sigurdsson. Four top bankers also came. The bankers said their present difficulties were due only to external factors, with no intrinsic problem that could not be solved, providing Iceland's position was strongly sold abroad. That, then, became policy. On February 24, Haarde praised Iceland's banks for being "bold but not irresponsible" and alluded to their big portfolios of assets. Ingibjorg Gisladottir took a similar line. When Danish media cross-questioned her, she replied, "The banks are doing fine." Haarde visited the Nasdaq exchange in New York, to beat the Icelandic drum, accompanied by Jon Asgeir and Sigurjon Arnason.

If Oddsson really did warn Haarde about the banks, then he did so late and in confidence. In public, he was a cheerleader. The foreign expansion of the banks, he said in one of many speeches in this vein, "was a very positive development which shows beyond all doubt the enormous force unleashed when the state entrusts individuals with freedom of action." If he had doubts, he kept them buried for most of the time. That was the case in 2008 and during the first collapse of confidence in 2006. Yet a public warning in 2006 would surely have steered Iceland away from national bankruptcy.

By the end of 2006, the banking crisis was already being dismissed as a harmless hiccup by both Haarde and Oddsson. If anything, they—and the masters of the Icelandic commercial universe—now felt unbeatable. The exchange rate had depreciated 25 percent, equity prices had dropped by a similar degree, and a barrage of international criticism had focused on the reliance on market funding of short maturities, on the quality of earnings, and on the fuzziness of who owned what. But the government had reduced this complex litany into three issues that needed action: expanding the deposit base, broadening the geographical range of maturities, and improving the "transparency" of the Icelandic economy. In return, the credit agencies—Moody's had in any case chosen not to follow Fitch in downgrading its outlook—made their peace with Iceland. Yet it was by and large a whitewash, an attempt to return as soon as possible to business as usual. The commitment to transparency entailed enlisting a handful of foreign and Icelandic economists to present the case that the bottle was more than half-full, rather than almost empty. As late as April 2008, Richard Portes of the London Business School was making the case in public that Iceland was a robust economy with a strong future. In a presentation he praised Iceland for its embrace of competition, he rated FME, the Financial Supervisory Agency, as highly professional, extolled the analytic reports of the central bank, and pointed out that unlike several EU states, it was implementing the directives of the EU Financial Services Action Plan. As for the current account deficit, one of the causes for concern for Fitch, it had fallen from 26 percent of GDP in 2006 to 17 percent in 2007 and was set to fall to levels sustained by Australia and New Zealand. Exports were rising (fish, aluminum), imports falling (because of the depreciation of the krona). There were a fully funded pension system and a fiscal surplus. It was, by any measure, an extraordinary example of the power of positive thinking.

As for answering international criticism that bank deposits were too low, that the banks had grown too fast in relation to their puny domestic market, Iceland was registering progress. The marketing of Icesave and Kaupthing Edge, the selling of Iceland as a lucrative place for ordinary foreign punters to park their money, had apparently adjusted the balance. At the end of 2006, Kaupthing's deposit ratio—that is, the relationship of deposits to customer loans—was 29.6 percent. By the end of 2007, it had improved to 36.7 percent. The most spectacular rise in deposits was recorded by Landsbanki (the mother of Icesave): from 47.5 percent in 2006 to 70.3 percent in 2007, outperforming the deposit ratios of other Nordic banks. Swedbank of Sweden, for example, had a ratio of 42.3 percent in 2006, 40.4 percent in 2007. But the underlying story, of course, was that the Icelanders were hoovering up foreign (British, Dutch, German) cash at a desperate pace, trying to keep from collapse.

Denial

By 2007 most of those in and around the banking world clearly saw that boom was about to turn to bust. Charles Kindleberger in his 1947 classic text *Manias, Panics, and Crashes* argued that seven stages exist between boom and bust. First comes an easing of liquidity. That happened in Iceland in the late 1990s when exchange controls were lifted. Anyone who wanted to take advantage of Iceland's stable and high interest rates was free to do so. That gave the Icelanders money to play with. Then came stage two: the euphoria when asset prices began to rise, when the Reykjavik housing market started to buzz and everyone on the island started to feel richer. Stage three in the Kindleberger cycle comes when the newly privatized banks started to offer equity release to anyone with a piece of real estate. Suddenly Iceland was awash with credit; the economy was being geared up. Then, according to the Kindleberger matrix, stage four begins: mania. A scramble begins to jump on the bandwagon; that was the moment when the celebrity oligarchs became role models for Icelandic schoolchildren, when girls imitated the clothing style of Ingibjörg Pálmadottir—distressed denim jacket over designer frock— and when three shopping trips abroad became part of the middle-class calendar. Kindleberger's fifth stage is the bubble: prices become ridiculous. At the level of the oligarchs, that was when they abandoned commercial logic and invested in trophy assets: when Jon Asgeir paid well more than he should have for Hamleys, the Regent Street toy store, not because it fit into his loose fashion-and-food retailing strategy, but because he remembered the delight of his daughter when she visited the dollhouse section. Hamleys was a symbolic purchase, supposed to signal to his British rivals that he was a presence to be reckoned with. However, according to one British retail expert, "It just showed Phil Green that Jon had lost his touch." Hamleys was a bubble purchase.

The sixth of Kindleberger's milestones is distress. Income from the assets begins to soften like chocolate in the sun. It could be rental yield or dividends; either way, it is the time that well-informed and still rational investors get out of the market, the last stop on the bus route. Initially, there are buyers. But it is no more than a hop, skip, and a jump to the seventh and final stage: when everyone realizes that the emperor has no clothes, that the asset has lost its value. That stage had almost been reached in 2006. Only the sheer force of collective self-delusion allowed Iceland to stay a player for another eighteen months.

But the signs were there to be read across the world in 2006. For Kindleberger's observations were not uniquely applicable to Iceland. Britain had the sense that it alone among the industrialized states had successfully surfed the waves since the popping of the dot-com bubble in the late 1990s. Vince Cable, the Liberal Democrat Treasury spokesman, recalls how in November 2003 he tried to raise the idea that Britain was only apparently doing well, since its success seemed to be based on bottomless household borrowing secured by rising housing prices. Cable was promptly slapped down by the then chancellor of the exchequer, Gordon Brown—the man who claimed to have abolished boom-bust cycles—and dismissed as an unpatriotic alarmist. The economy of the West was charging ahead like cavalrymen oblivious to the waiting, well-primed enemy cannons. It would have been unthinkable to rein in the horses.

In 2006, mortgage volume rocketed to record heights in the United States, to over $2.5 trillion. The financial engineers, the brightest of the backroom boys in the bank, had found a way in the 1990s of turning risky mortgages into products that would be attractive to investors. The investors didn't need to know anything about the underlying loans or to ask any of the salient, often awkward questions, such as who actually owned the properties concerned? How much did they earn? Instead, the mortgages—typically around three thousand of them with a face value of $400 million—would be bundled together, and a credit-rating firm such as Moody's or Fitch would give it a score. If the package on offer was awarded a triple-A top rating, then it was as plausible, as solid, as any other investment with the same gold-star classification.

It seemed like a foolproof way of shifting the mortgage business, the Rip Van Winkle of commerce, into a Wall Street instrument. No matter that the credit agencies did not analyze the precise structure of these mortgages—that, they argued, was the task of loan officers. Their task was to "securitize"—that is, to convert risk into an intelligent commodity. Many of these mortgages were subprime; that is, loans given to borrowers with dubious credit histories. Having no cash for a deposit, these borrowers had often taken out two loans. The task of the credit agencies was to number crunch, to provide a statistical aggregate that took into account factors such as how many borrowers had submitted a written statement of income, how many were buying their primary home, how many had taken out "teaser" loans, where the interest rate, having started out attractively low, could suddenly be hiked. The assessment, in short, had to make a call on the percentage of homeowners who were likely to default.

The package would be sold to corporations specially set up to take in the mortgage payments, and these bodies—SPVs, or Special Purpose Vehicles—would issue bonds using the mortgages as security. The credit-rating agencies' job was to determine whether the mortgage payments would cover the outgoing payments to bondholders. The SPVs floated different classes of bonds, from the desirable AAA to the almost ungradeable. The top bondholders had first call on the incoming mortgage cash. After they were paid, then the second tier would be paid, then the third, and so on. It resembled a molten-chocolate fountain in which the liquid is poured in at the top and then spills over to the next layer, and into the next. The bondholders at the bottom of the fountain were given higher rates of interest since they were the most vulnerable should mortgage payers default.

The subprime packages at least had some grounding in the real world: bricks and mortar in Florida or Pittsburgh. The next level of financial engineering, the collateralized debt obligations, or CDOs, were organized in a similar way, splicing up debt, but they were at one remove. The CDO market did not buy mortgages, it bought bonds that were supported by mortgages. The complexity of many of these new instruments was such that the CEOs could barely understand what was going on. The job of the clever people in the boiler rooms of the banks was to innovate, to find new ways of making a profit, and for this they were (a) rewarded handsomely, and (b) subtly ignored. Michael Lewis, who chronicled the trader culture in *Liar's Poker*, sums up the necessary wall of ignorance between corporate bosses and the real risk-takers tucked into their organizations. "The Wall Street CEO cannot interfere with the new new thing on Wall Street because the new new thing is the profit center and the people who create it are mobile." Slow them down, and they could leave to join a rival or set up a hedge fund. "He isn't a boss in the conventional sense, he's a hostage of his cleverest employees." This trend, this firewall of incomprehension, has accompanied every financial innovation.

"Traders only worked for banks, they never embraced their culture," says Stephen Fay, who has studied how rogue trading brought down Barings Bank in the 1990s. "Their loyalty was to their income streams, and the two words guaranteed to turn them on were compensation package." Sir Kit McMahon, who left the Bank of England to become chairman of Britain's Midland Bank, remembered how difficult it was to keep traders in the bank. One asked for a raise, and McMahon grudgingly agreed to an extra 20,000 GBP (this in the early 1990s). "That's a weekend's pocket money," he was told. The gulf of understanding has not narrowed; all that has changed in the past two decades is that the mercenary bonus culture of the trader has spread to all innovators within a bank, and relentlessly upward to include anyone in the senior hierarchy who may or may not have authorized some profitable risk-taking.

One of the smartest innovators was Ralph R. Cioffi, a fund manager at Bear Stearns in New York. When two Bear hedge funds collapsed in June 2007, questions were naturally raised about its exposure to the helter-skelter U.S. mortgage market. Cioffi and his team had devised an even more complex form of CDO that seemed to offer a higher interest rate than was normal for short-term debt, and which at the same time kept a lid on risk. Despite growing concern about risky assets, the Bear Stearns team put investors' minds to rest: Citigroup had agreed to refund the investor's initial stake plus interest if the market went haywire; it would do this through a "liquidity put." Citi believed it was onto a sure thing: it picked up commissions, could find buyers for its own mortgage-backed securities, and—since the credit-rating agencies gave the new CDOs triple As—assumed it would never have to fork over for its guarantees. Bear sold three batches of these new CDOs in 2004 and 2005 for over $10 billion, and banks and hedge funds loved this new new thing. Wall Street drummed up around $100 billion between 2004 and 2007 using the new CDOs. But as the U.S. mortgage market began to soften—house prices were slipping, defaults were up by February 2007—so did the value of some Bear hedge-fund holdings drop. Investors started to want their money back. Creditors wanted additional collateral. Confidence started to seep away; in nine months, after endless margin calls and shuffling of assets, of emergency board meetings squeezed between CEO James Cayne's bridge rubbers and golf rounds, Bear Stearns went under.

Well, there have been worse corporate failures in U.S. history, and Bear's demise need not perhaps have set all the alarm bells ringing; it was regarded in many European markets as a sideshow, even though Barclays and other big players were exposed. Some countries—Germany and Iceland among them—congratulated themselves for being more discriminating in their use of CDOs. Germany, however, was soon to find that the U.S. subprime market did indeed have global tentacles, prompting its first big banking bailout, of HypoRealEstate. It soon became clear that across the industrialized world, banks had taken on big chunks of risk, toxic assets that were now beginning to curdle the market. This was not, despite the initial smugness of the Europeans, an American mess. It mattered, it had always mattered, that homes were being sold in Kansas for inflated sums to people without savings or means of support. The signs had been there for the reading. It was being registered as early as the spring of 2004 that lending standards were slipping; Fitch had placed one major subprime lender on "credit watch" in the autumn of 2003; the Fed had collected data showing that it was becoming easier and easier to buy a house. By June 2005, Alan Greenspan, chairman of the Fed, was talking about imposing guidelines to curb irresponsible lending. Yet not until March 2007 was some protection offered to the most vulnerable subprime borrowers.

Thus it took more than three years from the initial recognition of the problem to its arrival on the political agenda. Too many vested interests were at play. It is difficult, then, to pin specific blame on the crony capitalist elite of Iceland for blocking out bad news, given the global, systemic neglect. Nobody wanted to hear that the good times were over. The question, though, is who was fooling whom? As frustrated societies scrambled to identify those guilty of squashing dreams and ransacking savings, they found themselves lost in an institutional labyrinth. Where do the responsibilities of the Fed end, and those of federal government begin? Who regulates the regulators? In Iceland these issues were easier to pinpoint. Indeed, Iceland's shareholder watchdog Vilhjalmur Bjarnason is adamant that precisely thirty men and three women were responsible for the Icelandic meltdown; thirty-three individuals with their own as well as institutional and corporate agendums. "All these people are connected in one way or another," he says, with an almost Cromwellian sense of outrage. "Some are friends, others adversaries." So, in a crisis that is top-heavy with brain-stretching numbers—schoolteachers in London reported that they were being asked for the first time by their ten-year-old pupils, "What is a billion? What is a million trillions?"—Iceland brought things down to scale. The mismanagement of risk and the encouragement of debt was the fault not just of remote and poorly controlled institutions, but also of humans: their petty feuds, their stored-up schoolyard resentments, their blunders, and their personal avarice. The human factor, as well as a systemic breakdown, blinded decision-makers to the warnings of disasters ahead.

Joseph Stiglitz's 2001 report for the Icelandic central bank—written in the light of the 1997 Asian crisis and the 1998 Russian crash—was full of foreboding: "On the basis of several variables that have been found to increase a country's vulnerability, Iceland currently does not fare well." The economy was overheated, the country had a large current-account deficit, banks that were rapidly expanding needed higher capital-adequacy ratios, stronger bankruptcy codes were needed. The lesson from Korea in 1997 was relevant to Iceland: "Rapid liberalization had forced changes in some parts of the system, while not giving time for other parts of the system to adapt," said Stiglitz. It was an appeal for intelligent regulation to shield a tiny economy in any forthcoming crisis.

But Oddsson did not act on the advice, neither as prime minister nor when he took over as chief central-bank governor in 2005. The reason was ideological. First, as prime minister he had clung to his belief in Milton Friedman's "perfect market model"—markets would always heal themselves. When Stiglitz shed doubt on the self-regulating and self-equilibrating power of the markets, Oddsson did not really want to listen. Second, although Stiglitz did not spell this out explicitly, the economist's thrust was that small, open economies with their own national currencies were likely to be the roadkill in any serious global crash. The report was written before the Eurozone had properly established its credentials. But by 2005, when Oddsson was installed in the central bank, the Black Fort, euro membership was viewed by many foreign economists as the only sensible way to address the vulnerabilities highlighted by Stiglitz. Yet joining the European Monetary Union—and by implication, the European Union itself—was anathema to Oddsson. Thatcher, his heroine, had urged him to stay out of the euro when he visited her after leaving office; his whole political orthodoxy rebelled against surrendering the country's fiercely defended fishing waters to foreign vessels. No, plenty of old-fashioned political reasons existed for rejecting learned counsel.

Most of all, though, the political and financial elite of Reykjavik was gripped by a siege mentality. Oddsson became convinced that Iceland was being targeted from abroad. Friendly economists—Richard Portes, but also Frederic Mishkin and the government economic adviser Tryggi Herbertsson—believed the Icelandic banks to be fundamentally sound and the economy robust enough to weather a new storm. And since the press, led by *Morgunbladid*, was even more upbeat than the popular mood, why should there be any doubts? Yet there were stirrings. Partly, it was a feeling of fin de regime: Geir Haarde, in Oddsson's view, was diluting the principles that they had both fought for since they were students. The government alliance with the Social Democrats was corrosive. Sometimes the two old friends would meet for a coffee and Oddsson would stay silent for fifteen minutes; it was an obscure punishment. Oddsson had even less to say to the young banking and commerce minister.

There was no dramatic schism, but by 2007 it was becoming clear that the Independence Party's time was running out. It had, even during short mini-recessions, branded itself as the party of growth and self-confidence, but that was coming to an end. One after one, foreign economists were coming to Reykjavik to voice their doubts. Robert

Aliber, a University of Chicago specialist on financial crises, became fascinated by the Icelandic bubble. In 2007 he drove around the capital counting the excessive number of building cranes and warned in a public speech, "You've got a year before the crisis hits." The level of borrowing implied by the construction sites, the frenzy of real estate speculation, could not be supported by the economy. "How should we persuade the government to listen?" asked a tweedy figure in the audience. "Just keep shouting louder and louder," Aliber replied.

In truth, though, there wasn't much shouting from within Icelandic society. Instead, experts on the Asian meltdown, such as the New Zealand economist Robert Wade, came to make their point. It was the summer of 2007. "I saw that Iceland was running world-record external-payments deficits," says Wade. "I saw that the krona was nevertheless appreciating, not depreciating, as it should have been, and I saw that many of my friends here were loaded up on debt denominated in foreign currency, leaving them vulnerable to a depreciation." When he told a meeting of businessmen, bankers, and government advisers in August 2007 that Iceland was "dynamite waiting to explode," he was dismissed as an alarmist. Dissident Icelandic economists who took up similar opinions were slapped down. One, Thorvaldur Gylfasson, warned that foreign short-term liabilities of the banking system had become fifteen times larger than the central bank's foreign reserves. This, he said, was gross negligence: "The government and central bank were warned, publicly and unambiguously, every step of the way." But the line had been that Iceland is not Thailand. Criticism was not welcome. Fridrik Baldursson, economics professor at Reykjavik University and Oddsson cheerleader, fumed that Iceland was being caricatured as an authoritarian, cliquish society. "Contrary to what a reader unfamiliar with Iceland might think after reading Professor Gylfasson, Iceland is a modern, Scandinavian-style democracy with all the institutions and social infrastructure of its Nordic neighbors," wrote Baldursson. "Iceland is among the least corrupted countries in the world."

But while Oddsson was irrational in his rejection of criticism, he was right to believe that Iceland was being targeted. Sometimes to be paranoid is to be in possession of the facts. At the very latest, after the collapse of the British mortgage lender Northern Rock in September 2007, hedge funds had begun to circle Iceland. Credit default swap spreads for Icelandic banks rose dramatically from mid-summer 2007 to March 2008: essentially a market bet that Iceland would default. At the same time the credit-rating agencies, led this time by Moody's, downgraded sovereign debt or put out a negative watch. The basic problem—or opportunity for short-selling hedge-fund managers—was the size of the banks in relation to the central bank. They were exposed by their heavy borrowing abroad. What if credit dried up—and all the signs were that this was happening worldwide—and beached the banks like the whales in the western fjords?

"Icelandic banks face the possibility of a run on their liabilities," the London School of Economics academic Willem Buiter and his wife, Anne Sibert, told Landsbanki in a paper in April 2008, "and if there were to be a run on their foreign currency denominated liabilities, there is no effective lender of last resort." Landsbanki asked Buiter and Sibert to keep their commissioned report under wraps: it was too market sensitive. Their warning could become a self-fulfilling prophecy. And what a prophecy! "In the current financial crisis, even fundamentally sound banks are threatened with illiquidity," the authors wrote. "In the U.S., a solvent but illiquid bank can count on its central bank to make it a loan against its fundamentally sound but illiquid or temporarily impaired assets. The same is true in the euro area or the United Kingdom. But an Icelandic bank has no such safety net: the readily available foreign exchange resources of the Icelandic authorities are too small compared to the short-term foreign currency exposure of its domestic banks. The market realizes this . . ."

Indeed, soon after New Year's 2008—fireworks were still embedded in the snow—a group of foreign hedge-fund managers met in 101, Ingibjörg Pálmadottir's hotel. According to various reports, they were there to think up ways of shorting Iceland. Why they physically needed to visit the Icelandic capital to do so—Bob Aliber having already done the crane-counting—is not clear. Perhaps they needed to be reassured that the Icelandic central bankers were in hibernation. If so, they could breathe easy. The central bank was still some way from taking the logical steps—taking up swap arrangements with the central banks of Sweden,

Norway, and Denmark (not actually done until May), with the European Central Bank, the Fed, and the Bank of England. This should have been a moment of concentrated, high-speed crisis management at the Black Fort, just up the hill from 101. There should have been an approach to the IMF to revive a contingency credit line. As Buiter and Sibert argued, "The government should be trying to borrow foreign exchange in the global capital markets by offering its national resource wealth, mainly hydro and geothermal energy, as collateral." The government considered such a move to be a sellout; politically unacceptable. And so Iceland in the crucial months—as the clamor of the crisis worldwide was taking on a Wagnerian brio—continued to sleepwalk its way to catastrophe. Which is just how the speculators liked it.

"All the people in the party, except me, of course, are out to short Iceland." That is how an Icelandic bank executive was greeted when he entered 101 one January evening. The encounter ended—how could it be otherwise in a room of hedge funders off the leash together with iron-stomached Icelanders—awash with Icelandic lava-filtered Reyka vodka. The actual outcome was uncertain. But significantly, the trip had been organized by Bear Stearns, which, two months later, on March 14, had to be rescued from bankruptcy by the Fed. A sense of desperation was in the air, a feeling that hedge funds might just have had their moment in history. It had been a remarkable run, with hedge-fund values rising from $38.9 million in 1990 to $1,864.4 billion in 2007. They were the very model of Anglo-Saxon capitalism—typically branded "locusts" by the German Social Democrat Franz Muentefering—raw and fanged and smelling blood. More than 4,800 funds were managed in the United States, 915 in Britain; the rest were bit players. And now their time was passing.

This was more than a bad patch. Academic studies showed that many hedge funds distorted their results as they scrambled to hang on to clients. Other research indicated that investors hoping to get above-average returns from the supposedly sharp-edged talent employed by hedge funds were likely to be disappointed. Many funds had just been counting on a rising market and collecting their 20 percent plus 2 percent fees. In volatile markets, they were proving to be less sure-footed. The mystery was evaporating. "It is extremely difficult to detect, from a fund's track record, whether a manager who is able actually to deliver excess returns is merely lucky, or is an outright con artist," concluded a report called *The Hedge Fund Game* prepared for the Wharton School. Later, when the Bernard Madoff scandal broke, with Madoff pleading guilty to a Ponzi embezzlement scheme whereby billions of dollars of new deposits were used to pay "interest" on investments that were never made, the public shock was muffled because it dawned on people that his methods, though criminal, were not that much different from the legal practices of supposedly aboveboard financial operations. The hedge funders dining in Reykjavik, camouflaging their desperation, forking out for the sushi of Icelandic bankers who were all too aware that they themselves were on the brink of bankruptcy, and together discussing the imminent collapse of the krona—that must have been quite a spectacle, a beggars' banquet.

Not that shorting a country's currency—that is, betting on its decline—is illegal. But David Oddsson's suspicion was that Iceland was being deliberately talked down, that a default was being made more probable by malicious rumor mongering. Richard Portes of the London Business School, having picked up signals that something was afoot, passed the word on to the Icelandic government. In his presentation in April 2008 he quoted Rossini's *Barber of Seville*—the aria of Don Basilio—to explain what was going on. *La calunnia è un venticello*— "slander is a little breeze"—he told the Icelandic Chamber of Commerce, but gathers explosive force in the retelling until it reverberates like a cannon shot, *come un colpo di cannone*. The aim:

> The miserable victim of slander,
> Humiliated, downtrodden,
> Under the scourge of the public
> By good luck, drops dead.

"If the current level of CDS spreads accurately estimated the probability of default, then Icelandic banks and indeed many others would be pronounced dead," argued Portes. But the CDS market was highly distorted. It had started as credit protection, then became a vehicle for speculation. "Now everyone wants to hedge the banks but no one wants to write protection—with very limited supply and rumors fueling demand, the price has gone way up, trading is thin and volatile." A classic hunting ground, in other words, for front-running speculators.

The Icelandic financial regulator opened an investigation. David Oddsson made plain that he thought the country was about to be stabbed in the back. Oddsson had always had an essentially operatic view of the world: emotions were writ large; politics was personal; feuds could not be settled in a single generation; traitors would be unmasked. The standard assessment of David Oddsson is that he is the product of the sagas; in fact, he was happy with the rhythms of Rossini. "There is an unpleasant odor of unscrupulous dealers who have decided to make a last attempt at breaking down the Icelandic financial system," said Oddsson.

All good operatic narrative depends, of course, on the convention of the duel: two men, representing good or evil or some more subtle forces, strut like peacocks and fight like bantams as the big story unfolds through the music. The global crisis has already yielded several such contests. One, between Richard Fuld of Lehman Brothers and Henry Paulson, the treasury secretary, was to shape David Oddsson's own duel with Jon Asgeir Johannesson. Both showdowns were messy.

Dick Fuld, nicknamed the Gorilla by his staff because of his tendency to answer questions with grunts, had risen through the commercial-paper department, on to fixed-income trading, to reach the top of Lehman Brothers. That was in 1994, and Dick Fuld is said to have had a forty-five-second panic attack on the evening before he took on his job. His first aim was to take business from Goldman Sachs; at that time, Henry "Hank" Paulson was a vice president there. By 2005, Paulson, now head of Goldman, was recording ever-larger harvests. "One reason for this," he said, "is that new financial instruments such as credit derivatives have helped us to better manage risk. That is a significant breakthrough." Dick Fuld, who now insisted on being called Mr. Chairman, put a stuffed gorilla in his office. When his people reported on trading loss, he flew into a temper. "It is us against them," he said of Goldman. In 2006 Paulson became treasury secretary and sold his Goldman shares to avoid any conflict of interest. Fuld, meanwhile, fired the head of his commercial-property division, who had suggested that Lehman needed to rethink its business model. Paulson said the main challenges for U.S. policy were in modernizing the global financial architecture.

In January 2007 both Paulson and Fuld were in Davos at the World Economic Forum. Fuld gave a lunch for economics commentators, warning that this could be the year the markets burst. He listed the reasons: the U.S. housing market, the excesses in debt financing, the rising oil prices. But Fuld ignored his own advice. In the autumn of 2007 Lehman bought the real estate giant Archstone-Smith for $22 billion. Paulson and Ben Bernanke, head of the Fed, pushed through a solution for Bear Stearns—J. P. Morgan Chase took it over, the Fed put up $29 billion—on the grounds that a failure in Bear would wreak chaos on the markets. Would Lehman be next?

Fuld held a crisis meeting on the Monday after the Bear takeover. Lehman convinced itself that it was solid, that it had intelligently spread its risks. The markets thought otherwise; its stock tumbled. By April 2008, Lehman clearly saw that it would register its first losses in fifteen years. Fuld and Paulson lunched together; the atmosphere was said to be icy. Paulson had saved Fannie Mae and Freddie Mac, the state-backed mortgage companies, to the tune of $200 billion and come under fire from conservatives, who accused him of creeping socialism. AIG, the insurance group backing Lehman, slipped in the credit ratings. Lehman's third-quarter losses were $3.9 billion. Fuld tried to call Paulson; there was no reply. "They hung us out to dry," said the Gorilla.

On September 12, Paulson summoned a meeting of all the top Wall Street bankers, plus Royal Bank of Scotland, Deutsche Bank, Credit Suisse, UBS, and BNP. "Every one of us is endangered by Lehman," said Paulson. He urged the bankers, in their own interest, to rescue the bank. "Why should we be the ones to bail out Fuld?" asked one of the participants. The Lehman books were studied. By September 14, a Sunday in Manhattan, only Barclays was still interested, providing the U.S. government backed the deal. "We're not giving guarantees," said

Paulson, and at that moment Lehman Brothers, the 158-year-old bank, was pronounced dead. In the list of men held responsible for the global crisis, Dick "Gorilla" Fuld and Henry Paulson now rank high up in the top ten.

The world's financial system was shocked; the markets posed the kind of questions one normally asked after a terrible train crash: Why does one passenger die and another survive? Why let Lehman perish but not Bear? Why one institution, but not the other? The inconsistency bothered investors and set off worldwide panic. That inconsistency derived in part from the breakdown in communication between two erstwhile rivals.

"We couldn't work it out—who would have expected them to let Lehman go?" Jon Asgeir Johannesson was as baffled as every other exposed investor in the world. It is of course a cartoon, crude reductionism, to shrink a crisis spanning several continents to a series of personal enmities. Paulson—if not much of the rest of the world—believed that the meltdown would have occurred with or without the cumulative failures of Lehman and Dick Fuld. The sudden drying up of credit, the breakdown of trust: these were complex processes. And in Iceland too. There, the end of the banking system, though a shock to the ordinary islanders, was being planned for by the bankers themselves. According to Icelandic press accounts, during the first six months of 2008, Landsbanki lent its own board members 40 billion Icelandic krona. And it took over 33 billion krona in liabilities stemming from the failure of XL Leisure. XL was one of Magnús Thorsteinsson's companies—he was a close business associate of Bjoergólfur Thor Bjoergólfsson, who had the controlling stake in Landsbanki. In June 2008 Landsbanki's capital base was 198 billion krona. In other words, the bank handed out some 36 percent of its capital to its shareholders in the few months before it folded. Kaupthing meanwhile lent its board members 39.2 billion krona over the same period. Glitnir passed on 17 percent of its capital.

The money was flowing out of the banks—and out of Iceland. Since the privatization of the banks, 136 Icelandic companies had been registered in the tax haven of Tortola in the Caribbean. The former head of Landsbanki's tax division, Kristjan Gunnar Valdimarsson, registered himself in 2007 as the manager of four limited companies on the tiny island. They in turn bought a chunk of Landsbanki. Kaupthing too served as an agent for 40 percent of the Tortola companies. True ownership was hidden behind the usual mist of dummy holding companies. On a more touching note, many top bankers discovered the virtues and merits of their spouses only days before the meltdown. Houses were suddenly registered in the names of their wives. True love?

As the crisis swirled around it—Merrill Lynch barely saved by a merger with Bank of America; AIG, the world's biggest insurance company, gasping for breath and government assistance—Iceland moved at two speeds. Ordinary Icelanders slumbered through their summer, celebrating the Olympic silver medal of the national handball team, clubbed, hot-tubbed, and pondered, without due alarm, why the krona had sunk from 100 to the euro in March to 140 in September. The commercial and banking elites meanwhile were cleaning out their safe-deposit boxes and renovating their London and New York residences for what could be a prolonged stay. Listen hard and one could have heard the scampering of rats exiting the ship of state. The Lehman collapse, however, marked the end of the summer for the Icelanders, those in the information loop and those outside.

"An unusually sharp-eyed journalist rang me up," remembers Urdur Gunnarsdottir, the diplomat who became one of the most influential figures in spinning the crisis for the government, "and wanted to know why there were so many cars outside the prime minister's office. After all, it was a Saturday and the place was usually dead." It was Saturday, September 20, five days after Lehman, and the world had clearly changed. The Icelandic banks were in big trouble. By the following Thursday, September 25, the chairman of Glitnir, Thorsteinn Mar Baldvinsson, requested a meeting at the central bank. Glitnir needed around $820 million of liquidity infusion. The Bayerische Landesbank of Munich, in trouble itself, had canceled a previously promised $200 million credit line. The Germans said they were overexposed to Iceland and were evidently in a panic (the bank ended up writing off about $1 billion of its $1.8 billion exposure to Iceland). Thorsteinn presented a portfolio of assets as collateral; the bank, he said, was in profit, its foundation solid. Oddsson waved away the collateral—"mere love letters"—and did not seem overly upset that the bank of his archrival was in trouble. The Glitnir team presented a second package, and by this time the shareholders of Landsbanki and Kaupthing were also growing nervous. They offered their own solution: why not merge Glitnir with Landsbanki?

Time was running out. Glitnir—whose main stakeholder, of course, was Jon Asgeir Johannesson—needed to stay liquid, needed to pay debts in October. But according to Thorsteinn, it was impossible to find a central bank staffer for most of the weekend. Eventually they found someone on Sunday afternoon. "Yes," said the official in a bored voice, "the package has arrived in the mailbox, but I haven't had a chance to look at it."

Glitnir was left to sweat until eleven o'clock on Sunday evening; it was September 28, with only hours remaining before the deadline. The Glitnir staff were led to a long table in the darkened canteen and told that the central bank would inject $750 million—in return for a 75 percent holding in the bank. This was less than half the market price of Glitnir. The agreement was already typed up, and Glitnir's executives were requested to sign on the dotted line. After all, everything had to be taken care of before the markets opened on Monday. Glitnir was being given the choice of a disorderly collapse or effective nationalization. The bankers discussed through the night; Glitnir made clear that no agreement would be valid without the signatures of the major shareholders. Early the next morning Thorsteinn headed off to get Jon Asgeir's signature. On the way he got wind of a planned emergency press conference at nine fifteen A.M. in which David Oddsson intended to announce the "saving" of Glitnir. Thorsteinn told the central bank to hold fire until he had obtained Jon Asgeir's signature. Oddsson assured him it would be postponed, then went ahead anyway.

The banks tumbled. The rating agencies immediately downgraded Iceland's sovereign rating. Landsbanki had been using Iceland paper as collateral for refinancing transactions with the European Central Bank. Now it had to find funds quickly—and the Icelandic central bank turned down its request for $200 million. The whole focus of the central bank was to save what was viewed as the strongest bank, Kaupthing, but

Oddsson unwittingly sabotaged even that by stumbling into a row with Britain.

At the heart of this bungling in the Black Fort was David Oddsson's antipathy for Jon Asgeir. Letting Glitnir go was Oddsson's final reckoning, the destruction of the entrepreneur's Great Gatsby–like posing. Without a bank in his pocket, Jon Asgeir's complex retail empire was bound to collapse. Central bankers argue that taking over Glitnir—it was formally nationalized along with Landsbanki on October 7—was a logical step and entirely in line with the international response to the liquidity crunch. Yet the strange unavailability of the central bankers, their sleight of hand, suggested something more: the dark undergrowth of the duel between two men who both claimed to be the true spirit of the capitalist revolution in Iceland.

Banking was traditionally built on personal trust. The giving of credit went beyond the figures in the ledger book to an assessment of character, of a lender's standing in society, his qualities as a man. It was about profit, mutual profit even, but it was also about psychology and morality. As late as the 1960s a British banker would ask of a potential borrower, "Is he a good egg?" Meaning, was he faithful to his wife? Was he a man of his word? Was he likely to conceal the truth? As banking became more sophisticated, from the 1980s on, these questions became less interesting. The giving of credit became institutional: criteria had to be fulfilled, rating agencies ticked boxes and delivered their verdict on who or what constituted a sound risk. Bankers started to see themselves as military commanders surveying the field of battle: they read Sun Tzu in the bath. The focus shifted away from subtle assessment of individual borrowers to the strategic picture.

What happens though to these banking brains when markets do not behave as they should? When the institutions break down, unable to react quickly enough to a collapse in the markets? Then the only recourse is to return to the old methods: calling up golf chums, meeting them, looking them in the eyes. The Lehman Brothers crisis saw a revival of face-to-face encounters. It suddenly became important to read faces again, to smell out nervousness. How close to failure were fellow bankers? The account books could no longer tell the complete story;

the credit-rating agencies were befuddled. Simple human observations, the gauging of character, became a necessary part of business again, the foundation of trust.

That is the moment when individual history matters, and when personal animosity plays a part in a crisis. Should Paulson have cut off Lehman Brothers, let it die? Perhaps not. Did he regret letting Dick Fuld fall? Almost certainly not. Part of the chemistry of the crisis is buried between these two statements. What if your commercial reflexes are dulled by personal antipathy? What if your emotions color complex decisions?

The Icelandic sagas teach us that the political is always personal. "In the end you have to go with your instincts," one platitudinous Icelandic banker told me. "The ship has sunk, you are on a lifeboat, you see two people struggling in the water, and you can take only one. Who do you take? The man you like or the man you don't? It's as simple as that. David understood that, but you know what? Everyone does."

11 : Panic

After all, money disappears, friends die, and you die yourself,
but your reputation remains.
Bjoergólfur Thor Bjoergólfsson, paraphrasing the *Hávámal*

Bankruptcy conjures up dark Victorian images of fire sales, of bailiffs splintering the doors of the dispossessed, of nighttime flight from creditors, of debtors' prison. The first blow to the Icelanders was to their pride. They were used to living with debt, the lot of all fishermen and farmers, but not under such public scrutiny. The frenzied fortnight that followed the takeover of Glitnir and the implosion of the country's financial system had exposed a private shame and made it global. The Icelandic government suddenly found itself the focus of interest in Japan, Australia, the United States: it had become a freak show. Fitting, then, that Geir Haarde chose to give his daily press conference in Reykjavik's theater house, the Idno, with its plush burgundy curtains and its creaking stage. The prime minister stood on the dais like a clumsy conjurer moving a little too quickly between tricks, while his tall assistant, Urdur Gunnarsdottir, prompted him from the wings. Sometimes the trim, boyish banking minister would act as warm-up, presenting the woes of the financial sector. For Iceland, it was an innovation: politics as performance was something new.

It was strange too for the visiting journalists. One had just come in from Afghanistan; two others I knew from covering the 1989 revolutions in Eastern Europe. Now here we all were again, on the Failed State beat. Under the mocking, bruised gaze of the Icelanders we searched the capital for signs of collapse. In truth, nothing resembled the revolutions and coups d'état that were our historical markers. There was no hoarding; this, after all, was the land of frozen food. As long as there was enough stored fuel, the trawlers would set out for sea. The farmers were still selling their sheep. The university year began as usual; there was no stampede of young people for the airport. Overhead, the corporate jets of the oligarchs seemed to be flying out rather than landing, but perhaps that was not so much an attempt at escape and evasion as a way to prevent those nifty Challengers and Falcons from being impounded. No, the Icelanders were in shock, internally taking stock. Does the government now own our houses? What has happened to our mortgages? More deeply, after a drink or two, and in the hope that the foreign guest would not pick up the anxious undercurrent: Who did this to us? Why are we being punished? Were we bad or were we good? Are we victims or perpetrators? Did this calamity come from outside, were we betrayed by our own business class, or did it all spring from deep inside us? Mainly, it was women among women who asked these questions. The men stayed silent and watched the drama unfold.

The government takeover of Glitnir, dubbed "the world's biggest bank robbery" by Jon Asgeir Johannesson, triggered a crisis across the Icelandic banking system. Although in competition, the three banks were intricately linked, just as the collapse of Lehman Brothers in New York impacted every other bank. Because their primary sponsors and borrowers were so connected through cross-ownership, a mutual collapse was almost inevitable. Bjoergólfur Gudmundsson approached the central bank for a $200 million liquidity loan shortly afterward on behalf of Landsbanki, the mother concern for Icesave. "There was substantial pressure on Landsbanki deposit accounts in the UK, and in response to this the British Financial Service Authority steadily tightened the demands it made on the bank," says Ingimundur Fridriksson, one of the three central bank governors. The cental bank turned down the request. The amount was too large, central bank reserves too small. Instead, after a meeting between the FME, the financial oversight committee, and the Landsbanki directors, it was decided that both Glitnir and Landsbanki would be nationalized the following day. An emergency-powers law, rushed through the Althing on that day, gave the FME the authority of a shareholders' meeting in the case of a threatened company. That is, it could dismiss the board of directors and appoint a receivership committee. Trading was suspended on the Icelandic stock exchange.

October 7, 2008, was a turning point for Iceland, the day when it fell off the cliff. The nationalization of Glitnir and Landsbanki was announced, leading to panic in Iceland. What was going to happen to everyone's savings? David Oddsson went on the evening news and tried to reassure the depositors: Icelandic taxpayers were not responsible for the banks' enormous debts, he said, and they would not be paying the debts of those who defaulted on their foreign obligations. The state itself was largely free of debt, and Iceland would stand strong when all this was over. The tone was defiant, and though it didn't have the same pathos as Haarde's "God save Iceland," it was aimed at pitting the island against the rest of the world. The appeal resonated on an island where bad harvests or erupting volcanoes have pushed people together in the face of an external threat. His key phrase was "We do not intend to pay the debts of the banks that have been a little reckless." Implicit in the statement was the promise, we will look after Icelanders first, deal with the foreigners later. The British, who had invested so much of their savings in Icelandic-run banks and holdings, were nervous. Landsbanki was not answering its service phones; many investors felt as if the bankers had run away under cover of darkness.

Alistair Darling, the British chancellor of the exchequer, phoned his counterpart Arni Mathiesen. What ensued was not so much a conversation as an attempt, on the British part, to extract a confession and a pledge from a government that was already in dazed confusion. An IMF team was in town; the empires of at least two oligarchs were falling apart; telephone landlines were jammed as depositers, foreign governments, and news desks tried to discover what was happening. The ruling machine was not equipped for a crisis with global dimensions, so it spent most of the day pretending that the issues touched only the islanders, that with a bit of help—a loan here, a loan there—everything could be settled within the family.

Then came the phone call from Darling. It was partly a clash of cultures between a hard politician flexing his muscles, impatient because the conversation was stretching beyond the twenty minutes he had allocated himself, and a tired small-town wheeler-dealer who plainly wished that everyone would just leave him in peace.

"This is Arni Mathiesen, minister of finance," said the minister as he picked up the phone.

"Hello, we met a few months ago, weeks ago," said Darling in a brisk attempt at small talk.

"No, we have never met. You met the minister of trade."

Ah, these Icelanders! So similar.

"All right, sorry," said Darling.

"No problem," said Mathiesen.

But somehow the exchange did not augur well. What follows is the entire transcript, leaked by the Icelandic authorities.

> Darling: Thank you for taking the call. As you know, we have a huge problem with Landsbanki, we have a branch here, which has got four billion pounds worth of deposits, and it has now been shut and I need to know exactly what you are doing in relation to it. Could you explain that to me?
>
> Mathiesen: Yes, this was explained in a letter we sent the night before last from the Trade Ministry. Since then, we have set out new legislation where we are prioritizing the deposits and where we are giving the FME, the Icelandic FSA authorities, the authority to go into banks, similar legislation to what you have in England, and the Landsbanki is now under the control of the FME, and they are in the process of working out how to do these things, but I think this legislation will help in solving this problem.
>
> Darling: What about the depositors you have got who have got deposits in London branches?
>
> Mathiesen: We have the insurance fund according to the directive, and how that works is explained in this letter, and the pledge of support from the government to the fund.

Darling: So the entitlements the people have, which I think is about sixteen thousand pounds, they will be paid that?

Mathiesen: Well, I hope that will be the case. I cannot visibly state that or guarantee that now, but we are certainly working to solve this issue. This is something we really don't want to have hanging over us.

Darling: People are asking us already, what is happening there? When will you work that through?

Mathiesen: Well, I really can't say. But I think it is the best thing that the FSA be in close touch with the FME about this to see how the timeline works out in this.

Darling: Do I understand that you guarantee the deposits of Icelandic depositors?

Mathiesen: Yes, we guarantee the deposits in the banks and branches here in Iceland.

Darling: But not the branches outside Iceland?

Mathiesen: No, not outside of what was already in the letter that we sent.

Darling: But is that not in breach of the EEA treaty?

Mathiesen: No, we don't think so and think this is actually in line with what other countries have been doing over recent days.

Darling: Well, we didn't when we had the problem with Northern Rock. It didn't matter where you saved money, we guaranteed your savings.

Mathiesen: Well, yes, that was actually in the beginning at least debated. I am sure you cleared that up in the end.

Darling: The problem, I do understand your problem, the problem is that you have people who put their money into a bank here, and they are finding that you have decided not to look after their interests. This would be extremely damaging to Iceland in the future.

Mathiesen: Yes, we realize that and we will be trying as much as we possibly can to make this not a problem. We are in a very, very difficult situation—

Darling: I can see that.

Mathiesen: —and just this week, since we can't cure the domestic situation, we can't really do anything about things that are abroad. So we must first deal with the domestic situation, and then we will certainly try to do what we possibly can, and I am personally optimistic that the legislation that we passed last night will strengthen this part of it. And we, of course, realize what could happen and don't want to be in—

Darling: Yes.

Mathiesen: But the point is also, Chancellor, that we have for months been trying to talk to everybody around us and trying to tell them that we were in trouble and ask them for support, and we have actually gotten very little support.

Darling: I understand that, but I have to say that when I met your colleague and these others, basically, what we were told turns out not to have been right. I was very concerned about the London banking position, and they kept saying there was nothing to worry about. And you know, with the position we are now in, there will be a lot of people in this country who put money in and who stand to lose an awful lot of money, and they will find it difficult to understand how that has happened.

Mathiesen: Well, I hope that won't be the case. I wasn't at the meeting, so I can't say—

Darling: Well, I know that. Can you tell me this, if the insurance fund you refer to, does it have money to pay out?

Mathiesen: They have some money, but as is with most of these funds, it is very limited compared to the exposure.

Darling: Yeah, so you don't know. See, I need to know this, in terms of what I tell people. It is quite possible that there is not enough money in that fund. Is that right?

Mathiesen: Well, yes, that is quite possible.

Darling: Well, that is a terrible position to be in.

Mathiesen: Yes, we are in a terrible position here, and the legislation we were passing through last night is an emergency legislation, and, as I say, we are just trying to ensure the domestic situation so that we can then secure other situations.

Darling: What I . . . I take it therefore that the promise Landsbanki gave us, that it was going to get two hundred million pounds of liquidity back into it, has gone as well.

Mathiesen: Yes, they didn't get that liquidity.

Darling: Well, you know, I do understand your position.

You have to understand that the reputation of your country is going to be terrible.

Mathiesen: Yes, we do understand that. We will try our utmost to avoid that. We need to secure the domestic situation before I can give you any guarantees for anything else.

Darling: Obviously, I would appreciate any help you can give.

Mathiesen: Obviously—

Darling: Sure . . . We would have to explain to people here what has happened. It will, of course, no doubt, have repercussions for others. It really is a very, very difficult situation where people thought they were covered and then they discover the insurance fund has got no money in it.

Mathiesen: Yes, as we said in the letter—

Darling: Okay, I will appreciate whatever help you can give.

Mathiesen: Yes, we will need for the FSA and FME to be in touch on the—

Darling: Oh, I know they most certainly will. I know you were not at the meeting and weren't part of it. We doubted what we were being told then, and I am afraid we were right.

Mathiesen: Yes, that can be.

Darling: Anyway, please keep in touch. Whatever you can do to help, that will be very helpful indeed.

Mathiesen: Yes. If there are any areas on your side, please be in touch.

Darling: All right. I will do that. Thank you very much indeed.

Mathiesen: Thank you.

Darling: Good-bye.

Mathiesen: Bye.

The conversation prompted Darling to freeze the assets of Landsbanki in Britain and set off a downward spiral that extinguished Iceland's last hopes of maintaining its role as an international banking nation. "The Icelandic government have told me, believe it or not, have told me yesterday they have no intention of honoring their obligation there," Darling told BBC Radio on the morning of October 8. Landsbanki had already stopped its Icesave customers from withdrawing or depositing money. Darling told the House of Commons he expected Landsbanki to be declared insolvent. The British FSA had decided that Heritable, a Landsbanki subsidiary, was no longer able to meet its obligations. So, that same day, Darling announced Landsbanki Freezing Order 2008, which froze not only the UK Landsbanki assets but also those belonging to the Icelandic central bank and the government of Iceland. The aim, he told Parliament, was to ensure that "no depositor loses any money as a result of the closure of Icesave."

The authority of the Freezing Order derived from the Anti-Terrorism, Crime, and Security Act of 2001—a piece of post-9/11 legislation in the UK that was supposed to monitor and block the flow of funds between terrorist cells and their masterminds abroad. The relevant passages were contained in sections 4 and 14 of schedule 3 of the act, which requires that the "Treasury believe that action to the detriment of the United Kingdom's economy (or part of it) has been or is likely to be taken by certain persons who are the government of, or resident of, a country or territory outside the United Kingdom." By this authority, Iceland was declared a terrorist nation. This blunt instrument immediately stigmatized all Icelandic operations in Britain and made it impossible for Iceland's third (and largest) bank to continue working. The FSA, said the chancellor, had declared that Kaupthing's UK subsidiary, Singer & Friedlander (KSF), "was likely to be unable to continue to meet its obligations to depositors." KSF was considered to be in default. Darling ruled that he was having KSF's retail deposits shifted to the Dutch bank ING, while the rest of the business would be put into the equivalent of Chapter 11, the breathing space given to companies to save themselves before bankruptcy. A Treasury spokesman said this was "the right cause of action to protect savers, ensure financial stability, and safeguard the interests of the taxpayer."

To the Icelanders, though, it was tantamount to a declaration of war. At one stroke Britain had placed the island on the same level as Al Qaeda, even though it was a fellow NATO partner, and crippled what seemed to Reykjavik to be a healthy bank. Kaupthing had to be nationalized on the same day: the transfer of deposits from KSF had triggered a technical default by the parent bank.

Darling was unrepentant about his dramatic moves, even though the transcript of his conversation with Mathiesen did not actually support his statement that the Icelandic government "have no intention of honoring their obligation" in Britain. Rather, Mathiesen was at pains to say that Iceland would try its best to meet its commitments, after first compensating the Icelanders. Under the directives agreed when Iceland joined the European Economic Area in 1994, Iceland was pledged to pay 20,887 euros to each depositor. The chancellor of the exchequer said, in testimony to the House of Commons Treasury Committee, that the move against Kaupthing had been taken purely on FSA advice but that the bank would have gone down anyway. Kaupthing had no chances of survival. "Anyone looking objectively at the Icelandic banks would find it difficult to come to that conclusion." In other words, Britain had not administered the decisive kick. As for the use of terrorism laws against a NATO ally, Darling argued that the act had been devised to be elastic enough to deal with other problem areas:

"Actually the legislation we used, although it does cover terrorism, also covers the powers that we have to protect the country's general economic interest. Interestingly, when you look back at what happened when the legislation went through Parliament, there was an amendment laid in the House of Lords to try and confine these powers to be used in the case of terrorism, and that amendment was voted down. I think it was contemplated at the time that those powers might be used more widely."

The alternative, he said, would have been to do nothing, and then he would have been asked, "How come you allowed all this money to be taken out?" What was strange, however, was the lack of consultation on the decision. While the Treasury and the FSA are the lead agencies in the UK regarding decisions involving potentially threatening movements of cash, the use of antiterrorist legislation would normally have involved other government departments. The Foreign Office, the security service, and the prime minister should have been brought in on a matter that was being defined, however dubiously, as being vital to national security. The Treasury Committee later rapped Darling's knuckles: "Although the Icelandic banking system was vulnerable to the crisis that has affected the international financial system since 2007, the actions of the UK government in making statements on the capacity and willingness of the Icelandic government to provide assistance to non-Icelandic citizens, whether or not such statements were accurate, turned the UK government from being a seemingly passive observer of events, to an active participant in the market. Given the volatility of the situation, and the vulnerability of Icelandic banks at the time, it appears that the Icelandic Authorities found the UK government's approach ultimately unhelpful."

"Unhelpful" was an understatement. The Icelanders were outraged. Gordon Brown and Alistair Darling were depicted not only in the Icelandic press, but all across the Nordic region, as swaggering bullies. The use of terror law set an uneasy precedent, since it could seemingly be used at will to smash the financial system of smaller states. It would be only a matter of time before the UK Treasury, like the U.S. administration, turned its ire on tax havens, branding them too as terrorist money launderers. The combination of a financial crisis and a security-obsessed world subtly pushed not only the UK Treasury but also the U.S. Treasury Department and the German Finance Ministry into key decision-making roles; foreign ministers and U.S. State Department officials began to appear marginal to foreign policy. Since the conversion of London into a major financial center, it had become the clearinghouse for the transactions of dozens of states. Yet at a critical moment, it elbowed its way to the front of the queue for the lifeboats.

Landsbanki had had 4.5 billion GBP of retail deposits outstanding in its UK branch at the moment of failure; not an insuperable number for Britain, which, like other major industrialized nations, was soon to issue guarantees for sums in the hundreds of billions. But the global crisis—despite the polite facade presented at the G-20 and other emergency summits—has overwhelmingly been a story of everyone-for-himself. When liquidity dries up, the first instinct is to reach for nationally defensive solutions. Darling's reaction was understandable, especially since the failure of Northern Rock: to define the possible removal of capital as a question of national security.

The Icelanders responded in a hostile tone not seen since the last of the Cod Wars. Britain, the imperial bogeyman, was depicted as the source of all of its problems. Ordinary Icelanders organized a witty online campaign featuring children, pets, grandmothers, and fishmongers asking Gordon Brown and Alistair Darling whether they really considered the islanders to be terrorists. Geir Haarde became passionate about the injustice of the British and garnered cross-party support. Meanwhile David Oddsson went on Icelandic television to declare that he knew why the British had used antiterrorist laws, but he could not say because that would be a violation of banking secrecy. What did he mean? That he knew the Icelandic oligarchs were trying to vacuum up the cash in the foreign deposits? That the Russian businessmen who liked to visit the island were making use of a poorly controlled banking system? Rumors had circulated in the London City and in Reykjavik at least since 2005 that the Icelandic banks had been used to recycle profits from Russian enterprises. But no hard evidence had ever emerged. And Oddsson certainly wasn't talking. His enigmatic contribution to the discussion was shrugged off in Iceland—after all, the country was under immense strain—because it was off-message; the point was not to wash dirty linen in public but to find a scapegoat for Iceland's woes, and find one quickly.

That too was to become a feature of the global response as the banking breakdown devolved quickly into a deep recession. Dick Fuld was assaulted in his gym; bankers, the Fed, the Bush administration, Margaret Thatcher, the owners of luxury boutiques, China—all became the butt of public anger. For the first time in history an Icelandic prime minister had to employ bodyguards. "I remember the moment," says Urdur Gunnarsdottir. "I had been receiving irate e-mails and phone calls from a Guernsey-based Icesave customer who had lost everything. The day he rang up and said he was going to kill himself in front of my house, that is when I decided to ask for police protection, and it became clear to me that others had been getting similar threats, that emotions were running high." Although Darling had promised to guarantee British Icesavers, that pledge did not stretch to British investors who had used offshore accounts—so Iceland had become a target, just as Britain had become Enemy Number One in Iceland. For a time it was easier to hate Gordon Brown and burn his effigy than to turn one's gaze inward.

"If old friends leave us in the lurch, it is natural that we turn to new friends," said Haarde. His press conferences in the Idno theater were divided into two. First, he would address the nation by briefing Icelandic reporters in Icelandic, delivering reassuring words to the camera. Then the state television team would leave and the prime minister would speak more freely, sometimes using more combative phrases, in English. Iceland, he understood in the first weeks of October 2008, needed to reach out to the world of suspicious creditors.

"Who does he mean by treacherous old friends?" whispered Marc Fisher of the German edition of *Vanity Fair*, which was itself to become a victim of the credit crunch. "Not just you Brits, surely?"

It wasn't clear; nor was it the Icelandic way to spell things out. Apart from Britain, Iceland felt deserted by the United States, by the Dutch, by the Germans. The Dutch had invested heavily in Icesave, and the Germans in Kaupthing Edge, the online banking service run by Kaupthing. None of them were inclined to rush into putting together an IMF package for Iceland until the Haarde government offered firm guarantees for disappointed savers. Haarde, though, declared that the IMF emergency loan and the Icesave problem were two separate matters. He was wrong. It was not just about the money—$2.16 billion, significantly less than Iceland needed to keep afloat—but about restoring international confidence. That entailed an open confession of all past sins, a gesture that was not part of the makeup of Haarde, Oddsson, or the Independence Party hierarchy. Everything was intertwined. Admit to the world that the banking system had been badly supervised, and the whole structure of power was likely to unravel. That, in turn, made it impossible to embark on credible and urgent reforms, which would, of course, be part of any IMF offer. So the government stonewalled. Iceland's even tinier neighbor the Faroe Islands offered a no-strings-attached loan. The Nordic countries, afraid of contagion, were ready to chip in. But there had to be at least a pretense of domestic concern about the government's role in the global crisis. Finally, grudgingly, Iceland, five weeks after nationalizing the banks, agreed to compensate at least some of the depositers at some time in the future. The result was the $2.1 billion package of loans from the IMF, and a separate $3 billion in loans from the Nordics (Norway, Sweden, Denmark, Finland, and the Faroes), Russia, and Poland, all intended to support a floating Icelandic krona.

But the idea of "negligent old friends" and "helpful new friends" was still part of the Icelandic worldview. And the white knight in the hour of need was no less than Vladimir Putin's Russia. Still flush with oil cash in October–November 2008, Russia suddenly showed itself to be eager to prop up the island. Central bankers, in that first troubled week of October, hinted that Moscow could come up with an additional $5.2 billion. An Icelandic delegation headed for Russia within days—and came back disappointed. But Russian interest had not faded; it had merely become more nuanced. What was going on? Iceland, after all, was a member of NATO; a major U.S. air base had left only two years earlier. The answer seemed to be this: in a financial meltdown when all the old certainties disappear, all that counts is geography, control of resources, and geopolitics. Across the globe, political alignments began to shift.

Prosperity built on easy credit had already changed international relations, shifting the terms of the U.S.-Chinese relationship. One priority of the new Obama administration was to bring China more closely into crisis management. Why? China was effectively bankrolling the United States. U.S. overseas borrowing needs in 2007 amounted to $800 billion; China was running a current-account surplus of $262 billion. China's economic success was dependent on exporting cheaply to the United States. To do so, it needed not only to hold wages down, but also to keep the Chinese currency low. That entailed buying billions of dollars. Niall Ferguson, the economic historian, calls this economic bonding Chimerica. China and America—Chimerica—made up a quarter of the world's population and more than half of global growth since the year 2000. "The East Chimericans did the saving. The West Chimericans did the spending. Chinese imports kept down U.S. inflation. Chinese savings kept down U.S. interest rates." But when the United States stops spending, China is in trouble. That is why the focus of U.S. foreign policy has been moving away from Europe to Asia; economic depression sometimes accelerates change that would otherwise have taken generations to achieve.

Few policy shifts, however, can have been quite as swift as that executed by Iceland in October 2008. The Independence Party, which had ruled Iceland for so long, nurtured a Cold War–era suspicion of Moscow. Others in the political class had a little more sympathy for the Russians: The former Communists in the Alliance Party, led by Olafur Ragnar Grimsson (later president), had come together with the pacifists to resist NATO membership. Some cultural and linguistic purists (such as the former president Vigdis Finnbogadottir) and the left-leaning intellectual elite resented the breadth and depth of American influence. But none of this had translated into a groundswell of sympathy. Only one Russian ambassador, Yuri Retchetov in the early 1990s, had ever made an impact: he had been fluent in Icelandic and reached the populace by appearing on talk shows. More typical was Alexander Rannikh. In a farewell reception in 2005, Rannikh laid into Iceland for being corrupt and having ideas above its station. "I happened to be standing with Thorgerdur Katrin Gunnarsdottir, who was minister of education and is now a big cheese in the Independence Party," recalls a NATO diplomat. "She leaned over and whispered in my ear, 'Asshole.' I assume she was referring to the Russian, not to me."

At the outset of the crisis, Rannikh's successor, Viktor Tatarintsev, floated the idea of a possible $5.2 billion loan from Moscow. Tatarintsev, said David Oddsson, had called him up at seven A.M. on October 7 and said that Kremlin leader Vladimir Putin supported the loan—tempting enough for the Icelandic government to openly announce Russian assistance long before any terms had been settled. By the summer of 2009, the deal had still not been struck. These, then, were Geir Haarde's "new friends," so much more trustworthy than the NATO partners, commented one journalist ironically.

Even in the white heat of the crisis, Iceland must have been aware that no loan from Moscow comes without strings. There is, of course, the mischief theory: that Russia wanted to teach the West a lesson, after NATO's public support for Georgia in the short summer war of 2008, by trespassing in NATO's own backyard. Haarde may meanwhile have been entertaining his own tactical thoughts: perhaps the West would show more solidarity with Reykjavik if Russia was paying court to the Icelanders. But possibly Moscow's interest had something to do with the profound change in the ordering of the north since July 2007, when the Russians planted a titanium flagpole on the floor of the Arctic.

With the northern ice cap melting faster than anyone had expected, the calculation is that global warming will thaw formerly ice-locked Arctic sea-lanes as early as 2015. Various studies suggest the whole summer ice cap could disappear by the year 2040. Since some 25 percent of the world's undiscovered oil and gas are estimated to lie under the Arctic Ocean (according to the U.S. Geological Survey World Petroleum Assessment 2000) there is a great deal to play or, perhaps, fight for. It is the equivalent to 375 billion barrels of oil (Saudi reserves, by contrast, are around 261 billion barrels). Diamonds, platinum, nickel, tin, and gold also lie under the ice. Canada, the United States, Norway, and Denmark (through semi-independent Greenland) also lay claim to a chunk of the Arctic seabed, but Russia has been the most active in restructuring its naval policies to guard and promote its interests in the north. The Arctic is already yielding fruit for Russia. "We obtain ninety percent of our gas, sixty percent of our oil, more than ninety percent of our nickel and cobalt, about sixty percent of our copper, and ninety-eight percent of our platinum from the Arctic area," said Admiral Vladimir Vysotsky, commander of the Northern Fleet, in June 2007. A senior member of the Russian Duma, Andrei Kokoshkin, made clear that the exploitation of the Arctic was above all a military task:

"We have to stand up for our interests in an active fashion, especially in the Arctic . . . We need to reinforce our Northern Fleet and our border guards and build airfields so that we can ensure full control over the situation."

For the Russians, this windfall from climate change has both an emotional dimension and a strategic one. Emotional because control of a newly accessible Arctic would in some way make up for the military humiliation of losing Eastern Europe. "In size and geographical situation, the Arctic could significantly compensate Russia for the losses she suffered as the result of the collapse of the USSR," wrote the military commentator O. Litkova in the naval affairs journal *Morskoy Sbornik* (June 2006). And strategically, Russia would, without having to plow through thick ice, be in command of some of the fastest and most efficient ways of moving goods around the world. Both the Northern Sea Route, north of Russia, and an ice-free Northwest Passage through the Canadian archipelago would open up far shorter routes between Europe and Asia. China would be able to move cargo to Europe via Russia's Arctic route and save more than 20 percent of the shipping time over other routes; the global supply chain would become faster. "You can shorten distribution times and the amount of inventory stored in advance," says Rockford Weitz, head of the consultancy Arctic Futures Initiative.

It will, in short, be a boom time in the Russian north, and Iceland, especially an Iceland resentful of its treatment by the West, its pariah status, can play its part. "Look at the map," says a senior NATO diplomat in Reykjavik, shoving a chart over the table. It shows the world as seen from the north pole, the frozen expanse and the soon-to-be-water areas. "Iceland is about to be where it always thought it was—at the center of the world." Actually, just fringing the arctic circle, it is not exactly sitting on the buried treasure chest. But it has become part of what is being termed the "respacialization" of the north. The Arctic has a function again, and that is transforming all the areas on its periphery. During the Cold War, Iceland's task, and its attractiveness to NATO, was to be part of the G-I-UK (Greenland-Iceland-UK) gap, which policed the movement of Russian submarines into the Atlantic from their all-year-round-ice-free base in Murmansk. Now that could quickly change. There will soon be huge transfers of energy not only from Russian ports but also from Norway. North of Norway's northernmost town, Hammerfest, lies the Snow White development, where liquefied natural gas is to be piped from under the sea, then shipped to North America, fifty-three hundred miles away, passing through Icelandic waters.

An acquaintance who works for the Icelandic coast guard accepts a beer from me at one of Björk's favorite dockside bars. "My job's safe," he says. "These banker kids will be queuing up for training." Sadly, I fail to find a banker-to-coast-guard convert, though a few have switched to trawler work. But Iceland's stake in this respacialization adds up to more than a bit of police work on the increasingly busy high seas.

Russia has been investing massively in modernizing harbors on the Russian Arctic shelf and developing an Arctic transportation system. It may need a refinery in Iceland, or a refueling and repair base. Iceland has again slipped into the strategic frame. Plainly it believes that it is in full control of its sovereignty, that it can adequately balance NATO membership with Russian cooperation. But in its desperation to escape failed-nation status, Iceland has in effect put its geography and its natural resources in hock. The combination of a huge debt, robbing future generations of hope, and an ambiguous international role is the worst of all options. But a year after the crisis broke on its shores, there were no good options. The scope of Iceland's downfall was so complete that all of its most valuable assets, including its natural resources, were beholden to foreigners.

One angry economist cataloged the misery: "The three banks are insolvent, the fishing industry is insolvent, the agriculture industry is insolvent, and most companies are on the edge of insolvency."

More: About 25 percent of home mortgages were in default. The government would be insolvent if not for foreign emergency loans.

"The currency would crash and be virtually worthless if not for currency restrictions and support by the central bank using foreign loans. So the currency is technically worthless," the economist concluded. "If you add up all the debt owed by individuals, companies, fishing, and agriculture, it adds up to twenty to thirty billion euros."

Good reasons for Icelanders to hide under the bedcovers. The government, naturally, could not take such an openly despairing line; having warned of possibly imminent bankruptcy, it spent much of the following months denying it was in default. But in truth Iceland was on a life-support system, with the breathing apparatus provided by an increasingly impatient IMF. Currency restrictions and laws limiting foreign ownership on the island merely masked the stark reality that Iceland had already lost control of its future.

The foreign debts were multilayered, but at the top of the heap of creditors were those foreign investors who held bonds issued by the three banks. These were secured against specifically named Icelandic assets—including Icelandic mortgages, fishing rights, factories, power plants, and income from future electricity sales. When the banks went down, those assets were automatically the property of the foreign bond-holders. The reorganization of the Icelandic banks switched the assets to so-called new banks—New Landsbanki, etc.—and the managers argued that foreign creditors could claim only against the old banks. This was illegal—the Reykjavik government could not unilaterally write off debt—and was little more than a survival reflex, along the lines of keep foreign hands off our assets. But unless one repudiated the whole system of international financing, these were clearly no longer "our" Icelandic assets. It was enough to fly on Icelandair, London to Reykjavik, in the spring of 2009 to sense the new underlying reality. Walking down the aisle, I saw a report, "Privatizing Icelandic Water: Chances and Pitfalls," heavily underlined, on one seat. A few rows down, a man with bags under his eyes had an analysis of Icelandic geothermal power snuggled on his lap. Foreign creditors wanted their slice of a shrinking cake. Iceland was well on its way to losing its sovereignty. Little wonder that the Russians were circling Reykjavik; it had become so vulnerable that it was on the brink of selling out its proud patrimony, its independent energy resources. Iceland had become internationally interesting for all the wrong reasons.

The economist Michael Hudson, sometime adviser to the Canadian and Latvian governments, organizer of the world's first sovereign debt fund, was treated as a welcome prophet when he declared in April 2009 on Icelandic television that the country was being deliberately smashed so that outsiders could carve up the place. "The U.S. and Britain are net debtors on balance," he said, "but when it comes to their stance vis-à-vis Iceland, they are demanding that it impoverish its citizens by paying debts in ways that these nations would themselves never follow." There was a plot, he said: "They know that it lacks the money to pay, but they are quite willing to take payment in the form of foreclosure on the nation's natural resources, land, and housing, and a mortgage on the next few centuries of its future."

In this scenario, the IMF becomes the enforcer of the financial crisis rather than the island's savior. "If this sounds like the spoils of war, it is— and always has been. Debt bondage is the name of the game." Hudson's advice? Icelanders should first assess the magnitude of their debts, assess their possibility to pay, then "toss the ball back into the creditors' court and ask the bankers to explain just how they propose that Iceland should pay, and what they anticipate will be the economy-wide effect of such payment." The Icelanders liked the sound of this advice. It smacked of fighting back rather than passive victimhood. "How can Iceland pay its debts without bankrupting itself, abandoning its social democracy, and polarizing its largely homogeneous population between a tiny creditor oligarchy, and the rest of the population?" It sounded good, rang true to many Icelanders. And yet, what would happen to the independence of a country, to its international standing and credibility, if it refused to pay its bills? That seemed to demand more courage than was available. These were not brave times, not in saga-land, not anywhere.

12 : Anger

*Coal miners used to put a caged canary in their pits. As long as
the bird sang, the air was fine. The Icelanders were the canaries of
international capitalism. And then the air started to disappear.*
Halldor Gudmundsson, writer

Along Skuggahverfi, in a narrow strip between downtown Reykjavik
and the northern coastline, lies a jumble of half-built high-rise buildings and a few older, derelict houses, shuttered, with wooden planks
blocking the doors. This was supposed to be the new Manhattan of
the north: high-ceilinged, big-windowed apartments looking out on
the sea, with state-of-the-art kitchens and underfloor heating, lovingly
finished for the New Rich. Now it is a ghost town. Iceland has had
abandoned communities for centuries, villages that died out when the
farming became too hard, when the young emigrated to Canada or
moved to Reykjavik in search of work. The modern fish quota system
made its contribution too; since the future fish catch could be bought
and sold, whole communities withered away as soon as a trawler owner
sold his fishing quota. The fish swam away. As for farmers living on the
most slender of profit margins, one bad year might bring financial ruin;
they quickly fell behind in payment on their inflation-indexed mortgages. If they were lucky, wealthy bankers would buy up the farmsteads
and use them as bases for hunting. But even that spelled an end to the
neighboring village. So Iceland knows about ghost towns and indeed
about ghosts. In the pre-iPod era children used to be sung asleep with
the lullaby:

Meltdown Iceland

Sofdu svinid thitt
Svartur i augum
Far i fulan pytt
Fullan af draugum

Which Auden translated as:

Sleep you black-eyed pig
Fall into a deep pit full of ghosts

The subpolar Manhattan became a ghost town for thoroughly modern reasons. The credit dried up; the developers ran out of money and so did the potential purchasers. The result was not just an eyesore but a social mess: the residents of the older houses interspersed between the skeletal high-rise blocks had strongly been encouraged to leave. They spoiled the picture; the houses would have to be demolished and so they were bought out. By the spring of 2009, with the days longer and wetter, the place had become an urban graveyard. Someone has scrawled CAPITALISM R.I.P. on the side of one of the buildings. Squatters have moved in. One group converted an abandoned house into a cozy café, the kind of place where you could strum a guitar and check your e-mails. The Reykjavikers cheerfully welcomed the return of some kind of life to Skuggahverfi. The developers, however, did not approve. So, just after Easter, the riot police were sent in, men in black, with a chain saw to hack through barricaded doors and pepper spray to disable the young squatters. The cleanup was nasty, brutal, and short: it was the official end of Niceland.

The Icelandic sense of live-and-let-live was the first real casualty of the meltdown. For centuries, island society had functioned on family lines. Yes, there were feuds and friction between family members, but there was tolerance too—as one might accept an eccentric or rude cousin or give a wayward brother a second chance, and a third. This clannish order had its weaknesses. It was too self-forgiving and encouraged the promotion of the mediocre and complaisant over the heads of the critical and the innovative. But it was cozy (*huggulegt* in Icelandic) and comforting and explained why so many Icelanders abroad yearn to return to the warmth of the native hearth.

The financial collapse, though, brought a rawness to everyday life and fear to the soul. While the Nordic rules still applied, no one was hustled out of the office on the day that the banks went under; no one stuffed the clutter of their desks into a cardboard box. But by November, dismissal letters were in the mail, and three months later the best and the brightest from the financial industry were out of work. Unemployment rose from under 2 percent in September 2008 to 10 percent by the spring of 2009. It was, as in other societies—in Greece, in Latvia, in Bulgaria—the speed of the collapse that whipped up the anger.

Iceland's ancient boom-bust cycles had seen a gradual acceptance of troubled times approaching: the boats returning with empty nets, a season of storms stripping the topsoil. When the bust came, it was plainly ordained by nature, not by man. The Icelanders became phlegmatic, accepting; the women became good housekeepers, bottling summer fruit for the dark months. That was the order of things. The financial crisis of 2008–9 was by contrast asymmetric: it hit the world's periphery faster than the core. Although for a decade or so Iceland had imagined itself to be at the center of the prosperous world, buying triplex apartments on Gramercy Park, tall Edwardian houses with servants' quarters in Kensington, the crash propelled Iceland back into the remote North Atlantic, into the subpolar regions.

Its pride was hurt. The bitter protests against Gordon Brown and his use of the antiterror laws reflected the feeling that Iceland had somehow been expelled from Eden. By what moral right did the British declare Icelanders to be the new pariah? Britain, which had evidently mismanaged its own debt and allowed its own bankers to run wild? Mainly, though, Icelanders were acutely conscious that they had been badly led, steered incompetently and corruptly into the abyss. Yet the political class showed no remorse. David Oddsson was quick to blame Jon Asgeir and the oligarchs; Jon Asgeir blamed both the United States for letting Lehman collapse and Oddsson for not responding intelligently; the Icelandic government blamed the British government. "There is no culture of ministerial responsibility here," says a senior official. "The prime minister will say, 'I didn't order this, I didn't cause that, so why should I step down?' And since the prime minister says that, so do the individual ministers and department chiefs." As a result, no one has an interest in discovering why mistakes were made.

In November, Geir Haarde set up a committee to investigate the causes of the crisis. By December, it had issued one press release. The main threads of Icelandic rule were too intertwined, matted together: The Independence Party had produced not only the prime minister but also the head of the central bank; the party had handed over ownership of one of the key private banks to party loyalists; the private banks in turn lent money to the Independence Party; oligarchs meanwhile paid into the coffers of all parties. The supposedly independent press was either dancing to the tune of the Independence Party or to the oligarchs who opposed it. Remove any one of these components—say, by an ill-judged confession of incompetence—and the whole edifice was likely to collapse.

The merging of the business and political class was not unique in Iceland but was an almost universal phenomenon of the 1990s and beyond, the very essence of modern power. Gordon Brown, after all, had made his left-leaning Labour Party acceptable to the City by virtually proclaiming a merger between politicians and bankers. His London speech to bankers in June 2007 was an extraordinary exercise in mutual congratulation, celebrating the apparent brilliance of his move to operate hand in glove with the financial elite. "This is an era that history will record as a new golden age for the City of London," said Brown. "I want to thank all of you for what you are achieving." The City, he said, was creative and ingenious. "The message London's success sends out to the whole British economy is that we will succeed if, like London, we think globally . . . and nurture the skills of the future, advance with light-touch regulation, a competitive tax environment, and flexibility."

After the financial and accounting scandals that brought down Enron, Britain was under pressure to toughen up regulation. But the prime minister and former chancellor of the exchequer resisted such pressure. "Many who advised me, including not a few newspapers, favored a regulatory crackdown. I believe we were right not to go down that road." Within a few weeks of these incredibly myopic insights, the world, including Britain, was slaloming toward a deep recession, and Brown was having to consider the cost of bailing out his former banking friends. The fusion of interests, of clans and loyalties, was just as evident in the United States. Forget Hank Paulson. Consider Tim Geithner, President Barack Obama's treasury secretary, who as head of the Fed had been offered (but turned down) the CEO job at Citigroup. As a *New York Times* investigation put it, "The Fed is charged with curbing banks' risky impulses, yet its president is selected by and reports to a board dominated by the chief executives of some of those same banks."

It therefore bordered on the hypocritical to attack Iceland's rules for concentrating power and shortchanging its citizens and depositors: a similar process was under way across the globe. Nor was there a flurry of unforced resignations as decision-makers faced the music. Iceland was, it could be argued, merely a concentrated form of the power structures that were in operation elsewhere. Yet the smallness of the society increased the risks of mismanagement: the humiliation of national bankruptcy, the speed with which the middle class was impoverished, the heaviness of personal debt, the almost instantaneous flip from being the world's happiest nation to being a place that could offer no future to its young. So Iceland became not only the first country to go broke, but also the first to chase its government out of power.

It began with a "citizens' meeting"—Icelanders reminding themselves that they could replicate Athenian democracy if leaders failed them. The novelist Einar Mar Gudmundsson opened his speech to that first citizens' meeting with an embittered joke: "A cannibal is flying in first class. The flight attendant brings a menu with several options. The cannibal is quite polite, as cannibals often are upon first impression. The cannibal scans the menu and then says to the flight attendant, 'I don't see anything appetizing on the menu. Would you be a dear and fetch me the passenger list?' I'm not going to compare Iceland's fat cats, who have landed our nation in these dire straits along with the government, with cannibals. Not literally. But after having got their hands on nearly everything, the banks and state enterprises, they seem to have said to the government and supervisory agencies, 'There is nothing appetizing on

this menu. Would you be a dear and fetch me the national register?' "
But Gudmundsson soon made it plain that he was not there to mock but
to stir Icelanders into action: "The government issued its guarantee for
an entire casino—Russian roulette—with the end result of destroying
the good name of an entire nation."

Soon, as living standards started to plunge and people took to the
streets, the uprising gathered force. It became known as the kitchen
revolution because demonstrators used wooden spoons to bang pots
and pans to drown out the proceedings of parliament. In one demon-
stration they hoisted the banner of the supermarket mascot Bonus—a
cartoon pig on a yellow background—onto the parliament building.
The point was to show that politicians showed more allegiance to the
oligarchs than to the Icelanders. These protests had plenty of pathos,
above all, the singing of the rather dirgelike national anthem. Mainly,
though, this was an ironic revolt. Banknotes bearing the image of David
Oddsson's head were distributed, free of course, since he was widely seen
as having betrayed the krona. The popular slogan, printed on T-shirts
and shouted out around the bonfires lit on Parliament Square, was not
exactly Byronic: *Helvitis fokking fokk*, which translates roughly as What
the Fuckety Fucking Fuck. Outside the central bank, a crowd in the
thousands heard a rock band play full volume to intimidate the workers
inside. On one occasion Oddsson had to be smuggled into the building
in the back of a gray van. He took to arriving extremely early.

Food also played a role in the protests. White buildings such as the
prime minister's office could be squirted with mustard and tomato
ketchup and pelted with eggs. One demonstrator, it was said with a grin
in Reykjavik cafés, had demanded his egg back from the government;
eggs were becoming more valuable than the krona. Raw offal and some
blue cheese was also chucked at government buildings—rat food—
but for the first few months the protest movement remained more or
less playful. In December 2008, Gurri, one of Iceland's many witches
(formally honored by First Lady Dorrit Moussaieff), led protesters
toward the central bank and entered the building, carrying a life-size
effigy of David Oddsson, his wild hair accurately represented by gray
yarn. Repelled by police, the short blonde witch, dressed of course

in black, started to spank her effigy—"You've been a bad boy!"—pronounced a spell, then stuffed it in a garbage bag.

Until this moment, Iceland's protest movement was an expression of hurt and a somewhat inchoate demand for change. Its ironic undertone was in part because many in the middle class, now being squeezed between higher mortgage debt and lower real wages, were half aware that they had allowed the political class to get away with their incompetence and bad deals. Now they were demanding that the same class be changed, yet no party was completely untarnished by the years of easy credit. No wonder one of the demonstrations consisted of holding up placards bearing either an exclamation mark (!) or a question mark (?).

The crowd wanted answers as much as action. The U.S. presidential election banging its big bass drum across the Atlantic seemed to rub in the desperation of the Icelandic dilemma. The Americans were preparing for change. What kind of change could seriously address the scale of the national crisis?

In Iceland, the Geir Haarde coalition was no longer really a government; rather it represented the husk of an Independence Party determined to hang on until the last lightbulb had expired in the bunker, and the junior Social Democrats anxious to distance themselves from Haarde without seeming undignified or unpatriotic. The result: instead of rebuilding trust, the government became an almost passive player. On October 24 the government formally asked the IMF for help, both to send a signal to other nations and to stabilize the currency. There was no rush to help: Britain and Holland were adamant that there should be no IMF package until they secured guarantees from Reykjavik to compensate Icesave depositors. Haarde eventually agreed because he had no choice: without the IMF loan of $2.1 billion, Iceland was finished. On November 16 Iceland announced that it would comply with the EU Deposit Guarantee Scheme's directive guaranteeing compensation for up to 20,877 euros for each savings account. The deal, cut in a UK Treasury visit to Reykjavik, was that Britain would compensate its three hundred thousand Icesavers (though not those with accounts in the Channel Islands), and Iceland would pay Britain back after its economy had been propped up by the IMF. "These accounts will be settled in such a way as to ensure that the nation is able to cope with the burden," said Haarde. Three days later the IMF said it would consider the loan.

The horse-trading showed the Icelanders that their government really had no choices and could not in any rational sense be described as a government anymore. More than fifty thousand people had their savings wiped out. The Salvation Army hostel began to fill up not just with alcoholics but with families unable to make ends meet. Car loans became like some obscure punishment from Dante's hell. Taken out in foreign currencies, the loan had to be paid back in a krona whose value was shriveling by the day. The only way out of the squeeze was to take out a newspaper advertisement offering thousands of dollars to anyone willing to take on the car and its bulging debt. A satirical ad appeared online:

> For sale:
> Range Rover (golden), one month old. Driven 200 meters.
> Available NOW—in exchange for food.

"The Range Rover and other SUVs have gone through an incredible transformation," a sociologist tells me. "First they were luxuries, then they were necessities—and you can see the point, you really need off-road vehicles if you hunt or fish or just for getting around in Iceland, it's a rugged place—and now they have become burdens; worse, kind of vampires sucking your lifeblood."

Like many revolts, the Icelandic uprising is a middle-class protest. Ted Gurr, the U.S. conflict theorist, talks of relative deprivation being the most common cause of social violence. Not poverty, but a short, sharp interruption in what was assumed to be a steadily rising curve of prosperity and well-being. This fracture shapes revolutionary movements. The crowd in postcrash Icelandic politics was made up largely of urban Reykjavikers, academics, doctors, poets, dissident economists, young mothers, better-off pensioners. To some degree they were swayed by that most bourgeois of emotions, shame. Shame that Iceland's standing in the world had dropped, that the country seemed to the outside world to be unreliable, that depositors at home and abroad had been betrayed. The stain could only be removed by a public expression of remorse.

In part, the global nature of the crisis allowed the Icelandic business and political class to believe that their troubles came largely from outside. But ordinary Icelanders knew that this crisis, the so-called Kreppa, was not an alien import; rather, it was of the very essence of Iceland, magnifying the island's social fault-lines. So why didn't someone apologize? Icelandic society could only be changed, be better managed, if politicians and businessmen were willing to admit to fundamental mistakes. The longer they were silent—or in the case of the oligarchs, merely absent, tucked away in their London and Copenhagen apartments—the more it seemed as if the discredited elite were trying to share the blame. Along the lines of, you wanted it this way! You wanted houses and cars you couldn't afford! Your demand created the problem! We were just enablers.

The Icelanders withdrew into their Christmas cocoon. In the two months following the meltdown, Icelanders had been in shock, and the shock had atomized the island. The traditional solidarity of Christmas and the long holiday break mutated into a political solidarity—and contempt for the seemingly guilty silence of the political class. When the demonstrations began again in the New Year, the tone was different. The aim was clear now: to bring down the government, to drive David Oddsson out of the Black Fort, even at the risk of seeing the whole architecture of power come crushing down. Now, for the first time, the government began to understand what was at stake. They were not just being barracked by communist agitators but were being brought to account by a nation.

So the atmosphere became raw, edgy. Those in power thought they were being confronted by lynch justice and allowed the riot police almost free hand to defend the institutions of state. Those demonstrating outside began to sniff every hint of weakness, like beagles scenting blood. There were many such pointers. Politicians were buckling under ill health, and although the medical conditions could not in all fairness be ascribed to the crisis, they did take on metaphorical significance. Foreign minister Ingibjorg Solrun Gisladottir, head of the Social Democrats, had been absent for most of the crisis because she was being treated for a brain tumor; President Grimsson underwent heart surgery; and Geir Haarde announced, as a reason for stepping down from the prime minister-ship, that he had developed cancer of the esophagus. All unfortunate diagnoses.

The demonstrators saw weakness politically too, of course; Iceland looked rudderless in the first few months of 2009, with the Icelandic parliament coming back from its Christmas holidays on January 22, after what might seem to have been an unusually long break in the middle of a world crisis. That day Geir Haarde addressed the Althing in his first detailed account of what the government had been doing since the October meltdown. It did not seem like much. Measures had been introduced, he said, to ease the pain of those tumbling into debt. Housing funds were to go easy on loan defaulters, child allowance was to be paid every month instead of every quarter, the unemployed were to be encouraged to study, employers nudged into offering part-time work instead of firing staff. Haarde stretched it out into a catalog of fifteen points, but it amounted mainly to a wish list, along the lines of one compiled by a child before Christmas.

The budget deficit could be financed in two ways, he said. First, the Treasury could make use of its credit balance with the central bank, "which fortunately is very sizable after budget surpluses of recent years." If too much was withdrawn from the Treasury account, he warned, then inflation would soar. Second, Iceland could issue government bonds, but this would boost interest rates. "Neither route is therefore without certain cost to Icelandic households and businesses." Sure enough, Iceland was already suffering from both high inflation and high interest rates. A familiar predicament for the islanders, but acutely painful at a time when the economy was already crippled. Haarde accepted that rebuilding the banking system should be the priority. "This is an enor-mous task, as around eighty-five percent of the banking system has collapsed, which is the most extreme shock ever suffered by any finan-cial system in the world." Haarde mumbled rather than declaimed these words, as a prelude to admitting that his government's policy on banks was to hand over the tricky bits to foreigners to sort out. A Swedish banking expert, long in the pay of the IMF, would supervise a special commission on bank reconstruction. A Finnish financial expert would look at what went wrong on financial regulation. The valuation of the new and the old banks—for they were to be split into two, with the "old" bank (Old Landsbanki) swallowing up the disastrous international liabilities, and the "new" bank (New Landsbanki) concentrating on domestic lending—would be handed over to the UK consultancy Oliver Wyman. This was part of the price of the $2.1 billion IMF loan: a steady surrender of control over the financial sector.

None of this pleased or satisfied the protesters outside parliament. The rallies grew and grew, to more than seven thousand protesters, an almost unimaginable number of people in Iceland, who gathered now every day and not just on Saturdays. They banged tom-toms and lit effigies of politicians until late in the night. There was something tribal about it, but at least they now had a goal: to unseat Haarde, to break the back of Independence Party rule. There were no more vague demands for apologies. "What do you want to happen next, after they've gone?" I asked the people in the crowd that January, and did not get a coherent reply. Some wanted a return to "fairness"; the more radical were so enraged that they went so far as to demand a kind of Nuremberg trial, with Haarde, Oddsson, and the oligarchs jailed on charges of defrauding the nation. The Reykjavik prison was not big enough to house the numbers of people mentioned on this mythical charge sheet. "This economic crisis has hit us with the force of a war," said Einar Mar Gudmundsson. "It will cost us more than a war, not just in terms of lost wealth, but in people—we will lose a generation, maybe two, to migration." By January 2009, having just received his cancer diagnosis, Haarde realized that he could no longer convince the nation that he was indispensable to its resurrection. Power had seeped away from him.

It was time to go. On January 23, a Friday, and the end of a long, noisy week of public protests, Haarde announced early elections and said that, for medical reasons, he would not be running. That was not exactly the triumphant defenestration that the protesters had been hoping for. The announcement of his illness—he left the country within days for treatment in Amsterdam—confused the protest movement and the country. There was sympathy, but also a feeling of having been cheated. "It was a bit cheap," said Gudbjartur Hannesson, a member of parliament for the

Social Democrats. "It would be very strange if you could simply leave behind all the things that have happened and all the bad decisions just by changing one name and one person." The pots and pans had been banged through the night with the aim of banishing a government that refused to show remorse; instead it had merely accelerated the retirement of a single leader. THE FIRST POLITICAL CASUALTY OF THE GLOBAL CRISIS! was the headline in Britain, but in Iceland it did not seem like that. "There was just a kind of emptiness," recalled Magnus, an economics student. But the crumbling of the establishment had begun. Many years ago, walking down a street in Germany, I witnessed a building collapse; underground excavations had weakened the foundation of the four-story (thankfully almost empty) house, and something had opened an undetected crack and pushed it from being into nonbeing. With a dark, deep-throated groan, like that of an aching Caliban rising from his bed, the house fell in on itself. A similar sense of expiry was in Iceland. The government stayed briefly in place, but within two days the boyish banking and commerce minister, Bjorgvin Sigurdsson, resigned and, just before doing so, fired the head of FME, the Financial Supervisory Agency. The great cannibalistic frenzy had begun within the Independence Party.

The interim government, intended to steer Iceland toward the election, was to be a coalition of Social Democrats and the Left Greens, led by the dour Johanna Sigurdardottir. The distinctly leftist administration did not necessarily express the popular mood, but was recognized for what it was: a symbolic act of purification. The Social Democrats had lost some of their innocence by agreeing to be a junior partner with Geir Haarde's compromised Independence Party; both parties had, for example, received a wad of party donations from the banks in 2006. Johanna, nicknamed Saint Johanna by Icelanders, was different. She was from the left of the Social Democrats, had been pushed aside in the contest for the party leadership in 1996 (leading her to declare grimly, "My time will come"), and had a reputation for talking directly to people rather than mouthing slogans. During election campaigns she would go to the huge dockside warehouse that housed Reykjavik's flea market. Next to the dried-fish stands, a scruffy café, much favored by the down-and-out, is warm, cheap, and only three minutes' walk from the Salvation Army hostel. Johanna Sigurdardottir would sit there and listen to their complaints and those of anyone else ready to draw up a chair. That, and her brisk, no-nonsense efficiency—she had worked as a flight attendant in her twenties and would sometimes raise her arms as if pointing to the emergency seats—was apparently what the Icelanders wanted. Not a dramatic shift to the left, but a political class that was willing to show solidarity with the weak. In the rush to prosperity and multiple-car ownership, this had been neglected.

The key requirement of this interim government was that it get rid of David Oddsson. He was the most hated figure in the country. Sitting with the economist Katrin Olafsdottir in her university office, I showed her the list of those deemed worldwide to be most responsible for the financial crash. There were the usual suspects: Dick Fuld, Hank Paulson, Alan Greenspan. A list that had little value except to put faces to aspects of a crisis that seemed so vast, so overwhelming. "If you had to replace these people with those guilty of bankrupting Iceland, whom would you choose?" I asked, spreading out the pictures from the international Wanted List. She singled out the oligarchs, Gordon Brown, Geir Haarde—and then she stabbed at a picture of David Oddsson. "Him!" she said. "Three times—as the premier who politicized the privatization of the banks, as the head of a party which maintained shady dealings with the private sector, and as the central banker who placed inflation targeting above all else." In Iceland's top-ten list of crisis-causers, David Oddsson occupied places 1, 2, and 3.

Not that he saw it that way, of course. He saw no connection between the stepping down of his protégé and his own future. He had a fixed term as bank governor. It was not for a (leftist) prime minister, appointed but not yet elected, to oust the head of the central bank. Had she not heard that the central bank was independent? But the focus of popular anger was shifting away from the government to the bank, and the prime minister, unable to have a telephone conversation with Oddsson (he hung up, claiming a bad line), sent him a letter urging his resignation. Johanna Sigurdardottir understood that she could not sack David Oddsson outright; she could, however, make it clear that if he did not go of his own free will, she could rush through a law stipulating, for example, that the governor of the central bank had to have economic training. Oddsson was a lawyer. Oddsson formulated a letter in reply: he was not going to budge from the Black Fort.

Oddsson's letter revealed much about the siege mentality in the central bank, but also the swagger with which he had dominated the Icelandic political scene for about twenty years. Referring to himself as the "Chairman of the Board of Governors"—to underline that the prime minister was attacking not a person but the representative of a state institution—Oddsson huffed and puffed. How dare she!

"At around the dinner hour on February 2, 2009," he wrote, "a letter was sent by messenger from the Prime Minister to the Chairman of the Board of Governors of the Central Bank of Iceland at the latter's home. The Chairman's place of work, of course, is the Central Bank, and this was a working day. The Chairman's wife, who was alone at home because the Chairman was abroad on business for the Bank, received the letter and laid it aside unopened, as it was addressed to the Chairman of the Board of Governors. An hour later, she learned from a television news program that the Minister had sent the Governors of the Bank letters requesting that they resign immediately from their positions with the Bank!"

Oddsson's letter, subsequently published in the Icelandic press, went on, "If they did not—or actually, in any case—she would present a legislative bill guaranteeing their removal and have it passed. Correspondence of this type, containing poorly disguised threats against government officials, is unique, not only in Iceland but in the Western world. The laws that are designed to guarantee the independence of the Central Bank and prevent political attacks on the Board of Governors have been violated. The responsibility borne by the Minister is therefore great indeed."

The prime minister's use of his noneconomic background as a way of levering him out of power was, he said, risible.

"It is absurd," he wrote, "to assume that a university-educated attorney with more broad-based experience in the administration of economic and monetary affairs than most people can claim is less equipped to carry out the duties of a central bank governor than a person who can present a particular academic degree—for example, a degree in monetary economics. It just so happens that, at the present time, public discussion implies that monetary economics may not be resting on solid foundations after the economic collapse that has occurred all over the globe. In these circumstances, it matters not whether the leaders concerned are Nobel Prize winners or can cloak themselves with other, less impressive credentials."

Why did Oddsson dig in his heels? Did he really believe that if left undisturbed he could have saved the krona? Probably not. But word trickled out of the Black Fort that the central bank governor would resign only after Baugur—that is, his archenemy, Jon Asgeir—was effectively closed down. The duel between the two men, it seemed, was doomed to continue right until Ragnarok, the Judgment Day of all Vikings. Whether or not this was a condition, it happened anyway. Landsbanki called in a loan, and the Baugur empire went under. Jon Asgeir suddenly found himself a pariah in Reykjavik—where he had been pelted with snowballs as he left his wife's hotel—and edged out of London's inner circle of retail millionaires. Baugur's goods and chattels, including its unremarkable but designer-branded office chairs, were put up for sale. Jon Asgeir was furious; as furious as Oddsson, chased out of the central bank. "Landsbanki has kicked me in the balls," Jon Asgeir said. "I am sure that Philip Green [the British fashion retailer] is now dancing in his living room, because he will get many of our companies for next to nothing."

Both Jon Asgeir and Oddsson were sure that they were absolutely essential to the recovery of their institutions, their country. It was a common cry across boardrooms and executive gyms: yes, we made mistakes, but we lived and prospered in freakish times. Now, though, came the cry, now we're indispensable to the solution. Partly they were driven by vanity, but also by a genuine sense that the difference between success and failure is as thin as gossamer. The Jon Asgeirs and David Oddssons had been successful, to an extraordinary degree, and though they were now failures—though failure, of course, was the responsibility of wider forces, or of malevolent conspiracies—they were convinced that their unique talents could turn fortunes around again.

But the true source of their downfall was not a chance shift in the trade winds. Rather, it was a blindness to new, adverse facts, a determination to follow a path that had previously brought results—and a love of risk that bordered on clinical madness. They possessed, one could argue, the wrong hormones. Certainly that is how some of Johanna's supporters saw the situation. She was not only the island's first female prime minister (although Iceland had a popular woman president, Vigdis Finnbogadottir, between 1980 and 1996), but also the first openly gay national leader in the world. Her relationship, in an officially registered union with a journalist and children's book writer, Jonina Leosdottir, was well-known to the Icelanders but attracted little curiosity. With only one gay bar on the island, Icelanders do not stay in the closet long. But to non-Icelanders Johanna's sexuality seemed important, a sign of a more fundamental shift in attitudes. Half of her cabinet were women—not unusual in Nordic societies—and more significant, the heads of new versions of two of the banks were women: Elin Sigfusdottir at New Landsbanki and Birna Einarsdottir at New Glitnir. Their brief was to create domestic-deposit bases, make a go of shaping a conventional, old-fashioned customer-oriented bank, and allow the formerly glamorous and now ruined international departments to sit in a kind of toxic-waste disposal unit.

The only Icelandic investment company to emerge from the crisis relatively unscathed was Audur Capital, set up by two women, Halla Tomasdottir and Kristin Petursdottir, to cater to female investors. "Our ground rule was simple," said Halla Tomasdottir, "we didn't invest in anything we couldn't understand." The economist Katrin Olafsdottir tells me that she is an admirer of the Nobel Prize laureate Muhammad Yunus, who set up a system of microloans targeted at women in emerging economies. "His logic is perfectly applicable to us," says Ms. Olafsdottir, who had been brought into New Glitnir (which would in the spring of 2009 be renamed Islandsbanki). "I don't want to lend to men, they take unnecessary risks, they get drunk and don't give back the money, that's what Yunus said. But if he lent to women, they used it sensibly and paid it back." In a sense the supposedly new orientation toward women echoes the Viking tradition, when the men would disappear out to sea for weeks on end, leaving women to run the households. This is when

Iceland's easy acceptance of bearing children out of wedlock was first established; there was no stigma because the women set the terms of what was socially acceptable while their risk-taking menfolk were busy with their foreign conquests.

The Icelandic approach to dealing with the crisis, essentially to let the women clean up after the party, is part of a broader feeling, though, that the Age of Testosterone may be coming to an end in the financial sector. Blaming the crisis on endocrinology is of course ridiculously reductionist. But some findings suggest a difference in male and female risk-taking. In 2008 a Cambridge University study of seventeen male City traders demonstrated that when they had high levels of testosterone in the morning, they tended to make profits throughout the day, but were also prone to impulsive and exhibitionistic behavior. High levels of testosterone turned risk-taking into a form of addiction. CERAM, the French business school, showed that companies with large numbers of female executives performed better than those run overwhelmingly by men. Companies with fewer female managers showed a more drastic drop in their share price in the first few months of 2008 than those with a large percentage. Michael Ferrary, author of the study "Global Financial Crisis: Are Women the Antidote?" concluded, "The feminization of management seems to be a protection against financial crisis."

It is quite a jump, however, from correlating low female participation with bad business performance to proving that something specifically male caused the financial crash. That is, above all, an ideological feminist assumption. In the United States, only 17 percent of corporate director-ships of companies were held by women in 2008. In Britain it was 12 percent. "Maybe if we had some more women in the boardrooms, we might not have seen as much risk-taking behavior," said Hazel Blears, another female member of Gordon Brown's cabinet. But it was only "maybe." The two Icelandic women who had been put at the helm of the new, "good" banks were not newcomers; they had risen under the ancien régime and were as much a part of the risk-taking culture as their male counterparts. One of the key proponents of credit derivative swaps, of the whole philosophy of segmenting and minimizing risk, was Blythe Masters, a female British economist on the J. P. Morgan derivatives team. She was credited with supplying the theoretical arsenal that was plundered by the people (men) who gambled away the global economy. The conclusion to be drawn from the (undoubted) genius of Ms. Masters and her ilk is that the crisis involved a complex interplay of personalities, institutions, and markets. The gender of the actors was not irrelevant, but it wasn't central. Common sense, however, suggests that a better balance between men and women, not only in the boardroom but also on the trading floors, would produce a more balanced approach to short-term risk.

At the heart of Ms. Sigurdardottir's shift for Iceland was not her feminism—even though one of her first legislative acts was to control sex work in Iceland (this in a country with only two nightclubs)—but a basic egalitarianism. Iceland had for centuries been a society without large income differences, that treasured literacy, socialized health care, and equal access to nature and its resources. Indeed, when David Oddsson took over the prime ministership in the early 1990s, Iceland bore a strong resemblance to a socialist society. That changed rapidly through privatization, and Icelanders came to believe that the egalitarian condition was unnatural. Johanna Sigurdardottir put egalitarianism back on the agenda; her promotion of women was not supposed to right some ancient wrong, a discriminatory imbalance, but rather ease the way back toward a society that treasured solidarity. Women understood Johanna's aims better than men and confirmed her in power in the general election on April 22. By that time, after only a few months in government, Johanna had convinced society that it had to reach deep into itself and fish out special Icelandic virtues: modesty, hard work, a rugged respect for each other.

That was not enough, however, to dispel the anger, the sense of betrayal. On election day, protesters broke into the grand villa of Bjoergólfur Thor Bjoergólfsson in Frikirkjuvegur, Free Church Street. Thor had bought the house from the city council years earlier. The villa had originally belonged to Thor Jensen, his great-grandfather, who had founded one of the country's most influential trading dynasties. Since the current Thor was ensconced in London's distant Holland Park, the protesters were able to climb onto the front balcony of the house, hang some life-size

Viking dolls from the balustrade, and hang a banner declaring WE WERE NEVER ELECTED TO ANY OFFICE, YET WE RULED EVERYTHING. The sentiment was shared by the voters, who elected the Social Democrat and the Left Green parties with a thumping majority.

Seven months after the meltdown, Iceland was still a seething, frustrated, unhappy nation. Hildur Helga encountered a normally mild old woman as she left city hall after casting her vote. "What were these people thinking when they bled their own country dry?" the woman said. "They will never be able to show their faces in this country again, nor will their children, or their children's children." Gurri, the blonde witch, could not have produced a better curse.

13 : Trauma

We peel the skin from the darkness
and cut the head off misery.
Einar Mar Gudmundsson, "A War Cry from the North"

At a certain moment in the Icelandic calendar, night disappears, is whited out. You can read a newspaper at three o'clock in the morning on the deck of a boat—only the silence of the gulls gives a clue to the time—with darkened glasses to protect your eyes from the sun's glare. Not that you really do that, of course; newspapers are too urban to be taken on board the trawlers. The fisherman novelist Jon Kalman Stefansson has a character in his book *Himnariki og helviti* (Heaven and Hell) who after being up with the nets for twelve hours, then goes down to the sleeping quarters to read a translation of Milton's *Paradise Lost*. Many Icelandic writers have done their time on the boats.

Working the Atlantic trawlers is like a performance onstage: everyone knows his part; the timing has to be precise, the physical commitment total. Too many trawlermen die because they briefly forget their lines. No wonder that actors and fishermen are the most superstitious professions. It does not just sap you physically, but also emotionally, no more so than in the summer white haze.

On Icelandic trawlers these nights-turned-day are times of strange spiritual renewal. Belowdecks, bone-tired teenagers hear from the older crewmates about what is demanded of men; about courage and risk. Some read their books aloud. There is talk of foreign places, of what should be done in life, of duty, of the weather and its meanings. Stefan Alfsson, sailor and banker, started out like that. He came from a family of farmer-fishermen in northern Iceland and first went to sea at the age of sixteen. Since then he has worked on dozens of freezing or ice-fish trawlers. "I remember one month-long trip in particular, which was on the *Malmey SK*—my share was around one and a half million Icelandic krona. In 2001 that was worth twelve thousand pounds sterling—the salary in those days of a CEO of a medium-sized company." Stefan went onshore to study navigation and get his captain's certificate, all the while studying business at the University of Iceland. Trawler work paid for the business studies. "But I wanted to start a family and so I decided to stay on land for a bit," he says. He is thirty-six, bright-eyed, intense. "In 2005 I was offered a job in Landsbanki in risk management but switched later to speculative investment, to currency trading." Landsbanki liked that he was a sea captain. "There were similarities between speculative trading and the uncertainties of the sea—both jobs are about tackling the unknown!" He enjoyed the banking, he enjoyed the fishing. "The future is open—I could go back to the financial sector, I could go back to sea, I could go into fisheries management—or I could get my own boat."

The assumption that the island would turn in on itself—that has proved to be false. Stefan's story was taken up by at least one visiting writer as a metaphor of Iceland's amateurish adventurism: from fish to finance and back to fish again—a retreat from the world. Yet, Stefan's story is not unusual in Iceland, where farmers became fishermen and vice versa, where people have often held down two jobs simultaneously (if only to service escalating loans), and where the community is so small that clan structures rather than an artificial class system provide the mechanical workings of the social clock. The sea does not represent a lower civilizational plane for the Icelanders. Rather, it is the essence of the island and defines the place at a time of crisis, just as it defines it during calmer times.

The immigrant workers, above all the Poles, were returning home, and though unemployment was rising above 10 percent in 2009, there was a creeping shortage of people ready to do manual work in the supermarkets, to fix sinks, scrub the fish, and wash the dishes. For the Poles a collapsed currency meant no money could be sent home to pay their mortgages; just as "hot money" leaves a country during a crisis, so too do the new migrants. Suddenly Poland seemed richer than Iceland. A few Icelanders took their turn on the migrant wheel: some were recruited into the Norwegian police force; others worked the ferries between Sweden and Finland. Unlike the emigration wave in other troubled times, however, people had no single, obvious destination; casual work was drying up across the globe. The Icelanders became prisoners of the crash, frustrated that their revolt, their kitchen revolution, had not actually changed their lives. In May 2009, state television featured the case of a disabled single mother of three children; she had been able to buy her own apartment five years earlier for ten million Icelandic krona ($44,444). But due to the inflation indexing of all personal loans and mortgages, her mortgage had risen, despite years of regular payments, to eighteen million krona ($80,000). She was no longer able to keep up with payments and faced eviction. Debts were mounting across Icelandic society, and in contrast to the rest of the world, interest rates—near zero in the United States—were going through the roof as Iceland struggled to batten down 12 percent inflation.

The new Social Democrat–Left Green government seemed unable to deal with housing debt, the issue that most concerned the nation. Instead, it appeared to many Icelanders to be losing its bearings in an ideological fog. One of its first measures was to impose a tax on fizzy drinks to improve the dental health of the nation. The new sugar tax was absurd: soft drinks were already 63 percent more expensive than the European average because of the weak krona, inflation, and tariffs. The Icelanders wanted to be liberated from debt, not be given lectures about tooth decay. But the Icelandic government was faced with the double bind affecting all governments in the crisis: it had been forced to take a more interventionist role in the economy (nationalizing the banks), yet found itself marginalized, unable to shape society because of the sheer force of the crisis. It had responsibility without power. The problem with the banks—in what seemed to be the worldwide consensus—was that they had elevated profit above client service. The idea of profit as something that resulted from satisfying the customers had been inverted in the 1990s. The effect was a dangerous concentration of profit-generating activities in a single institution. "What was Bear Stearns doing investing so heavily in in-house hedge funds?" asks the former broker Philip Augar in his book *Chasing Alpha*. "What was Lehman Brothers doing investing so heavily in commercial property and in being so highly leveraged? What was Royal Bank of Scotland doing running an unbalanced funding book, chasing growth through ill-judged acquisitions, and getting to a size when an accident threatens the whole system?"

The Icelandic banks had swollen to such enormous proportions that they continued to dominate the state even after they had failed. In theory, Iceland followed the good-bank, bad-bank model, with the "good" versions of Kaupthing, Landsbanki, and Glitnir running domestic business, and the contaminated international departments being placed in quarantine. Yet this did not alter the mentality in the banking world. A country facing bankruptcy naturally called in loans, and the three big banks did so, driving Baugur toward bankruptcy and shaking the empire of magnates such as Robert Tchenguiz. Landsbanki pulled the plug on Jon Asgeir; Kaupthing turned on its biggest customer and onetime shareholder, Tchenguiz. The bank claimed to have extended loans of 900 million GBP to offshore firms controlled by the Tchenguiz Discretionary Trust—equivalent to 46 percent of deposits held by the bank. Under state management, Kaupthing pushed for repayment. TDT surrendered some of its assets; Kaupthing sold them at bargain prices. The nationalization of the banks thus fractured the relationship between the banks and the oligarchs.

Yet the informal connections continued. The wives of Agust and Lydur Gudmundsson—the owners of the frozen-food company Bakkavor and former co-owners of Kaupthing—decided they needed a break from the crisis and traveled to a party in Oman. They belonged to the same Champagne Club, a jet-set holiday club, as the wife of Kaupthing ex-CEO Sigurdur Einarsson. Other oligarchs meanwhile found enough cash to buy distressed companies and property that had reverted to the banks because of loan defaults. The real estate agent Högni Kjartan Thorkelsson discovered that banks were resistant to change. "I found three tenants for a large property that had been represented by the banks," he says. "The place was empty, making no money and in effect costing the taxpayer money. Yet when I suggested that they come down with their rent, they stubbornly stuck to prices pitched for the market in summer 2007—as if nothing had changed in the world."

It would be naïve then to think that banks can heal themselves, or that a state-run banking system could somehow become an engine of reform. The core of the financial crisis was that the integrated-investment-banking model had created giant institutions; this jeopardized independent, objective advice, made for conflict of interest. Several countries, such as the United States and the UK, not just Iceland, gave banks extraordinary political clout. It was, after all, under Britain's New Labour Party, and its then chancellor of the exchequer, Gordon Brown, that the political and the financial classes officially declared themselves to be partners for life. Under New Labour, the City of London was dubbed in government "the big end of town." The financial sector had become the national wealth creator. Essential for a modern left-leaning government: you cannot pursue social democratic goals if there is no wealth to redistribute.

In the United States, with its right-leaning government under George W. Bush, the same market revolution occurred, with similar effect on the ability of banks to dictate the political agenda. The essence of this market revolution was a compact between political leaders who were willing to soft-pedal on regulation and tolerate an extraordinary bonus system, and financiers who offered a form of national resurgence that went well beyond old-fashioned manufacturing and old-fashioned values. The unhappy result, when the market revolution failed, was that political leadership was discredited. It had allowed the bankers to become a state-within-a-state and had, in so doing, abdicated from one of the prime tasks of government: to protect and encourage the stability and well-being of its citizens. Little wonder then that governments came tumbling down in Latvia and Iceland, that Greece and Bulgaria looked shaky, that the Brown government found itself in the political doldrums, and the Republicans in the United States were trounced.

The coziness between the business and political sectors made change difficult; more important, it confused the necessary debate about how we should be living our lives. One earnest discussion concerned the long-overdue end of the rule of Milton Friedman and his disciples at the University of Chicago. Their belief in the "rational expectations hypothesis," which posits clearly defined and universally understood economic laws stemming from the market economy, had, it was claimed, misled a generation of decision-makers. The assumption was that government spending would increase inflation. Since everyone accepted this as an immutable law, no stimulus program could ever boost employment; "rational expectation" led everyone to raise prices and wages as soon as the government intruded in the marketplace, and that in turn meant no jobs could be created. That sounded like an ideological conclusion, and indeed it was; the Friedmanites wanted the state kept at bay.

David Oddsson had embraced the Friedman philosophy; indeed, even Milton's son David Friedman was awarded junior-hero status after writing a paper celebrating the way that Iceland had privatized its justice system in the thirteenth century. "Icelandic institutions might almost have been invented by a mad economist to test the lengths to which market systems could supplant government in its most fundamental functions. Killing was a civil offense resulting in a fine paid to the survivors of the victim." Not all the leaders of the Western world were Friedmanites. Ronald Reagan's aphorism ("The nine most terrifying words in the English language are 'I'm from the government and I'm here to help.' ") had been treated as received wisdom. But for three decades, market-as-ideology was a reaction to the apparent failure of the mixed economy, the stumbling, chaotic 1970s. And it had seemed to be going so well: inflation had been tamed, Communism made redundant, and Eastern Europe, and more important, China, had become active players in global capitalism. These thirty years could, on reflection, be seen to have been a heroic epoch.

The trick was to retire early enough; a trick missed by David Oddsson. The failure of the model should have become progressively obvious as the crises multiplied (the 1987 market collapse, the 1994 bond-market crash, the 1997 Asian currency crisis, the 2000 dot-com failure); when rational expectations were no longer quite so rational, the American business model no longer such a surefire thing. Only the 1930s had seen such frequent financial upheavals. Paul Volcker, a champion of the system that imploded, had to admit in a 2008 speech, "Simply stated, the bright new financial system—for all its talented participants, for all its rich rewards—has failed the test of the marketplace." Those words were the rhetorical equivalent of the felling of Lenin's statue in Eastern Europe; an act of ideological surrender.

Yet to admit dysfunction, to accept that the maximization of share-holder value might not be the best way to guide business, was not quite the same as peering into the deep recesses of the soul. Something had gone amiss with the way of the world. Bringing back Maynard Keynes, turning back the ideological clock and rustling up trillions of dollars to prevent a repeat of the Great Depression, was certainly a sign of government resolve. It answered a popular need for assertive political leadership. And about time too! said the global crowd. The state had become a kind of night porter, sleepily watching over the vacated premises, while the bankers went off to their lavish banquets. But the sudden reawakening of government initiative did not address the strange brew of emotions felt by ordinary people: the sense of victimhood, guilt, self-hatred, and anger. We had, it seems, been cheated and at the same time let ourselves down.

What had happened, not only in Lutheran Iceland, was that people had deserted the Protestant work ethic. This ethic, as formulated by Max Weber, was that happiness should be earned and therefore deferred. By saving for the future, the good Protestant created the capital that was needed not only for social prosperity but also for an individual sense of worth and well-being. But in the modern postwar world the capitalism of the small saver—trusting in the permanence and honesty of big banks—was undermined by the rise of consumer fetishism, the urgency of purchase artificially stimulated by the media, advertising, and indeed the banking industry. Daniel Bell, the U.S. sociologist, called this a "cultural contradiction of capitalism," but he was writing in 1976, before this work-save-spend conflict had been raised to new levels by debt-driven capitalism. I remember, as a child in Britain in the 1960s, how déclassé it seemed when the neighbors bought a television set on layaway; in those days, it was a no-no and seen as vulgar, a sign of decline.

The Icelanders understood debt because banks have to support fishermen out of season, the collateral being as-yet-uncaught fish. This debt was not regarded, as in some other Western societies, as a spiritual burden, but rather as a kind of compact between bankers and fishermen. The unspoken duty of the fisherman was to live soberly and within his means when he was not at sea. This latter obligation was guaranteed by the women who ran the household budget. That domestic ordering went haywire when banks encouraged debt—aware that debt was profitable—and helped remove the guilt of spending the revenue from what had not yet been fished out of the sea. Something similar was happening across the industrialized West. The savings rate in the United States fell to around zero by 2007, when it needed to be closer to 30 percent to pay the pensions of a population that was living longer. The fully funded state-pension scheme made it easier for Icelanders to believe that their debt-driven behavior was not a betrayal of future generations. That, nonetheless, is what it remained: delusional short-termism, a delight in the present.

That capitalism has contradictions does not mean it is doomed. The Marxist narrative—that technology would set the forces and relations of production against each other, that an increasingly impoverished proletariat would hurtle toward revolution—does not take into account the way that capitalism has spread wealth. The people of Iceland even now, with the ball and chain of debt pulling at their ankles, are incomparably better off than their fathers and grandfathers. The nation-bonding myth's claims that the grand- or great-grandfathers of many Icelandic businessmen grew up in turf cottages may be exaggerated, but the fact remains that a capitalist Iceland has modernized fast, reducing poverty.

Iceland may therefore be showing some superficial signs of returning to traditional values—a boom in knitting and homemade bread, an exhibition of love letters plastered in the windows of bankrupt shops—but it has not embraced a postcapitalist ethic. Financial crashes have always formed part of social learning. Carlota Perez, the Venezuelan economist, traces a pattern whereby innovation holds out the prospect of great wealth, which in turn generates speculative investment. Stock and asset prices soar, finance rules, and anything inhibiting its ascendancy is seen as antisocial. Then comes the crash: in 1797, 1844, 1893, 1929, or 2008. There is social upheaval. New, better-adapted institutions then arise, followed by a period of creative growth. Bismarck's creation of a state pension scheme was in response to a fear of revolution. The foundations of the modern welfare state were laid in response to the Great Depression. Thus crisis—even in Iceland, where individuals are the most deeply affected—will naturally create opportunities, not only for sharklike entrepreneurs smelling bargains, but for social change.

Capitalism has both failed Iceland and not failed it. An MIT study in 2003 examined fifty-six countries and concluded that states that had liberalized their financial sector and had encountered serious financial crises had a higher long-term per capita income than those that had protected their markets. One indicative comparison is between Thailand and India between the years 1980 and 2002. India took the path of steady growth and only gradually liberalized its capital markets. Thailand by contrast had enormous growth, punctuated by crisis and heavy losses. Per capita growth in Thailand was 163 percent in the study period, while India's was 116 percent. True, Thailand was hit particularly hard by the 1997 Asian crisis, but it also recovered with astonishing speed. "Iceland is not Thailand," Thorvaldur Gylfasson was told by complacent central bankers when he warned of a meltdown in Iceland. But what if Iceland really is an Atlantic Thailand, falling hard but bouncing back, exactly because of its openness to the world? The prediction that Iceland would now undergo a radical change in mind-set and embrace the cautious, prudent growth models expounded by Nordic capitalism seems to be off the mark. Although Reykjavik's financial system in 2009 was in the hands of we-told-you-so Norwegian and Finnish custodians, the Icelanders were still pondering how they could best exploit the openness of their economy. And it seems to me, from my strange vantage point in the nightless summertime of Reykjavik, that their instincts are correct. There was no point in creating a culture of victimhood. No point either in trying to turn back the clock and reinvent the island as an appendix to Norway or some other well-wishing Nordic neighbor. Iceland needed the regenerative power of capitalism, the kind of solutions that can only come from freeing the entrepreneurial spirit. The difference, after the meltdown, is simple: capitalism had to become a servant rather than a master.

Part of this adjustment means thinking more deeply about the uses of capital. Iceland felt itself strong and happy—not always a natural combination—when it found out that its GDP per capita was higher than that of the United States. What did that GDP statistic signify? Very little, though the sense of prosperity certainly contributed to the bubble psychosis. Iceland, like many other societies, had misread the meaning of GDP. Rating the success of a society requires other, more significant measures. Just as Iceland was hit hardest and most rapidly by the financial crisis, so it may now be the first to understand that rebuilding a damaged society entails more than restoring the traditional growth indicators. It was at the top of well-being charts not just because it had accelerated out of poverty, but because it had a smoothly functioning, state-funded health system and a developed ecological awareness. These elements—pure water, clean air, geothermal energy—are what anchor Iceland and ensure that it will not simply allow the return of a new generation of Viking-oligarchs. These natural resources cannot become gambling chips in bubble activity.

Bankruptcy or near-bankruptcy does, nonetheless, force a country to lay its wares out on the counter of the pawnshop. Many of Iceland's natural resources are in hock to foreign creditors. The glass-clear rivers, it seems, have been given a market value. That offends the Icelander, hits at the essence of his sense of nationhood—and defines the limits of capitalism. "The ruling Independence Party thought that harnessing Iceland's natural energy and selling it to huge companies such as Alcoa and Rio Tinto would solve the problem," says Björk. "Now we have three aluminum smelters, which are the biggest in Europe—and they want to build two more in the next three years. That would require new geothermal power plants and the building of dams that would damage untouched wilderness, hot springs, and lava fields." The danger, says the singer, who is regarded as a near-prophet by younger generations in Iceland and as a naïve irritant by right-wing politicians, is that Iceland's economic malaise will make industrial growth—effectively the selling off of the island's natural habitat—seem to be the only option. The future, she argues, is rather in developing innovative green technologies than in sucking up the lifeblood of the nation. "We missed out on an industrial revolution, and my hope was that we would be able to skip it immediately and go to sustainable high-tech options."

The singer has set up a nature investment fund, earmarking some of her royalties for green start-up companies. Starry-eyed perhaps, but the search is on in Iceland for an alternative to industrialization, rather than a world without banks; capitalism as servant, not master. For all her music-world idealism, though, Björk had caught the zeitgeist not just of an Iceland determined to hang on to its rugged, unsellable beauty, but of developed societies that suddenly felt the need to anchor themselves on land. Predictably, fewer people flew abroad on long-haul holidays after the crisis, but this was more than a nod to shrunken budgets and carbon neutrality; it seemed to express a genuine need to stay in and cherish familiar terrain; a return not so much to basics, to carpentry and gardening, as to modesty, and to localism.

The crisis had been oversold as a global disaster; it was not quite like that. The acceleration in changes to the climate—that was global. But the economic meltdown was rather a worldwide phenomenon, an interlocking of different financial, economic, and social crises across the planet. The crisis had at least four levels, and they hurt varying societies in varying ways. First, a credit crunch spread out from the United States and crippled the banking sector in much of the developed world. Second, the housing market sharply contracted, especially in the United States, the UK, Spain, and Ireland. Then, capital and debt problems were caused by the rapid withdrawal of foreign-bank lending, with exchange-rate volatility for people who borrowed in foreign currencies. Latvia and Hungary were on the brink of following Iceland into a national breakdown. Finally, the collapse of global demand struck every export-dependent society.

The United States was able to muffle some of the impact of this multiple shock, but the Icelanders were rocked by all four crises. As a result, every one of its institutions came under scrutiny and was found wanting. This process happened across the planet—a desperate struggle to keep up with, and understand, the pace of decline—and again Iceland was a microcosm. One could not hide from this crisis, not even on a chunk of volcanic rock in the northern Atlantic. The first question in Iceland, as in the United States and the UK, was, why did the markets, and the high priests, fail us? The overtrusting, underskilled shepherds of local-government financing, who threw away taxpayers' money on bad investments? The school governors, the guardians of retirement funds for policemen, firemen, park rangers, and teachers? Did they lose our savings? Or was it the bankers and fund managers, the investment elite, who exploited our eagerness to make a profit, then sold us a dud product or a berth in the investment fund of a failing country? Or the financial regulators who waved through decisions made by institutions that needed closer scrutiny? The accountants? The auditors? The press? Or has government let us down?

These seem like pertinent questions, and studying Iceland brings one closer to understanding the institutional failures. But the search for the guilty deflects from the more awkward question, why did we fail ourselves?

Iceland shifted faster than most societies from the baying pursuit of its discredited leaders to a discussion about values and a reappraisal of policies. It was small and had wished itself big; this, a year after the meltdown, seemed clear. But apart from an acknowledgment of the hubris of it all, the slightly unhinged ambition to be a global player, practical issues had to be faced. A trading island had to stay open to the world. There was no serious protectionist option, no prospect of autarchy. Yet, as Stiglitz and other economists had warned, smallness in an interlocked world was usually a liability at time of crisis. Why did a community of three hundred thousand need its own central bank? If Iceland could get by without an army, then why not without its own currency? And what did independence really mean in a world where sovereignty was being constantly eroded?

At a time of crisis it meant gritting teeth and abandoning entrenched positions. For decades Iceland had resisted joining the European Union because of the danger that foreign fleets would fish its waters dry. By July 2009, though, the Icelandic parliament voted (albeit narrowly) to open negotiations with Brussels. The result could still be overturned by a referendum, but a start had been made: the price of national sovereignty had been cut. And the government took the first steps to restoring the credibility of its banks by injecting some $2.1 billion in the summer of 2009, an attempt to build up foreign-exchange reserves. Iceland, it seemed, was waking from its crisis-induced coma.

The meltdown made Icelanders think more deeply about what was important to their lives and to their nationhood. What if Iceland joined the EU and took over fisheries policy? Iceland had rational policies to tackle overfishing; the EU did not. The apparatchiks in Brussels shook their heads: the Icelanders, they said in a discreet yet audible undertone, were still in the grips of megalomania. Not content with buying up the

British high street and biting chunks of American Airlines or Saks Fifth Avenue, now this tiny country—with a population equivalent to that of a mere suburb of the Belgian capital—wanted to overhaul the fishing habits of twenty-seven other countries! And announced their intentions even before being admitted to the magic circle.

The Icelanders brooded on the alternatives. One could, for example, adopt the euro without joining the European Union—Montenegro had made a similar unilateral move, and Ecuador had declared itself to be part of the dollar zone. The drawback would be that Iceland would be unable to influence directly the European Central Bank. These were the deliberations of a small nation, all but broken by crisis, and they revealed a great deal about how the meltdown made all affected countries think more carefully about their identity.

In the United States the crisis accelerated a self-questioning, revived a sense of curiosity about the world that helped bring about a change in the presidency. The 9/11 assault had exposed the vulnerability of the United States, and it had responded by growing an armadillo shell. The global meltdown prompted a different kind of introspection. The conclusion this time round was not that militant Islam, the Foreigner, was threatening the American way of life. But rather, a question: Are we living our lives correctly; what makes life worth living?

Iceland too had felt its vulnerability and had been scared by the insight. Geologically on the fault line between Europe and America, Iceland thought of itself as a founding European culture with American esprit. Its road to a modern economy had largely come through America; its continuing development, its future stability, seemed to be linked with Europe. Ultimately, though, Icelandic identity had to be found within the confines of the island; in the often baffling relationship between the submetropolitan sophisticates of Reykjavik and the inland wilderness where, barely two hours' bumpy SUV drive from the headquarters of failed banks, you can lose yourself among the scree, where water meets rock, and where in the lunar vastness of it all not a human is to be seen, nor evidence that a man or a woman has ever set foot on the lava stone. You can bring a megaphone out of the trunk of the car and shout your anger and your voice will disappear, caught up like a kite in the wind.

Acknowledgments

Natasha Fairweather, my agent, and George Gibson, my U.S. publisher, hatched the idea of writing about this extraordinary island and its role in the rupture of the financial system. I am grateful to them for introducing me to a society that has shown real grit in the face of ruin. I stayed at the Reykjavik house of Hildur Helga Sigurdardottir, a formidably well-connected commentator who fed me enough meatballs and stories to last a lifetime. Sigurdur Jokull Olafsson, a bright investigative journalist and researcher, deftly steered me around the island and its powerful clans; this book really could not have been written without him. Alp Mehmet, the best British ambassador to Iceland since Andrew Gilchrist, read the manuscript as it took shape, opened his contacts book, and made shrewd suggestions; he is a good friend of Iceland. With his usual crisp efficiency, Tom Whipple looked into the way that the Icelandic crisis tangled up so many lives and gummed up so many institutions in the UK.

I have talked to, and been entertained by, scores of Icelanders over the past year. The conventional wisdom that all Icelanders know each other is wrong; it is a complex place with all sorts of invisible walls. I was alerted to them by Gylfi Magnusson, Katrin Olafsdottir, Thorvaldur Gylfasson, Urdur Gunnarsdottir, Halldor Palsson, Stefan Alfsson, and many others who have either been named in the text or whose identities have been masked. Some have become friends.

Books written at speed need a support team. Mine included Heike Cornelsen, helped in the later stages by Silke Schneider, who put the book on the screen. Nancy Miller edited with real intelligence. My son Philip kept feeding me links. Ruth Elkins made some shrewd suggestions about the narrative structure and stuffed me with vitamins. James

Harding, editor of the *Times*, gave me the necessary time off and was never less than enthusiastic. Richard Beeston, my benign foreign editor, stopped the wolves attacking my sledge. This book is dedicated to Mary Hammond, a dearly loved and respected aunt, and her late husband, Alan, who first sparked my curiosity about Iceland back in the 1960s, in a different world.

Thanks to you all. Any errors in the text are, of course, of my own making.

Dramatis Personae

The Oligarchs

Samson Group: banking, pharmaceuticals, and football
Bjoergólfur Gudmundsson, his son Bjoergólfur Thor Bjoergólfsson, and
his friend Magnús Thorsteinsson
(Company portfolio: Landsbanki, Straumur Investment Bank, Novator,
Actavis, Eimskip, XL Leisure, West Ham United)

Baugur Group: banking, food, and fashion empire
Jon Asgeir Johannesson and his father, Johannes Jonsson. Kristín
Johannesdottir, sister of Jon Asgeir. Ingibjörg Pálmadottir, wife of
Jon Asgeir
(Company portfolio: Baugur Group, Gaumur Holding, Glitnir, FL
Group, Hamleys, House of Fraser, Bonus, Hagkaup, Mosaic fashion)

Fons Group: investments in banking and airlines
Palmi Haraldsson
(Company portfolio: Sterling, FL Group, Glitnir, Stodir)

Oddaflug: airlines, breweries, and banks
Hannes Smarason
(Company portfolio: FL Group, Icelandair, Finnair, American Airlines,
Royal Unibrew, EasyJet, Glitnir)

Bakkavor and Exista: the frozen-food kings, and bankers
Brothers Lydur and Agust Gudmundsson
(Company portfolio: Bakkavor Group, Exista, Kaupthing bank, Siminn,
VIS)

Samskip: investment banking
Olafur Olafsson
(Company portfolio: Samskip, Kaupthing bank)

The Bankers of Reykjavik

Kaupthing (including Kaupthing Edge)
Sigurdur Einarsson and Hreidar Mar Sigurdsson, CEOs of Kaupthing
  bank

Glitnir
Bjarni Armansson and Larus Welding, CEOs
Thorsteinn Mar Baldvinsson, chairman of the board

Landsbanki (including Icesave)
Halldor J. Kristjansson and Sigurjon Arnason, CEOs
Bjoergólfur Gudmundsson and Kjartan Gunnarsson, chairman of the
  board and vice chairman

The Godfather and His Independence Party Consiglieri

David Oddsson, PM and central-bank governor
Geir Haarde, finance minister and PM
Kjartan Gunnarsson, vice chairman of the board at Landsbanki
Styrmir Gunnarsson, editor in chief of *Morgunbladid*
Jon Steinar Gunnlaugsson, lawyer and now Supreme Court judge
Hannes Holmsteinn Gissurarson, professor at the University of
  Iceland
Kari Stefansson, CEO of Decode

Dramatis Personae

The Opposition

Olafur Ragnar Grimsson, president, and his wife, Dorrit Moussaieff
Ingibjorg Solrun Gisladottir, former foreign minister
Halldor Asgrimsson, leader of the Progressive Party and former prime minister
Johanna Sigurdardottir, now prime minister and member of the Social Democrats
Steingrimur J. Sigfusson, now finance minister and member of the Left Green and former opposition leader

Bit Players

Jon Gerald Sullenberger, former business associate of Jon Asgeir's and key player in the Baugur court cases in Miami and Reykjavik
Jonina Benediktsdottir, former girlfriend of Johannes Jonsson of Baugur
Tanni (Toothie), David Oddsson's German shepherd
Gurri, blonde witch

The Pots-and-Pans Revolutionaries

Björk, singer
Hördur Torfason, singer and musician
Einar Mar Gudmundsson, writer and holder of the Nordic Council's Literature Prize
Andri Snaer Magnason, writer and opinion maker—green activist

The Dissident Economists

Katrin Olafsdottir, lecturer at Reykjavik University
Thorvaldur Gylfasson, professor at the University of Iceland
Vilhjalmur Bjarnason, chairman of the Icelandic independent investors

Gylfi Magnusson, professor at the University of Iceland and now
  minister for business affairs
Jon Danielsson, lecturer at London School of Economics

Notes

CHAPTER 1: FALL

The most accessible history of Iceland for the non-Icelandic reader is Gunnar Karlsson, *Iceland's 1100 Years* (London: Hurst, 2005).

2   perched at the top of the international happiness and satisfaction scales: According to the Human Development Index, Iceland was the "best developed" country in the world for 2007–2008. Its GDP per capita between 2001 and 2008 fluctuated between fifth- and tenth-highest in the world.

CHAPTER 2: PRIDE

12   "Two thousand out of a Reykjavik population": Alda Sigmundsdottir is founder of the influential blog icelandweather report.com.

13   "We have no concept": Author interview, January 2, 2009.

13   Robert Wade's Reykjavik speech can be read in full at http:// www.economicdisasterarea.com/index.php/uncategorized/ robert-wades-speech-in-reykjavik/.

15   Celtic wives and slaves: Recounted in Magnus Magnusson, *The Vikings* (Gloucestershire, England: The History Press, 2003), pp. 179–208.

17   "The Nazis have a theory": W. H. Auden and Louis MacNeice, *Letters from Iceland* (London: Faber and Faber, 1937), p. 117.

18   On the expulsion of Jews from Iceland, see Vilhjalmur Orn Vilhjalmsson, "Iceland, the Jews, and Anti-Semitism, 1625–2004," *Jewish Political Studies Review* 16, no. 3–4 (Fall 2004).

19   "A young Icelander at North Quay": War diary for 146th Infantry Brigade, April 4, 1942, Imperial War Museum, London.

20   "Well dressed, well fed, and virile": Amalia Lindal, *Ripples from Iceland* (Akureyri, Iceland: Bokaforlag Odds Bjoernssonar, 1962), p. 150.

21   Halldór Laxness's experiences taken from Halldór Gudmundsson, *The Islander: A Biography of Halldór Laxness* (London: MacLehose Press, 2008), p. 135.

23   "Couldn't we have done it without the Americans?": Andri Snaer Magnason, *Dreamland: A Self-Help Manual for a Frightened Nation* (London: Citizen Press, 2008), p. 120.

24   "Obviously we would have wanted to observe the base": Arnaldur Indridason, *The Draining Lake* (London: Vintage, 2008), p. 85.

26   The conversation between George Bush and David Oddsson from July 6, 2004, is quoted in full in Magnason, p. 147.

CHAPTER 3: CARVE-UP

29   "*Something* went wrong": Tina Brown, "Did We All Go Mad?" *Daily Beast*, December 15, 2008, http://www.thedailybeast.com/blogs-and-stories/2008-12-15/did-we-all-go-mad/p/.

34   In the 1950s one of Loftleidir's ramshackle DC-3s . . . crashed into Vatnajökull: John Griffiths, *Modern Iceland* (London: Pall Mall Press, 1969), pp. 84–85.

37   "Russia's new capitalist elite": Chrystia Freeland, *Sale of the Century* (London: Abacus, 2006), p. 16.

37   "For decades": Author interview with Thorvaldur Gylfasson, February 2009.

Notes

Chapter 4: Respect

46 "The rich weren't just getting richer": Robert Frank, *Richistan* (New York: Piatkus Books, 2007), p. 3.

47 "Now we are seeing a rampant re-feudalization": Peter Sloterdijk, "Unruhe im Kristallpalast," *Cicero*, January 2009.

50 According to Illugi Joekulsson: See Illugi Joekulsson, *Ísland Í Aldanna Ras 1976–2000* (Reykjavik: JPV Forlag, 2002).

51 "This is about respect": Luisa Kroll, "Thor's Saga," *Forbes*, March 28, 2005.

52 For more on the privatization of Russian breweries, see Chrystia Freeland, *Sale of the Century* (London: Little, Brown, 2005), pp. 81–83.

Chapter 5: Duel

59 "There's a hall called Glitnir": Snorri Sturluson, *Prose Edda*, trans. Jean I. Young (Berkeley: University of California Press, 1954), p. 55.

60 "He compensates for inadequate information": Quoted in Robert Misik, "Das Ende des heroischen Unternehmers," in *Blätter für deutsche und internationale Politik*, February 2009, pp. 63–64.

61 "She got to know people": David Cannadine, *Class in Britain* (New Haven: Yale University Press, 1998), pp. 171–76.

65 "The newspaper industry is the marketing arm": Daniel Bogler interview with Danny Schechter, "Financial Crisis: A Media Failure?" available at http://www.editorsweblog.org/analysis/2008/11/financial_crisis_a_media_failure-print.html.

67 The FL-Icelandair share dealings follow the account in Oli Bjoern Karason, *Stodir FL Bresta* (Reykjavik: November 2008).

72 The *Thee Viking* case draws on documents presented to the Circuit Court in Dade County Florida, case no. 02–29149 CA11, *Gaumur v. Jon Gerald Sullenberger*.

76 "And when the banks were less cooperative": Author interview with Katrin Olafsdottir, February 2009.

Chapter 6: Bonus

79 "In the '80s double-digit inflation rates": Kristof Magnusson, "Inflation Will Pay," *Financial Times Deutschland,* October 13, 2008.

80 "Welfare in Iceland": John Griffiths, *Modern Iceland* (London: Pall Mall Press, 1969), p. 93.

82 "In a future age": Quoted in Griffiths, pp. 80–81. Apart from building the earliest automatic calculating machine and being prescient about Iceland, Babbage invented the ophthalmoscope and, in 1827, the logarithm table. In his later years he waged a war against organ-grinders.

84 "The war saved us from the Depression": Andri Snaer Magnason, *Dreamland,* p. 155. His film was shown in Reykjavik in the spring of 2009 and was regarded as a powerful call to reject the aluminum industry.

84 "The other Nordic cultures have the concept of *lagom*": Author interview with Urdur Gunnarsdottir, January 2, 2009.

86 "If you wanted to borrow even a piffling sum": Author interview with Högni "Huck" Kjartan Thorkelsson, February 2009.

Chapter 7: Delusion

94 The John Cleese Kaupthing commercial is available on YouTube, youtube.com/watch?v=nc1eRmk7ijc.

98 "I was screaming blue murder": Phil Green interview, *Sunday Times,* September 8, 2002.

105 For more on Dorrit Moussaieff, see interviews in the (London) *Sunday Times* (Rosie Millard, "Dorrit Moussaieff: How to Revive Iceland," February 1, 2009); and *Portfolio* magazine (Joshua Hammer, "Ice Storm," February 2009).

Notes

109 For Dorrit and Stephen Schwarzman, see Trista Kelley, "Female Nudes Crafted from *Financial Times* Lure Bank Barons," Bloomberg.com, June 22, 2008, bloomberg.com/apps/news?pid=newsarchive&sid=a7mg06V9WPH8.

Chapter 8: Bubble

112 "Membership of the EEA" Gylfi Zoega, "Iceland Faces the Music," *Vox*, November 27, 2008, voxeu.org/index.php?q=node/2621.

113 "The global financial crisis of 1998–99": Joseph Stiglitz, report for the Icelandic central bank, "Monetary and Exchange Rate Policy in Small Open Economies: The Case of Iceland," Central Bank of Iceland, Working Paper no. 15, November 2001.

114 "When I raised these issues with top central-bank managers": Author interview with Thorvaldur Gylfasson, February 2009.

114 Grimsson speech to the Walbrook Club, "How to Succeed in Modern Business," October 10, 2008, can be accessed at http://www.grapevine.is/Author/ReadArticle/How-to-Succeed-in-modern-business-Olafur-Ragnar-Grimsson-at-the-walbrook-club.

121 "None of us had ever heard of them": Comments recorded in "Banking Crisis: The Impact of the Failure of the Icelandic Banks." House of Commons Treasury Committee. London, Stationery Office Limited, April 2009.

Chapter 9: Invasion

126 "We were hoping to open all six beds": Author interview with Khalid Aziz, April 2009.

130 "a Scot, defiantly playing the bagpipes": Sir Andrew Gilchrist, *Cod Wars and How to Lose Them* (Edinburgh: Q Press Ltd, 1978), p. 85.

134 The school board in Whitefish Bay, Wisconsin: Charles Duhigg, "From Midwest to M.T.A., Pain from Global Gamble," *New York Times*, November 1, 2008.

135   "Risk and Return": London Audit Commission, "Risk and Return: English Local Authorities and the Icelandic Banks," March 2009, available at www.audit-commission.gov.uk.

141   Catherine Cowley: *The Value of Money: Ethics and the World of Finance* (Edinburgh: T & T Clark Ltd., 2006). Also see an interview in the (London) *Evening Standard*, April 15, 2009.

Chapter 10: Denial

147   *Manias, Panics, and Crashes*: Charles Kindelberger, *Manias, Panics, and Crashes: A History of Financial Crisis*, 3rd ed. (New York: Basic Books, 1978).

148   Vince Cable: Vince Cable, *The Storm: The World Economic Crisis and What It Means* (London: Atlantic Books, 2009).

149   "The Wall Street CEO cannot interfere": Michael Lewis, "What Wall Street CEOs Don't Know Can Kill You," in *Panic!: The Story of Modern Financial Insanity*, ed. Michael Lewis (New York: Penguin, 2008), p. 341.

155   "Icelandic banks face the possibility of a run": Willem Buiter and Anne Sibert, "The Icelandic Banking Crisis and What to Do about It," Centre for Economic Policy Research, Policy Insight no. 26, October 2008, http://www.cepr.org/pubs/PolicyInsights/CEPR_Policy_Insight_026.asp.

157   "The miserable victim of slander": Richard Portes, "The Icelandic Financial Sector and the Markets," presentation to the Icelandic Chamber of Commerce, April 2008, available as a .pdf document at http://faculty.london.edu/rportes/Iceland%20international%20financial%20sector.pdf.

Chapter 11: Panic

168   The transcript of the Darling-Mathiesen conversation from October 24, 2008, can be accessed at http://www

.icelandreview.com/icelandreview/search/news/Default. asp?ew_0_a_id=314205. The Icelandic government has released correspondence with the British and Dutch governments and a collection of official memoranda. An index of the documents can be found at http://eurooffice.is/news/?p=400&i=14. My thanks to Mar Kristjonsson for providing access to the documentation.

175 "Actually the legislation we used": Comments recorded in "Banking Crisis: The Impact of the Failure of the Icelandic Banks," House of Commons Treasury Committee, London, Stationery Office Limited, April 2009.

179 Chimerica: Niall Ferguson, *The Ascent of Money* (New York: Penguin Press, 2008).

Chapter 12: Anger

186 "Sleep you black-eyed pig": W. H. Auden and Louis MacNeice, *Letters from Iceland* (London: Faber and Faber, 1937), p. 143.

Chapter 13: Trauma

206 "What was Bear Stearns doing": "The City of London's Golden Decade Went Wrong; Interview with Philip Augar, author of *Chasing Alpha*," *Financial News* (London), April 27, 2009.

Index

Note: Icelandic names are alphabetized by the forename followed by the patronymic.

Index

Bank of America, 161
Bank of England, 156
Bank of Japan, 125
bankruptcy of Iceland
    approaches to solving, 9–10, 216
    Britain and, 167–175, 187, 191–192
    David Oddsson on, 144–145, 167, 178,
        187
    debt and, 144, 152, 182, 183, 184, 206
    duels of, 163, 199
    early warning signs of, 4, 124–125, 139,
        147–148, 154, 161
    effects of, 213, 215–216
    Geir Haarde's announcement of, 2,
        142–144
    global financial crisis of 2008–2009 and,
        3, 193
    interim government and, 196–200
    journalism and, 65, 145, 165–166, 167,
        173, 175, 177, 180
    mismanagement of risk and, 152
    national pride and, 165, 187, 189, 192
    oligarchy and, 58, 167, 176, 184, 188, 193,
        197, 207
    opportunities for social change and, 211
    panic and, 167
    political class and, 4–5, 7, 8–9, 12, 54, 187,
        193
    radicalizing effect of, 7–9, 12, 14
    responsibility for, 197
    sovereignty and, 183
    tolerance as casualty of, 186–187
    villains versus victims of, 127–128,
        135–141, 152, 160–161, 166, 176–177,
        214–215
    welfare state and, 13
Barings Bank, 150
Baugur Group
    acquisitions and, 96–103
    bankruptcy of, 207
    dominance of, 108, 109
    fishing expeditions and, 95
    Glitnir and, 117, 119
    Jon Asgeir Johannesson and, 60, 62, 72–73,
        74, 199
    Jonina Benediktsdottir and, 74–75
    Kaupthing Bunadarbanki's alliance with,
        116
    leaders of, 48
    media bill and, 108–109, 110
    Reynir Traustason and, 66
    Unity Investment and, 118

Bayerische Landesbank of Munich, 161
Bear Stearns, 150, 151, 156, 159, 160, 206
Bell, Daniel, 210
Benediktsdottir. *See* Jonina Benediktsdottir
Benediktsson. *See* Bjarni Benediktsson; Einar
    Benediktsson; Hallgrimur Benediktsson;
    Svein Benediktsson
Bernanke, Ben, 159
Big Food Group, 97, 99, 105, 120
Bill's Dollar Stores, 62
Birna Einarsdottir, 200
Bismarck, Otto von, 211
Bjarnason. *See* Vilhjalmur Bjarnason
Bjarni Benediktsson Jr., 35
Bjarni Benediktsson Sr., 35
Bjoergólfsson. *See* Bjoergólfur Thor Bjoergólfsson
Bjoergólfur Gudmundsson
    acquisitions of, 100
    bankruptcy and trial of, 50–51, 54–55, 57
    bottling plant of, 51–53
    David Oddsson and, 63
    Hannes Smarason and, 118
    Independence Party and, 49, 55, 56, 58, 63,
        65, 71
    Landsbanki and, 44, 54–55, 56, 71, 139,
        166
    Morgunbladid and, 65, 66
    ostentation of, 48–49
    Samson Group and, 48, 68
    Thors family and, 49–50
    Verslunarskoli and, 61
Bjoergólfur Thor Bjoergólfsson
    ambition of, 53, 56
    arrest of father, 51
    birth of, 50
    bottling plant and, 52–53
    Britain as rival, 129, 130, 131
    critics of, 58
    David Oddsson and, 63
    Eimskip and, 57
    Hannes Smarason and, 117, 118
    Landsbanki and, 139, 160
    ostentation of, 48–49
    protests against, 202–203
    Samson Group and, 48, 68
    Viking identity of, 59
Bjoernsson. *See* Sveinn Birkir Bjoernsson
Bjorgvin Sigurdsson, 145, 196
Björk (singer), 40, 80–81, 83, 108, 111,
    213–214
Black, Conrad, 106
Black Fort. *See* Icelandic central bank

Index

Index

Index

Index

Index

Index

IATA (International Air Transport Association), 34
Ibudalanasjodur, 89
Icelandair, 33, 34, 35, 67–69, 108, 117, 118, 119, 183
Iceland Express airline, 48
Icelandic banks
  assets of, 6, 43, 44, 120, 122, 145, 183
  bonds issued by, 183
  bonuses in, 87, 93, 116, 120–121, 123, 150
  and Britain, 121, 126, 127, 128, 132–133, 135–141, 167–175, 176
  business class and, 108
  capital ratios of, 139
  collapse of confidence in 2006, 145–146
  credit default swap spreads for, 155
  credit ratings of, 124–125, 127, 138, 139, 146, 155, 163–164
  crippling of, 11
  David Oddsson on foreign expansion of, 145
  deregulation of, 13, 55–56, 68, 85, 86, 121–122
  disproportionate size of sector, 6, 144, 207
  economics of, 86–87
  exclusion of foreign banks, 43, 44
  Glass-Steagall Act and, 85–86
  growth of, 122, 146, 155
  homeownership and, 93
  loans in foreign currencies, 123
  modernization and, 93
  power of, 13, 58, 85
  privatization of, 6, 32, 37, 42, 43, 44, 46–47, 55, 68, 76, 85, 86, 87, 90, 115, 120, 160, 197
  profit and, 206–207
  rebuilding of, 194–195
  self-enrichment of banking class, 90–92
  women as heads of, 200
Icelandic central bank
  analytic reports of, 146
  bankruptcy of Iceland and, 58, 188
  David Oddsson as governor of, 6, 30, 31, 114, 116, 117, 119–120, 121, 122–124, 125, 152, 162, 164, 197–199
  Fitch and, 139
  inflation targeting and, 123–124, 197
  liquidity of banks and, 161–163, 164
  memorandum on state of banks, 144–145
  protests against, 190, 193
  siege mentality in, 198
  size of, in relation to banks, 155

state power and, 71, 80, 112–113
Stiglitz on, 113, 152
swap arrangements and, 155–156
warnings unheeded by, 154
Icelandic economy. *See also* bankruptcy of Iceland
  boom-and-bust cycles of, 9, 23, 78, 85, 187
  as bumblebee economy, 80
  competitiveness of, 30, 31, 38, 48, 67, 112
  government's interventionist role in, 206
  growth of capitalism in, 48–49
  as ideologically driven, 115
  independence of, 111
  inflation and, 23, 32, 33, 38, 62, 66, 79, 112, 123, 194, 206
  liberalization of, 65, 67, 112, 152
  oil crisis of 1970s and, 79
  openness of, 212
  regulation of, 37
  Russian economy and, 55–56
  size of, 14, 111, 113, 144, 153
  transparency of, 116, 146
Icelandic founding myths, 15, 84
Icelandic parliament. *See* Althing
Icelandic Stock Exchange, 44, 90, 113, 167
Icelandic temperament, 10
Icesave, 127–129, 132–133, 146, 166, 173, 177–178, 191
Illugi Gunnarsson, 108
Illugi Joekulsson, 50–51
independence
  conditional nature of, 16–17, 22, 23
  history of, 15–16
  modernization contrasted with, 14, 15, 23
  occupation and, 17, 19, 20–21, 23–24
Independence Party
  bankruptcy of Iceland and, 178, 179, 188
  banks and, 43, 44
  Baugur Group and, 108
  Bjoergólfur Gudmundsson and, 49, 55, 56, 58, 63, 65, 71
  coalition with Social Democrats, 38, 153, 196
  David Oddsson and, 33, 38, 47, 51, 63–65, 67, 71, 77, 89, 109
  election of 1996, 89
  FL Group and, 95
  H. Bens family and, 35
  influential families of, 35
  Keflavik air base and, 25–26
  Kjartan Gunnarsson and, 56
  Morgunbladid and, 64, 89

Index

Progressive Party and, 50, 89
protests against, 195
siege mentality in, 77
waning power of, 153–154, 191, 196
India, 212
Indridason. *See* Arnaldur Indridason
ING, 174
Inga Jona Thordardottir, 117
Ingibjörg Pálmadottir
    Baugur Group and, 48
    fashion knowledge of, 103, 104, 105, 107, 147
    Hannes Smarason and, 119
    101 hotel and, 48, 104–105, 106, 107, 155
Ingibjorg Solrun Gisladottir, 145, 193
Ingimar Haukur Ingimarsson, 51–53
Ingimarsson. *See* Ingimar Haukur Ingimarsson
Ingimundur Fridriksson, 166
International Air Transport Association (IATA), 34
International Monetary Fund (IMF), 156, 167, 178, 183, 184, 191
Islandsbanki, 35, 68, 118

Jackson, Robert, 143
Japan, 4, 88, 125, 165
Jarry, Alfred, 31
Jensen. *See* Thor Jensen
Jews, 18
JJB Sports, 99
Joekulsson. *See* Illugi Joekulsson
Johanna Sigurdardottir, 196–200, 202
Johannes Jonsson, 61–62, 72, 74–75
Johannesson. *See* Jon Asgeir Johannesson
John, Elton, 2, 48
Johnson, Samuel, 93
Jon Asgeir Johannesson
    American business model used by, 70, 76
    on bankruptcy of Iceland, 187
    Britain as rival, 129, 130, 131, 132, 147
    critics of, 58
    as David Oddsson's nemesis, 42, 43, 60, 63–65, 67, 69, 70, 71, 73, 75, 76, 77, 107, 108–109, 116, 158, 163, 187, 199
    fashion industry and, 48, 72, 96, 99, 103–105, 107, 118, 147, 199
    fishing expeditions of, 95
    Geir Haarde's trip to New York and, 145
    Glitnir and, 43, 59–60, 76, 116, 119, 139, 162, 166
    Hannes Smarason and, 69, 116–119
    international market and, 62, 76, 77, 96–104, 107, 109

investigations of business practices, 71–74, 77, 96, 98–99
    Landsbanki and, 207
    Lehman Brothers and, 28, 160
    media interests of, 64–66, 108–109, 110, 116
    as mold-breaker, 46
    as New Viking leader, 48
    philanthropy and, 98
    supermarkets of, 61–62, 63, 66–67, 72, 96–97, 99, 101–103, 105, 147
    trophy assets of, 147
    Viking identity of, 59–60
Jonasson. *See* Hermann Jonasson; Palmi Jonasson
Jon Helgi Gudmundsson, 69
Jonina Benediktsdottir, 74–75
Jonina Leosdottir, 200
Jon Kalman Stefansson, 204
Jon Olafsson, 42, 116
Jon Sigurdsson, 12
Jonsson. *See* Johannes Jonsson; Trygvvi Jonsson
Jon Steinar Gunnlaugsson, 31, 33, 73, 75
Jon Steingrimsson, 4
journalism
    bankruptcy of Iceland and, 65, 145, 165–166, 167, 173, 175, 177, 180
    business class and, 35, 65–66
    global financial crisis and, 65–66
J. P. Morgan Chase, 159

Karahnjukar dams, 83
Kari Stefansson, 31, 40–41, 69
Katrin Olafsdottir, 76, 81, 87, 93, 112, 116, 197, 200
Kaupthing
    acquisitions of, 118, 121, 126, 128
    architecture of, 11
    assets accumulated by, 6, 43, 44
    Baugur Group and, 120
    Britain and, 127, 133, 174
    capital base of, 160
    celebrity ads of, 95
    commercial practices of, 115–116
    credit ratings and, 139
    deposit ratio of, 146
    growth of, 122
    liquidity of, 162–163
    loans and, 90
    merger with Bunadarbanki, 48, 116
    nationalization of, 90, 174

239

Index

Index

forms of, 10
Icelandic banks and, 93
of Icelandic society, 22
independence contrasted with, 14, 15, 23
poverty reduced by, 211
U.S. as modernizing force, 21–23, 25–27,
216
Monroe Doctrine, 20
Montenegro, 216
Mont Pelerin Society, 69
Morgunbladid, 64–65, 66, 67, 75, 92, 153
mortgages
bankruptcy of Iceland and, 166, 183, 191
bundling of, 148
debt and, 90, 206
inflation indexing of, 206
subprime mortgage funding, 65–66, 87,
139, 148–149, 151
Mothercare, 99
Moussaieff, Dorrit, 105–108, 109, 115, 190
Muentefering, Franz, 156

National Cat Protection League, 127
national identity
bankruptcy of Iceland and, 216
Björk and, 81
as Cool, 2, 3, 58, 66, 80, 85, 93, 109, 127
David Oddsson and, 77, 85
modernity and, 25
NATO membership and, 15
National Power Company, 83
NATO
Cod Wars and, 131
Iceland's membership in, 14, 15, 22, 83,
174, 178, 179, 180, 182
natural resources, 3, 15, 182, 184, 213
nature, privileged access to, 95
Nazi Germany, 17–18, 19
Nazi Party of Iceland, 17–18
New Vikings. *See also* oligarchy
acquisitions and, 100, 102
clans of, 47–52
cross-ownership and, 48
David Oddsson on, 47, 70
privatization of banks and, 46–47, 68
U.S. market and, 63
New Year's celebrations, in Reykjavik, 1–2, 3,
4, 7–8
New Zealand, 146
NI oil company, 35
Nordica, 72
Norse mythology, 59–60

Northern Lights media group, 108, 116
Northern Sea Route, 181
Northern Travel Holiday (NTH), 117–118
Norvik, 69
Norway
Arctic claims of, 180, 182
bankruptcy of Iceland and, 178
Icelandic immigrants to, 206
Icelandic resistance to, 15–16
Iceland's banks and, 133
Laki volcano's effects on, 4
market of, 63
proposed Icelandic currency union with,
215
settlers to Iceland from, 15
swap arrangements with central bank, 156
Nutmeg Ltd., 101
Nykaup, 62

Obama, Barack, 179, 189
Octopus families
Bjoergólfur Gudmundsson and, 49, 50–51
business practices of, 46–47
cross-ownership and, 36, 67
Eimskip and, 33, 34–35, 68
Independence Party and, 35, 70
Jon Asgeir Johannesson and, 65, 67–68, 105
Nordic market and, 62–63
Orca group opposing, 116
privatization and, 33, 36, 42
structure of, 35–36
Oddaflug, 68
Oddsson. *See* David Oddsson
OECD (Organization for Economic
Cooperation and Development), 111, 113
Olaf Haraldsson (king of Norway), 15–16
Olafsdottir. *See* Katrin Olafsdottir; Kristin
Olafsdottir
Olafsson. *See* Jon Olafsson; Olafur Olafsson
Olafur Hardarsson, 131
Olafur Olafsson, 44, 48
Olafur Ragnar Grimsson, 89, 106, 107, 108,
109, 114–115, 179, 193
Olafur Thors, 23, 49
oligarchy
acquisitions and, 95–96, 117–118, 128–129
as advance guard of new order, 63
bankruptcy of Iceland and, 58, 167, 176,
184, 188, 193, 197, 207
banks and, 44, 58
as feudal class, 47
Icelandair and, 67–69

241

Index

Independence Party and, 65
international market and, 96, 108–109
members of, 48
protests against, 195
salmon compared to, 94, 102
trophy assets of, 147
weakening power of, 95
101 hotel, 48, 104–105, 106, 107, 155
Orca SA group, 42, 116
Orwell, George, 32
Oxford University, 127

Pálmadottir. *See* Ingibjörg Pálmadottir
Palmi Haraldsson, 117
Palmi Jonasson, 103
Palsson. *See* Thorstein Palsson
Paulson, Henry, 158–160, 164, 189, 197
PepsiCo, 52, 53
Perez, Carlota, 211
Petursdottir. *See* Kristin Petursdottir
Pharmaco, 51, 53
Planet Pulse, 75
Poland, 178
Poles, in fishing industry, 5, 82, 92, 205
police, riot units of, 14, 193
political class
    bankruptcy of Iceland and, 4–5, 7, 8–9, 12,
        54, 187, 193
    business class and, 57, 58, 75, 95, 188, 208
    centralization of political authority, 111
    guilty silence of, 193
    obligations of, 41
    political cronyism of, 54–55, 69, 77, 151
    presidency and, 107
    protest culture and, 193–197
    protests against, 191
    rebuttal of Den Danske Bank's analysis, 125
    Reykjavik grammar schools and, 30–31
    as ruling elite, 46
    as rurally based, 22–23
    Russia and, 179
    siege mentality of, 153
    wealth transfer in fishing industry, 39
Portes, Richard, 146, 153, 157–158
privatization
    of banks, 6, 32, 37, 42, 43, 44, 46–47, 55,
        68, 76, 85, 86, 87, 90, 115, 120, 160,
        197
    David Oddsson and, 6, 26, 32, 33, 36, 40,
        42–43, 47, 63, 79, 83, 85, 112, 115, 202
    flaws in, 41, 43–44
    of state assets, 29, 36, 41

Progressive Party, 42, 43, 50, 89
prosperity
    business class and, 58
    credit availability and, 179
    creditor/debtor relationship and, 93
    David Oddsson and, 32
    interruption of, 192
    NATO membership and, 15
Protestant work ethic, 115, 210
protest culture
    citizens' meetings and, 189–190
    industrialization and, 83
    kitchen revolution, 190, 206
    middle class and, 192
    passion of, 14
    pervasiveness of, 13
    political class and, 193–197
    riot police and, 14, 193
    size of, 12
Putin, Vladimir, 178, 180

Ramsay, Gordon, 127
Rannikh, Alexander, 179–180
Rawkins, Paul, 124
Rawle, Ron, 19
Reagan, Ronald
    David Oddsson and, 26, 32, 63
    Friedman and, 29–30, 36, 209
    Gorbachev and, 76
    individuals as market players and, 134
    inflation and, 112
    Octopus families and, 36
    personalized style of government and, 70
    political cronyism and, 41
regulatory boundaries
    bank deregulation, 13, 55–56, 68, 85, 86,
        121–122
    in Britain, 188–189
    capitalism and, 7
    in U.S., 6
retail, property, banking axis, 102
Retchetov, Yuri, 179
Reykjavik
    architecture of, 11–12, 32
    financial elite of, 45
    Hotel Borg riot, 8
    New Year's celebrations, 1–2, 3, 4, 7–8
Reykjavik Energy, 95
Reynir Traustason, 66
Rich, Denise, 106
Rich, Marc, 106
Rist, Rannveig, 105

Index

Index